Va'

Estha Hayes
From her teach
E. B.

1924

Travels in
The Old World

Illustrated.

BY

REV. J. M. ROWLAND
Editor Richmond Christian Advocate, Richmond, Va.

Author of:
"Blue Ridge Breezes" and "A Pilgrimage to Palestine."

APPEALS PRESS, INC.

Richmond, Va.

1922

The Author.

Dedication

To my wife who followed my journey
with her prayers and met me
when my ship sailed in

and

to the party of genial sunny souls
who helped me all they could to
make the Pilgrimage of 1921
all that heart could wish

These pages
are tenderly inscribed.

PREFACE.

When my first book was printed, I did not dream by this time six thousand would be sold. Little advertising has been done. The folks who read them, have sold them. I have yielded to the many calls to issue another book on Travels in The Old World, and I send it forth with a tender wish that it may receive as warm a welcome in the world as the others have. To my old friends—known and unknown—who have read my pages and sent me greetings, I herewith return the best greetings of my heart.

Part of the first book,—the historic facts—appear in this book but the most of it is rewritten. It makes no claim to stateliness and dignity and none to scholarship and literature. It will shock some. It goes the Pilgrim Path with a smile and a hop, but with bared head and bowed heart it approaches softly Holy Shrines and Truths. It is written in the writer's own way. If he writes at all, he must write that way. It goes forth with a prayer that it may cheer and help and make people more interested in the Pilgrim Path.

THE AUTHOR.

Travelers Rest,
3812 Hawthorne,
Richmond, Va.

INTRODUCTION.

By Dr. G. T. Rowe,
Book Editor of the M. E. Church, South.

Let me say right at the beginning that the reader who takes this book in hand has a delightful treat in store. The next best thing to taking a trip abroad is following the meanderings of a man who knows how to travel with his eyes open and to describe the things the reader would have noticed, if he had been along. As I have read some books of travel I have wondered why the writer left his comfortable home, when all of his material could have been gotten from Baedeker and the Encyclopaedia Britannica, and have not been surprised to learn that such productions are not in general demand. It takes more than a succession of facts to make a book of travel interesting. The writer must have sympathy and humor and imagination. These the reader will find in Mark Twain and J. M. Rowland. I do not hesitate to couple these two illustrious names together. The broad humor of exaggertion of the former enlivens the account of the purchase of a pair of gloves in Paris or the description of the appetite of a camel in the Holy land, while the sly touches of the latter relieve the soberness of the narrative at every turn.

The value of a book of this kind depends as much upon the kind of man that does the traveling as upon the extent and duration of the journey. The Author of Travels in the Old World acknowledges that he is described in his passport as "red-headed," and while that color of hair was not supposed until recent years to enhance the pulchritude of either man or woman, it has always been taken as an indication of alertness of mind. Everybody knows that red-headed people are unusually bright. Moreover, everybody loves a red-headed man, because his heart goes out to everybody. J. M. Rowland took to Europe and the Near East a genial soul, enriched by divine grace, and his candid manner was a passport to the hearts of the people everywhere. Hence the book abounds with human interest. One glance convinced the most suspicious officer that he was not a spy, or a fomenter of revolution, and even the custom houses took his word for what was in his baggage. Having steeped his mind for years in the history of the lands that he had long hoped to visit, he was prepared to appreciate the significance of sights and scenes, and to adorn his narrative with historic allusion and incident. Consequently, the reader will find, as he goes along, that he is being instructed, as well as entertained.

Travels in the Old World will advertise itself. No one will be able to read it without quoting from it and relating incidents recorded in it, and the reader of each copy of the book will create a demand for others. My excuse for complying with the author's request for a word of introduction lies in the fact that I was a member of the company on the return end of the European part of the journey, and I am rather proud to have my name carried far and wide by the nimble pen of so ready a writer. The other members of that congenial group will be glad to be assured that, although the author threatens to write of their pranks and foibles without fear or favor, he really does exercise a judicious reserve, which prevents any one of them from suffering in the eyes of his fellow-countrymen. And yet, if he had told all, it would not have been so bad, for while that party followed to some extent the old adage, "when in Rome do as the Romans do," they did not do all that the Romans do—or the Parisians either. And while all of them heartily despised each other in turn, as travelers are wont to do, every one would desire to take a second trip with the very same crowd, and have as their leader the same red-headed and red-blooded American, who did not hesitate upon occasion to show his contempt for a head waiter or to stand up for his rights in the face of the whole French army.

GILBERT T. ROWE.

Nashville, Tenn.

CONTENTS.

PROLOGUE.

Have you ever had Travel fever? Did you feel the germ creeping in your blood and wings beating against your heart doors as you longed to fly up and out and on? Did you ever hear the call of the sun as He flamed the East with morning glory, chasing out the dark and as He threw his good-night kiss back at you as He dipped his red chariot in the distant blue? Has the long white winding road held out beckoning hands and pled with you to go on and on to find its end? Is the clank of the train wheels on the jointed rails sweet music to your soul as the fields and woods rush by? Has the rainbow begged you to go on to the place where its radiance kissed the ground in search of the pot of Gold? Or has the moaning tides coming in at your feet sung songs of lands afar where voices were strange and dress and manners weired and varied? And has the sails of boats called you to come on to ports beyond where your feet would walk strange paths, your ears hear strange sounds and your eyes see strange sights? Have you felt the urge in your soul to go to ancient shrines and historic places where the race was rocked in its cradle, and you could dig in ashes of buried empires and see relics of dead dynasties and remnants of ancient glory and forgotten lore? And have you longed to put your feet in the foot prints of the great priests and prophets of the past and come at last walking softly to the spot where the Son of Man and God was born, lived and died and lived again the blessed life?

Then come on—

A FOREWORD.
(To the first book).

There is no reason why this book should be written. Perhaps my friends should have secured a restraining order from the courts to prevent my attempt at a forcible entrance into the Literary World, but they did not, and the book is from the press. A book without a demand! It is true three friends have said they would buy it, but that was before they saw it.

I read the other day the Introduction to a Book of Travels by a lady. She said her reason for printing the book was self-defense. She had given the travels to the papers in a series of articles. The people had urged her to put it in book form, but she declined. Then the people were in the act of committing bold trespass and printing her writings whether or no. So to keep the people from forcibly publishing it in undesirable form, she had, after long and careful contemplation, decided to publish the book herself; not because she wanted to, but because she was forced to.

When I read this, I waited patiently for developments. I had given a number of articles on my travels to the papers, and I had lectured in a number of places. So I waited for a deputation of aroused and enthused citizens to come in great zeal and determination, demanding that I write a book: but they have not come. A number of publishers and book men have been to see me, but they did not come with a pistol in their hand to force me to publish a book. They all seemed to have more books than they could manage already. Their offer usually sounded something like selling me "Kilpatrick's Universal Encyclopedia and Compendium of Science and Literature," illustrated, with index, and covering every phase and form of life from how to raise babies to how to become President of the United States (neither of which the agent could do). This wonderful set, which was endorsed by Dr. C. W. Elliott and W. H. Taft, they would sell me for five dollars a month—for nine hundred and ninety-nine months (my main reason for not buying things this way is it makes time fly so fast)—and throw in a lot in San Diego, California, and a new war atlas.

They came with such offers as these, but never to try to make me write a book. And I never dreamed I would write a book of my travels, until awhile ago in reading that admirable book, "Out of Doors in Palestine," by Dr. Henry Van Dyke. In giving his reason for writing it he said he knew many books had been written on Palestine and people might say there were no more needed, but he thought there were flowers enough on the Holy Hills for every one to come back with a bouquet. So here I come with these pages—flowers in a little bouquet which I place in the hands of my friends.

I know some of them are wilted flowers, and in some of them there are thorns. I know some of them are such common-place blossoms that many people will cast them aside as unworthy to be put on their table. But if any of these pages should

chance to be a flower that brings any beauty or
fragrance to the heart of any of my friends, my
heart will be glad and my labor will be rewarded.

No attempt at scholarship has been made, and
no effort at literary attainment has been undertaken.
These pages are rather the plain musings of a humble soul and the impressions of a heart that has been
touched. It is written in that heart's own way, with
nobody for a pattern and no other hand guiding the
pen. It is withal the plain, frank words of a heart
that believes and feels, and therefore speaks.

Special appreciation is extended to Rev. J. J.
Wicker, D. D. and Mr. J. J. Wicker, Jr., of Richmond, managers of the Wicker Tours, whose courtesies and friendship was invaluable; to George Jallouk the best of Guides and Dragomen; to Dr. Squires
of Norfolk, who allowed me the use of some of his
pictures; to the members of my churches (Rivermont Church, Lynchburg, and Laurel Street Church,
Richmond); to Miss Janie Lipes of Lynchburg my
efficient secretary—for the interest they took in
my travels; and last but not least to the members
of our party whose fellowship, patience and good
nature made the trip a success.

MY PILGRIMAGE.

In the far-away land of Egypt
I gazed on the setting sun,
As I stood on the sand, with my staff in my hand,
At eve when the day was done.

I stood in the courts of Rome,
And thought of her days so great,
When in her gold and her glory she wrote her own
story
In the sin that sealed her fate.

I walked through the city of Zion,
So hallowed in life and in lore,
Where her priests and her king made all her hills
ring
In praise to the God we adore.

I walked where the Master went
By the side of the far-famed sea,
As the winds blew o'er the wave-washed shore
Of beautiful Galilee.

I walked in the Garden of God,
That men call Gethsemane,
And the moon shone bright, that beautiful night,
Where Christ won Heaven for me.

CHAPTER I.

It is a great sport. Seeing Babe Ruth hurl the ball is tame and an old southern fox hunt with forty hounds in full cry on the heels of old Red is a second class show. Charles Chaplin and a meeting of the Board of Stewards together cannot furnish as much fun.

It seems it would be an easy task to leave your native land for a little trip to see your cousins over seas but the telephone girl gave you the wrong number when she thus connected you with information.

You will find your wife and all the neighbors glad to see you go and all their little niceties are done to show it. If you are a preacher, the Board of Stewards will hear your plea for travel and study with as much gravity as the Hebrew Sanhedrin selecting the scape goat that is to be driven into the wilderness. Then Col. Grimes and Bill Stone will gravely speak and say that they do not see how in the world the church will get along without you and that you will be missed more than Woodrow Wilson was when he went to Paris. But in all their hearts, they are thanking the Lord you are going and are vowing they too will have a rest and not go to church until you return, not even the Sunday the Elder preaches.

But the strange thing is, your Uncle Sam seems gravely concerned about your departure and has

Philadelphia lawyers and the experts, who muddle railroad time tables, and the doctors, who write unreadable prescriptions, all to combine and work in full committee designing a series of entanglements and manufacturing a quantity of red tape that would have made Julius Caesar say something else besides "Gall is divided into three parts."

This is what I found when with all my comrades I tried my little trip. I received all due information with exhibit a b c from D'an to Beersheba so to speak and set about the task of getting my passport.

I was told the first thing was to produce a birth certificate to convince my Uncle on my Father's side that the alleged owner of the name I was reputed to bear was really and truly born one time, somewhere and was therefore the party of the first part.

Here I was to speak for myself but they would not take that as evidence. I did not remember where nor when I threw my hat in the ring but felt I had reasonable evidence that I was born somewhere and in the days of my coming, birth certificates like Fords were unknown. Folks had something else to do besides filing affidavits and sending out perfumed announcements every time there was such a trivial occurrence as another kid born into the flock.

Then I was told that I would have to get some reputable citizen to swear in the presence of a Notary Public where and when to the best of his belief the accused was born if at all, and if so, why not? I thought of a friend, who would thus swear

Teorge Jallouk. The best of guides, kindest of friends.
The more you see of him the better you love him.

When is daddy coming home?

for me. He will swear on slight provocation and
didn't mind doing it in the presence of a Notorious
Republican for he will even swear in the presence
of gentlemen. So he came forward and swore I was
born Jan. 9, 1880, at Rowland, N. C., according to
the best of his knowledge and belief, tho both of these
things with him were scant. He has never been to
Rowland and does not know whether I saw the light
in frozen Siberia or the Fiji Islands.

This being fixed, I was told I would have to have
my boss to swear why I was going and give his
permission. I got my Presiding Elder to do this
swearing for me.

Then I had to go to the photographer and have
a full face pcture taken to put on the passport and
take some extra ones along to put in foreign rogues
galleries. I always feel and look like a nut having
my picture taken and rather have a back view than
full face but I had to do it. Then I had to get the
picture man to swear it was my picture so they
would take it.

Armed with these things I went to the clerk of
the court, who sat me down and looked at me as if
I was "particeps criminice" in the Wall Street explosion and demanded me to answer the following
suggestions describing myself.

I was asked of my age, which I told. Since I
was not responsible for it, I was not ashamed of it,
and I told it. Then he asked my height and weight.
I measured my height and got that right. He called
my forehead high, tho I dislike the term high headed
and big headed as much as anything I know.

My eyes were blue and my nose he called medium, whatever that means. My chin he put down as medium and my hair as red and gray, the last of which made me sad. My complexion was fair. But the last two things stumped us and it was here we almost had a fight and seemed dangerously near calling off the whole thing.

He had to record the kind of a face and mouth I had. He could not tell and he asked me. Now reader if you are reading and did not get disgusted long ago, you do not know how hard it is to put down on paper in a sworn statement the kind of a face and mouth you have unless you have tried.

Some friend in the room suggested I had an ingrowing face and I told him I would see him later. Another said it was a sneaking face and the look I gave him was good evidence.

Someone said my mouth was of the Henry Cabot Lodge variety and another thought it was of the George Harvey brand—just runs without knowing where it is going.

But reader what kind of a mouth have you? A kind and gentle one that cheers and helps and comforts and encourages or one that cuts and knocks and hurts and growls and complains? Finally he put mine down as medium, whatever that means, and I wonder if he was right. It seemed he was getting me too much in the medium class. But I hope that in doing the real service a normal mouth was meant to do, mine is even medium. My face he said was oval which sounds better than saying it was square, oblong, three cornered or mule faced. But between us it is not oval.

Then I paid him $9.00, war tax and post mortem expenses and we went on to Washington to do some more red tape stunts. We had to run the gauntlet of the state department for extensions and begin that marvelous and interesting game of having it visaed before all the foreign consuls whose countries we were to visit and there receive a stamp with the King's photo and license to be skinned in that particular land and for this privilege, pay what altogether made $33.00 more which went to buy more war ships to whip some future king, who might try the "Me and Gott stunt."

The first was the Italian office and after waiting in line and measuring enough Italian red tape to throttle an octupus, we came out with proper endorsement signed by Hon. Guisseppelesante Vetes bearing this significant statement "Deriti hero ono assuguanto" which cost $10.00.

Then we did the same preliminary stunt over at the office of the Swiss Legation and an official with more dignity than George Harvey has of brass filled out a little pamphlet that looked like Blums' Almanac, pasted it neatly in and signed his name D. C. Jenny, Secretaire de Legation Suesse, Washington, D. C. and $2.00 we paid and told Mr. or Mrs. Jenny as the case may be good-bye and made for the other red tape mills. At the Greek office when our turn came, he wrote on a place after affixing stamps—"Bon pour serendere en Grese Le Direct our D. C. Le St Joe 121 and signed L. Koundoumauke—which in English may mean Jim Jones.

Then likewise to the French, the Belgium, Eng-

lish, Holland and all the others. The last thing was
the picture of King George which cost $5.00.

Then we were told we must get another reputable man to swear if we never came back, he would
pay our income tax and also get a sworn statement
from the Collector of Revenue saying we had already paid up. This enabled us to get a sailing
permit, which with our baggage and a certificate
that we had been vaccinated for several diseases
enabled us to board a steamer for the land of waiting pirates, who would skin us of what hide the
diplomats had left.

CHAPTER II.

THE EFFECTS OF TRAVEL.

There are a great many effects that come from travel. We are told it broadens folks. It sometimes narrows folks and belittles them. It is exhausting to your pocketbook, your patience and the opinions your friends have of you. It makes some folks love the old world more and makes some others hate it. It causes some people to think they know everything and others to think they know nothing.

One of the far reaching effects of travel and one fraught with most danger, is the close association that will make us know too much about one another by living together at close range. We find out who snores, and who eats onions and who chews gum, who has any divorced relatives, who belongs to different churches, who are Republicans and Democrats, who says "ither and nither" and in all this private and detailed information comes trouble and disaster.

There is a fine looking woman we have honored and admired and three days out, it leaks out thru her roommate, who remarked in the profoundest secrecy to the wife of a friend in the party that she has false hair and false teeth. There is a dignified Doctor of Divinity, we honored and respected but we have to eat by him at the table and soon learn he does not put on the muffler when he eats soup and that he insists on rehearsing the smart antics of his baby boy. This ruins him forever.

There is a beautiful young woman sweet as an Elberta Peach and as fine a picture as an artist could paint. We classed her as among those beyond this earth when in less than a week, we saw her turning up her nose at everything and pouting like a swell toad.

Here is a man we thought the personification of chivalry, when we discover he picks over a dish to get the best portion for himself, slips into the best seat first and considers no one but himself.

The tragedy of life is in seeing one another at close range. It is a hazardous thing to do. The old proverb says, no house is big enough to hold two women and like Postum "There's a Reason." They learn too much of each other.

It is sad to see some folks at close range. The microscope brings out the defects. Close gazing at the canvas reveals a gob of paint on a cloth and not the fine lines of a masterpiece. The beautiful face of the sweetest woman under a powerful magnifying glass reveals great black spots and hairy horrors like a briar patch.

Our wives know all about us but with them charity covers a multitude of faults. She will read to us all our defects and short comings but she will raise a rough house if another woman even finds out one of them and speaks of it. She will to the whole world then proclaim us perfect.

But the difference is when we know other people at close range like this there is no love that covers a multiude of faults, but a criticism that magnifies them. Whoever heard of one man or woman loving and respecting their roommate who snored! All they would want to lynch the offender would be for someone to start the mob.

What a pity we have to know so much about one another when we travel. If there was some way to stay in glass cases a good deal of the time and not force our personality on our comrades, how much better it would be. You are not long out when you hear the different ones saying, "He is not the man I thought he was." "I am certainly surprised in her." "Who would have thought."

But there are some folks—we hope a large number of folks who like a shoe feel better on the foot the more you wear them. They improve on close acquaintance. Not that they look prettier and more perfect under the high power glass of close inspection, but that they show up to be real humans the more you know them. You have found some of these —the real true travelers of life. Happy are you if in the road of life as you jog along with your friends you are one of those who wear well, and more and more at close contact prove yourself real human and not polish even of the highest quality or worse still cheap veneer.

And herein lies one of the best things of travel. I would never have known how real, how true, how human some of my friends were if I had not travelled with them at close range—and listen a minute— much of the wrong was in me for magnifying the short comings and not magnifying the virtues.

It is interesting to study the distinctive products of different cities you visit when touring the old world. These old cities may hold all sorts of things but each one will claim some products distinctive above the others.

In Naples you buy Roman Pearl beads. In Rome you look for cameos, while in Florence your hunt is for mosaics—the finest in the world. Then in Venice, you go wild over Venetian glass.

Of course, you can't be a tourist without being a nut and while you will travel all the main methods of locomotion, by boat, rail, auto, carriage, tallyho, donkey, camel, gondola, aeroplane your main method of getting about will be riding hobbies. You may never have developed any special mania for hobbyriding at home save when you took the children to the park to ride the hobby-horses. Your wife with the assistance of your mother-in-law may have saved you from the hobby mania. You may not be wedded to red flannel under shirts, derby hats and patent medicines. If you are a school teacher, the Board of Trustees and the scholars saw to it that you were saved from the hobby mania.

But once you join a tourist party, you get the hobby mania. The lady from South Carolina had the disease when she got to New York and it being contagious everybody caught it. Conspicuous in the list is the kodak hobbiest. You see him with the little black case strapped on his shoulder and you know the jig is up. Morning, noon and night, he must be busy taking pictures. He never thinks of anything else. Forty times a day he insists on lining the whole party up like they are to be shot and making them go thru the ordeal of looking pleasant while he takes your pictures. He must take the guide's picture, the horses' picture and get snap shots of all the tombs, dogs and cats you pass.

Then you have the germ hobbiest. And of all the poor nuts of the seven hundred and fifty seven varieties classified in the Blue Book of who is who among nuts, there is none so miserable and incurable as the nut who thinks some little bug will get you if you don't watch out. Sometimes these nuts are women and sometimes men. They are afraid of disease. They insist on having the pedigree and family history of all the cheese and macaroni. They protest about the bread being hauled about like wood. They are always looking for cooties. They want the water boiled and are always afraid of catching something.

Then you have one or more whose hobby is the diets of the lands you visit. He attracts attention by what he pretends to know about the things they serve to eat. He claims he knows what it all is and pretends to like it. He eats garlic and diseased cheese, and snails, in the presence of all the others and pretends to relish it when in reality he is punishing himself just to punish other people.

Of course you will have the souvenir hobbiest. He or she will risk life and reputation to secure a relic from every place he visits. He loads up on rocks from many places and does not know where they come from. He will steal or do anything for a souvenir.

Some go crazy over cameos and some over beads, some over mosaics, and some over silks, some over walking canes and some over—but all go crazy over something.

But doubtless the most detested nut that travels in tourist party is the one who tries to tell you everything about the places you are to visit. If there should be a mob that should tar and feather this culprit, they should be excused. Happy are you when going Abroad if you do not fall in with some one who has been before and wants to tell you everything.

It will take you a long time to get over your crazy spell when you get home but when you do get normal, you will be glad you went.

CHAPTER III.

Outward Bound.

(1914)

I cannot remember the time in my life when I did not long to visit the old world. Especially did I hunger for travel in the parts of the world from which we get our Bible and all that is worth while in our civilization and religion. With the passing years this dream became a passion and a prayer. I did not see much prospects to overcome barriers and go, for time and money and a family that needed me, came first. But God seemed to open the way and move some hearts to open doors.

When I found the Wicker party was going right in Richmond where I was living, I took the matter up with my official board at Laurel St. Church. It was asking a good deal to expect them to let me off the whole summer, but when they heard me timidly make my plan, with one accord they voted, they would be delighted for me to go. I have learned better since then that church boards are far more willing for the preacher to go than people think. If Col. Grimes the Chairman says he does not see how they can possibly live without him, the Colonel is hoping in his heart the parson will leave and give him and the rest of the board a chance to play hooky from church all summer.

Then I went to the Sunday School and when they heard my plea, they voted with one accord they would be highly pleased for me to go. Then at last I mustered courage to tell my wife I had decided to put the wide ocean between us and journey to lands afar where I might be like Jonah swallowed by a whale or like the man on the Jericho road fall in the hands of custom officers who would take all my souvenirs and breaking my heart, depart leaving me half dead. Instead of protesting tears, she smiled her sweetest smile and said it would make her heart ring with joy for me to do so.

Then I had to go, for I had burned the bridges. The folks had a farewell service and presented me with a handful of the root of all evil, a steamer rug and a suitcase to take a clean shirt over there and bring back all I could smuggle in. When they opened the suitcase a mouse jumped out and made for the Sunday school entrance embarrassing the ladies, who wore hobble skirts and therefore were hampered in retreating under fire. A wise one said this meant bad luck, and his warning was certainly well founded for the world war broke out that summer and an Arab stole Bro. L. T. Williams' best coat.

The trip of that summer was a rare and gracious privilege and brought into my life more than pen could write or tongue could tell. There are many rare incidents of the voyage I would preserve and rich treasures I would treasure. They are preserved in the first book, "A Pilgrimage to Palestine." This volume will give some of these but the most of it will deal with the second tour of 1921.

SOME INCIDENTS OF THE FIRST TOUR.

The majestic boat is ready to turn her nose to the open sea. The whistle has blown, the gang plank hauled in and the tug boat takes her like an ant lugging a huge thing and turns her toward the channel. Handkerchiefs wave, tears are falling, the shore receding, the waters churning, the wide sea calling, and the sun sinking in the reddening glory of the west, while in the deepening shadows the shore line of our native land fades in the gathering night and the majestic Statue of Liberty with exalted torch waving to nations beyond, is lost to view and the boat with her great heart of fire and quivering life settles herself to the long and eventful journey.

This ocean journey was interesting for many reasons. One of the most attractive things on board was the large amount of eating that was done. That has always been interesting to me. I formed the habit early in life and have never been able to break myself of it. I like to be around when it is going on. We had breakfast at 7, forenoon lunch at 10, noon lunch 12 to 1:30, afternoon tea at 3 and dinner from 6 to 7:30. There is a simple reason for so much eating on a sea journey. You cannot always keep what you eat and you need some more handy when you want it.

A story was told of a Kentucky gentleman on our boat. In a storm when the sea demons roared and the wind raged at eighty miles an hour, he was found on the outer deck praying to the God that holds the ocean in His hands and confessing all the sins he had ever done. As a friend bent over his prostrate form, he whispered,

"Jim when it is all over, take my remains back to old Kentucky where the grass is blue and the women true."

There came another surging of the boat as she pitched from a high wave into the trough of the sea as if she was headed for the regions below and when the sufferer recovered sufficient strength again, he said in a voice more feeble,

"Jim, you needn't bother about the remains. There aint goin ter be enough to take to Kentucky."

Another reason the trip was interesting was because the boat was a German boat and the crew and many passengers of that Nation. They were very interesting folks that summer and the longer we stayed with them, the more interesting they became until we were almost unable to tear ourselves from them and return home.

It is hard to live in peace with the Germans as the following incident shows. My room-mate was Rev. L. T. Williams of the Virginia Conference. There is no truer man and like Nathaniel under the fig tree he is almost—mind you, almost a man without guile. But he has other things to take its place. He was a fine room mate and ever kind to me. When time came to send our laundry to the laundry woman, he took mine in his bundle and went on a hunt for her. The bundle was small, for we were restricted in our dry goods and notions, since all we took went in one big suitcase to avoid trouble and extra expense. But it is wonderful how well you can get along thus limited. The ladies would come down every day with something new or the old fixed in a new way. But give a woman a powder puff and a varnish brush for her nose and she —but—

Williams came back saying he feared we would never see our duds any more for the laundress was a German with no English on her tongue. I suggested if there was any question, we would use the sign language on her, an accomplishment in which we were making honorable mention. And when he brought the bundle back to the state room, there was a question, for my shirt was missing and a fellow needs such an article away from home. I told him to go to the laundress and make complaint as she might remember him, but would never remember me. He went and in a minute, I heard him talking louder and louder in English and a German woman answering back louder and faster in German. It seemed like diplomatic relations would soon be severed if some intervention did not take place, and I went with all speed to help my friend. But I was too late. I met him coming in full retreat with a big double jointed kraut eating female hot on his trail. I retired to my state room doubled my fists with all the Protestant blood of the Stuarts charging the crimson tide of my ancestral veins, ready to defend my private quarters from the invasion of any Teutonic intruder. I looked her in the eye and told her no offense was meant either to her or to the House of Hohenzollern but the whole crux of this international altercation hinged on my lost shirt which I thought she had and since she could not wear it (she seemed to require twice that size) and I could, I would be grateful to her to produce it since it was rather trying on a man of dignity to be away from home without a shirt.

She flashed a Hunish and evil eye on me and directed a finger near my nose, telling me in a language I understood that we had made a mistake for she was not the laundress but a passenger on the boat—I drop the curtain.

That afternoon I saw a German mother and an American mother. Each had babies about the same age. Said the American mother (it was before the war) to the German mother.

"He was a purty little tootsie wootsie." Said the German mother to the American mother,

"He vus not a he, he vus a she."

And then I knew baby talk was the same the world over.

A brother could not get his food fixed right. And of all the folks, who have a pay day coming, the traveler in a party who makes demands and complaints is on his way to his. This man was rich and had servants coming and going. He had his way and all his taste called for. His choice hobby was kicking because the coffee was not hot. He complained all the time and to everybody. One morning as the waiter boy came behind him with a waiter full of coffee, the gentleman was absorbed with his snout in his oatmeal dish, eating without puttng the muffler on. Someone touched the boy's elbow and he deposited two cups of coffee down the gentleman's neck. He leaped in the air, knocked over his chair screaming,

Our girl. Miss Estelle Warlick, the best of travelers—never late, never complained, never sour. She has since become the wife of Rev. E. L. Hillman, pastor of the Methodist Church in Scotland Neck, N. C., and is eminently qualified for the "Traveling Connection."

Ready for the Customs Officers.

"Dog bite (?) it. I'm scalded, I'm scalded."
Before I thought, I said,

"Well Colonel, I am glad you got it hot once."

When folks go abroad, they must have a guide
book and a bottle of quinine. The book has many
foreign phrases that are used by tourists to give
the impression of scholarship and learning. I heard
many using these things and felt lost without them
so I got a book to find some. I was reading about
the retinue and pompous pedigree of the Duke of
Luxumberg when a dude walked by. Like all English
Americans and Irish, I have a deal of prejudice in my
blood. Some things and folks I do not like. The
reason why I cannot always tell, but this I know
and know full well, I do not like you Isabel. I do
not like dudes and poodle dogs. I like most all other
dogs—both human and canine—especially hounds
and pointers, but don't like dudes and poodles. I
do not know just why I class them together but
since I think of it, I let them stay there.

This dude wore a monocle over one eye and nothing over the other. The reason they do this is they
can see more with one eye than they have sense
enough to understand, and they need not use the
other eye. As he passed a lady asked me who the
distinguished looking gentleman was. I swelled up
like the Professor of Bontology in Boston University and said in a voice lke a bishop—

"He looks like he might be Duke Von Sternberg
of Luxumberg."

I did not say he was it, but said he looked like
he may be it, and he did for he looked like he might

be most anything. A girl heard me say that and spread it over the boat that he was Duke Von Sternberg of Luxumberg. The next time I saw the duke he had a lady on each arm and for the rest of the trip was the most popular man on board. In those pre-war days, a duke and a pedigreed European nut stood higher than they do now.

Sitting near us was a German girl bright and sunny, who had a good English tongue. She helped us as an interpreter. Her name was Miss Marie and the second name was as long as a broom and had the sound of Limberger and Garlic. I asked her one day who that fellow was and her eyes shone as she replied with animation,

"Why, he is Duke Von Sternberg of Luxumberg."

"No," I said, "He isn't that. I don't know what he is but that girl at the post with a brown cloak knows him from the way she talks to him. Go and find out who he is."

Of course if you send a woman off on a trail like that, she will tree something before night, and in a few minutes Miss Marie returned, smiling, saying she she had his number in the phone book. His name was Isaac Ernstine. He was a German Jew who had been in the fruit business in New York and was on his way home to see his mother.

Having journeyed over forty thousand miles, mingling with people of many tongues, we found no difficulty in talking with foreigners on their native heath in their own language. There is but one rule to remember. Make a fuss in your goozle like you gargle your throat for tonsilitis and then make signs to express your meaning. I will never believe all the pig gruntlng, goose quacking sputtering, I heard in foreign lands is language. We are the only folks who have a language. They just jabber and make signs.

Sitting near us on the deck was a woman of leisure and means, who was traveling the world over. She had just returned from China where in the port of Hong Kong, she purchased a Pomereen pup. He was the only child she had and he very much resembled his mother. I have long known the best way to win a woman's favor is to notice her child and we paid attention to the pup. Bro. Williams tried to ask her if the pup would bite but she could not understand what "bite" meant. He put his finger toward his lips and then toward the pup's mouth to try to ask her in the sign language if the dog would bite, and suddenly the light of understanding flooded her face. She thought he wanted to kiss the pup and she put the pup's face up towards his.

We landed in Germany and traveled this country. Much could be written about it, but what is the use? In those days, the Kaiser ruled in splendor, receiving about $6,000,000. a year all told. It is hard to get accurate information from the place where that arch fiend of the human race hides behind the skirts of the Queen of Holland whither he fled in beastly cowardice—to keep the hands of an outraged world from getting him by his devilish throat and bringing him out to the justice his bloody crimes against God as well as men, women and little children—deserve—but it is safe to say his salary has been considerably reduced since that day.

But the Hohenzollerns have fallen and their glory departed. The storm has swept proud monarchs from their gilded thrones; crowns corrode in the dirt; moths eat the ermine; the blood of the Romanoffs stain Siberian snows, while Charles of Austria dies in lonely exile. Ah! The strange new day that has dawned! The civilization of Europe, we saw in 1914 has crumbled to the ground, and men work desperately to build again in the wreckage that was wrought.

A COLLISION AT SEA.

Today there is little that modern ocean boats need dread. Mortals are safer on the sea than trying to dodge automobiles in Richmond for now we are all divided into two classes, the quick, who get out of the way, and the dead who do not. Those majestic ocean liners defy the raging winds and dashing storm, as they ride the rolling waves unafraid. Seldom does one perish in a storm. Barring the devilish submarine—the most fiendish invention ever made, save mustard gas and liquid fire —there is but one thing that is dangerous. It is when fog comes dark and heavy on the water that danger is near.

Going the northern road, we come near the ice zone and the fog comes down upon us. It was not far from where the Titanic made her deadly plunge to her watery grave and shocked the world, and it was not long after that awful tragedy. We went to our beds listening to the fog horns every five minutes. You think you wouldn't sleep, but you would for the great good God has put something in the roll of the ocean's wave that is like your mother's hand on the cradle of your childhood, and he has put something in the moan of ocean wind that is like her lullabies in your tired ears. It lulls you to sleep. In after months men slept like babes when the sea was full of death and they never knew as they laid down at night whether they would be on the boat or in eternity in the morning. About 2 A. M. June 13, 1914—and it was on Friday—I was hurled from sweet repose in my upper berth to the floor and as I crossed the great divide out of the other world where we sleep into this world where we are awake, I heard a sound such as I never heard before and I pray God, I will never hear again. It was the smashing of timbers and the grating of iron, mingled with the crying of the women and children and the hurrying of the officers. The boat shook and quivered and felt as if she was going head first to the bottom of the deep. In after months when Germans torpedoed *helpless* boats and the white faces of the women and little children looked up at the stars as the swelling floods of death rushed on them, I could hear their cries—Oh that cry of the women and the children in a sinking ship in the dark. Then came the voice of the officer—

"Collision! All passengers on board with life preservers on."

Fixing our life belts, we climbed to the outer deck and looked out in the dark to the dim decks of the

New York of the American Line inward bound. A hole was torn in her side just above the water 35 ft. x 4—The hole in our boat was 10 x 4. Both were just above the water and after ours was repaired, we proceeded.

During the war, I met a man who was on the New York. He was mail clerk, and he told how he prayed as he had never prayed before and said he well remembered how they sang, "Nearer My God to Thee," as they thought the boat was going down.

Looking back, there comes a sweet remembrance of the beautiful hymn and its prayer that was gently hummed and ever since it has been sweeter than before,

> "Jesus Saviour Pilot Me
> Over Life's Tempestuous Sea."

CHAPTER IV.

THROUGH AUSTRIA-HUNGARY AND THE BALKAN STATES.

June 28, 1914.

For a long time we will not forget that fifteen hundred miles from Dresden, Germany, through Southern Europe to Constantinople. We were on the train, the Continental Express, which is a good train, for two days and nights. Our party numbered fifty and we were unable to secure but twelve berths in the sleeper. We adopted a rule that only the older ladies would be entitled to sleep, and never in my life have I seen ladies age so rapidly. We finally modified the rule by allowing men who were both old and infirm a few hours in bed. The rest of us sat up with the corpse.

And well we might sit up for there was no sleep on that trip. We were passing through countries, recently shaken by war, with battle-fields much in evidence, while seething, surging all about us the caldron of the nations was about ready to boil over again. It seems a shame that a section of the world so rich in possibilities, wide and fertile fields, hills heavy laden with boundless ore, should be settled by a people so restless and so turbulent. Such a nervous condition would be hard to equal. Soldiers and guards were everywhere. We had to snatch a little nap beside a soldier whose form was decked with guns and swords and whose eye watched your movements. At every little thing he would start and his hand would seek his gun.

At every turn guards and officials of vicious mein and piercing eye came stalking through the train in gaudy uniform and clanking steel. They overhauled us, scrutinized us, looked at our passports, fumbled through our baggage, examined our eyes and talked to one another about us in words we could not understand. They gesticulated over us and made many signs and motions. They looked through the car to see if we had anything concealed. They would leave us for a while and go off only to return presently with others more vicious looking than the first and men of higher rank who wore more things on their bodies and carried longer swords. Again they would gather about us, jabber, and motion, looking first at us and then at one another. At every station crowds of soldiers and citizens of every kind and shape and style would gather about the car windows looking in and likewise talking about us, expressing their opinions of us in a language like the barn yard. Often they would bring their friends to peer at us and say what they thought about us. Sometimes we dozed from sheer exhaustion soon to be aroused by approach of armed guards and heathen hands upon us and we started over the routine we had dropped but a while ago.

Since then I have had sympathy for a monkey at a zoo gazed at by the crowd. I have been one myself.

One night at two o'clock they stopped the train and examined the wheels. We learned they proposed to put off our car and leave us with it in the heart of the Balkan mountains for there was no room in the rest of the train for us. We pleaded but it did no good. The leader, being inspired by a Methodist impulse to get out of a tight place by taking a collection, raised a few dollars and handed it over to the heathen. They smiled, and after examining the wheels again, reported that three more francs would make the train in condition to travel. They got the money and we went on. After that when language failed us and our country's flag was of no avail, we passed the hat and money talked us through. After all, there is no language like that of silver and gold.

We passed through the town in which the Austrian prince and his wife were murdered the very day of the crime. Little did we think what a great matter a little fire would kindle. But the fire was already there and it took only that to fan the flame. From what we heard of the man we do not think he was worth what he has cost the world.

During this trip we had tme to stop for a short visit to Vienna and Budapest. We found these cities far more beautiful and attractive than we had expected. Vienna is called one of the most beautiful cities of the world, and it sustained its reputation. The capitol and royal buildings were indeed attractive. Many of the people made a fine appearance, some of the women being the most beautiful we saw. Constantly we observed ever

changing costumes, both of men and women, but
none were more marked than those of the young
ladies at Budapest. Their feet were bare and their
skirts reached their knees. Such skirts we never
saw before. Some of them were twenty-five feet
around and they wore many skirts one over another. They were of various shades all ruffled and
arranged so when they walked it looked like the
whirl of the rain bow. Some of them must have
had on two dozen skirts. The social rank of a lady
is shown by the number of her skirts and on that
count I think we butted into an international ball
of the royal swells.

We were greatly impressed with the names of
some of the people and the places of these countries.
I copied in my note book some of the merchants.
It may be in order to recommend to the mothers
who read these lines the advisability of keeping
their children out of mischief by having them pro-
nounce these names. These are some of them,
noted citizens of Vienna and Budapest; Zum Zuck-
erlkonig, Mr. Puperkoniggim, Mr. S. Tibersver-
sicherungs, M. Schrierbmosher, T. Schrunmachier-
meister, C. Wasserlolanger, T. Sputuosenschonk, Z.
Vizzygyintzete, V. Cyogykisyeltetnek, A. Zcegtulo-
jdonos, M. Meghoditotiuk, S. Arczfinomitoers, and
Zim Zuckerbuckeri. How would ou like to do business with men of such names in the rush of this
fast day? How would you like to be secretary of
a Conference over there and try to call the roll? I
met some of these gentlemen and when I introduced
them I said, Allow me to present Mr," and then

I sneezed. The allies will have a time taking places and people with such names as these.

I dare say if some of these folks come to our land we Americans will treat them like a certain section of North Carolina once treated a son of Italy who came in their midst to settle, with a hand organ, a monkey and a name as long as the monkey's tail. Not being able to call the name with much speed or satisfaction, the Tar Heels called him "Old Man Turney" because he turned the organ for the monkey to dance and Turney it had to be. He raised a big family and the people called them "The Turney youngens." In the public school they registered as Joe Turney, Jim Turney, Pete Turney, etc., and the last time I was in the town I heard Joe stand at the window of the post office and ask if there was any mail for any of the Turneys. I doubt if Joe knows that awful thing the priest called his daddy back in Sunny Italy, when he made the cross and put the holy water on his head in that far off day before North Carolinans brought his family through the reformation.

Through fertile valleys, well watered and rich, we made our way to the south. In the valleys we found it hot while high up on the peaks of the Balkans we saw, in mid summer, mantles of snow. Our hearts grew sad as all about us we saw unnumbered hosts of men, women and little children bereft of all that makes life worth living in home and human society, subjects of a tyranny and despotism that knows no bounds, torn by ceaseless wars and internal strife, cursed by a religion far worse than darkest heathenism. The number of souls in these countries seems without number. Their lives are pathetic beyond the power to tell. What could they do in this great country with our civilization and religion?

Did ever a brighter day dawn for the race than when God guided Columbus to our shores? Should any people be more happy than we whom the Lord has so richly blessed and so tenderly cared for? These nights about our firesides with our loved ones, surrounded by peace and heaven's blessings of a Christian home and the gospel of Jesus as we think of the horrors of war, famine, pestilence, superstition, heathenism and sin that sweep the hills of Europe and Asia, let us kneel and thank our God for our lot. It required an effort to keep the troubles of these souls from taking the pleasure out of our trip.

CHAPTER V.

AMONG THE TURKS.

The sun was rising from over the cliffs of Asiatic Turkey and flooding the blue waters of the Bosporus with a bright and welcome light as our train came into the station of Constantinople. A strange feeling came to us as we realized where we were. This great old city, capital of the Ottoman Empire and one time capital of the world lay about us, teeming with its more than a million souls. The uncanny and treacherous looking Turks moving in every direction about us, strange, varied and hideous costumes, seas of bobbing red fezs, create an atmosphere heavy with history and many odors, when you enter this land of prejudice, passion and darkness. If you were to travel the world over you would not feel just like you do in Turkey.

We had often heard Constantinople was the most charming city of the earth from a distance but the dirtiest and most repulsive when you were within its gates. We were not there long when we found it even so. As we beheld the city that morning in the golden light of the southern sun, with its houses stretching for a great distance along the front of the beautiful Bosporus whose waves lapped the steps, it looked like a necklace of pearls about a fair lady's neck, but once beyond the border and into the city of the Turks, we felt we were in the garbage can of creation with Judge Taft sitting on the lid.

The Bosporus is a wonderful body of water, very narrow, separating the continents of Europe and Asia, connecting the Black Sea up near Russia with the Sea of Marmora. It is twenty miles long. Along its European shore almost to the Black Sea are rows of beautiful houses intermixed with luxuriant gardens and old towers from the time of Constantine. Within these walls men, women and little children have often paid the price of being Christian with the warm blood of their loyal hearts.

On this shore is the palace of the old Sultan where, with his many wives he lived in splendor and shame, drawing a salary of sixty million dollars a year from the brawn and blood of his ignorant, suffering subjects. Out there in the Bosporus old Abdul Hamid used to sink a wife now and then with a rock tied to her neck like an undesirable cat because he tired of her. He would watch from the porch of his mansion while the boatman took the unfortunate woman out upon the moonlit water. When the old fiend was ready he would raise a light and at that signal the boatman would drop his charge into the water, while the Sultan in his palace, would smilingly go on his Satanic way. The rising of the young Turks banished old Abdul a few years ago. When he left he sold some of his wives to settle a few debts; others he gave as presents to his friends while to his island of exile he carried the four that remained after he had in a fit of jealous rage murdered the youngest and fairest of them at all.

Sixty million dollars a year this old fiend received for the place he held among the rulers of the earth so long. He was the highest paid sovereign of the world; His pay being five million dollars a month, four hundred thousand dollars a day!—nearly three hundred dollars a minute! When the President of the United States received one dollar old Abdul Hamid got six hundred, and then had to give some of his wives to pay his debts. He must not have been wise in his expenditures. But his day is done. On his little island he is waiting the time when his blackened soul will be consigned to the lowest depths of an orthodox hell. The above facts were told us and vouched for by prominent Turkish officials we met.

The Bosporus has made much history along its shores. Many Christian martyrs were faithful unto death beside its waters. Here Xerxes undertook to build a bridge and cross from Asia into Europe on a mission of conquest. The sea became rough and tore his bridge away, whereupon he had the builders killed and ordered the waters lashed for their bad behavior, showing what a fool he was. Here Xenophon crossed on a pontoon bridge with ten thousand men, as many youngsters have tried to translate from that Greek book he wrote, as in sweat and toil they expended more strength than did old Xenophon in doing the deeds they tried to read about. Here Jason came in 1400 B. C., rejoicing with the Golden Fleece.

The Golden Horn is the bay running from the Bosporus and the Sea of Marmora where they meet, back into the city. It gets its name because of its **horn shape, being large at its mouth and curving**

to a point like a horn back into the heart of the city.
The sun shining upon its waters gives it the name
"Golden Horn." Also its name comes because it
is the meeting place of the nations on the highway
of the seas and into its horn-shaped mouth the nations of the earth pour their golden treasures. When
the power of the Turk is broken and civilized
nations get this country it will indeed be the Golden Horn and the greatest harbor of the earth.
A brdge crosses the Golden Horn connecting Stam-
boul, the old section of the city, with the new city.
Over this brdge daily moves the greatest mixture
of mortality the world can show you. Every class
and clan, creed and crowd, color and costume pass
before you. It is interesting to watch as far as
your eyes can see the stream of red fezes with black
tassels mixed in the mass of other things. This
is a toll bridge and yields a tremendous revenue
to the government.

It is impossible to realize the living conditions of
Constantinople. It must be seen to be understood.
The poverty, filth and degradaton is beyond the
telling of tongues. The streets are full of filth.
Thousands of dirty dogs are sleeping on the side-
walks or lazily pursuing their canine way as though
they owned the town. In returning to our hotel
one day we counted ninety-nine dogs in a few blocks,
and as we started in the door the hundredth one
trotted by. These dogs are full of fleas and are
very generous in distributing them. A Turkish official informed us that when the young Turks came
into power, among other reforms they had a dog

Jerusalem from the Mount of Olives. A shepherd and his sheep are seen at the bottom of the picture.

The River Jordan. It was near here that Israel entered the Promised Land and Jesus was baptised.

killing and dispatched thirty thousand canines to the "happy prowling ground" in one day. He also added with a smile that sausage was cheap the next week. There certainly must have been a few dogs in town before the killing time. These dogs belong to nobody. They are looked upon as sacred animals and are reverenced and protected. They are called the Sultan's street cleaners and perhaps to them is due some credit for keeping down some of the filth that might otherwise entirely destroy the people.

The town is full of beggars, dirty and ragged to a degree beyond description. Donkeys, camels and goats are everywhere in sight. The streets are full of venders of every class and kind, calling, crying, moaning out their wares. All these strange weird sounds pouring into your ears in the early morning when you awake make you feel you are surely in a strange land.

One very noticeable thing through all the Turkish realm is the burdens the people bear. Instead of having drays for hauling, the people become the beasts of burden. Men, women and children are seen carrying loads on their heads and backs that it seems impossible to carry, and it seems only exaggeration to tell it. When we landed men carried our suit cases to the hotels. They were big double suit cases and certainly some of the women had theirs full. I could carry mine but a little way. These men strapped seven and eight of these heavy cases on their backs and went several blocks to the hotel with them. Constantly this stream of burden bearers goes by you—men with loads of lumber, rocks, trunks, barrels of vegetables and every conceivable kind of burden; women with loads little lighter; children heavy laden, the stream goes on.

Often did we think of that beautiful verse of the Master's we had told to many troubled hearts, "Come unto me all ye that labor and are heavy laden and I will give you rest." But Jesus has not yet had the chance to lift the burdens from the bodies or the souls of Turkey's millions. It seems strange it has never occurred to them to harness their donkeys and haul these burdens instead of carrying them. As they have done through centuries they go on with pack saddles on their backs and heavier loads on their souls.

One of the most interesting objects to the tourist is the mosque of St. Sophia. It is imposing and beautiful, but its interor decorations are rather gaudy. This building, now the most noted Turkish temple of the city, was a Christian church built by Emperor Justian who cried when it was complete, "O Solomon, I have surpassed thee." In the fifteenth century it was captured by the Turks and turned into a Mohammedan Mosque. A hundred thousand christians fled to this their place of worship for refuge when Mohammed rode triumphant into the city. He charged upon them and many thousand of them were killed. Over their dead bodies he rode his horse into the building and striking his hand-dripping red with the blood of the Christians he had murdered upon the side of the wall, he cried, "There is no God but Allah and

Mohammed is his prophet." For hundreds of years millions of deluded mortals have sent on that cry echoing over their deeds of blood and shame.

We were shown the bloody print of Mohammed's hand upon the wall. We were not supposed to notice the print was so high on the wall that a man would have to sit on the head of a giraffe to reach it and that the hand was no larger than that of a very small child. We were also shown the holy carpet and the prayer rugs which are carried on long and arduous pilgrimages to Mecca, where, by touching the grave of Mohammed they received the magic power to heal and save all who kneel upon them for months following. We also looked upon the precious Mecca stone which fell down from heaven to Mohammed. To touch this stone and rub your finger on any diseased part of your body will surely work a cure. The constant rubbing of a ceaseless stream of superstitious fingers for five hundred years has worn great grooves in the stone.

Many pigeons—sacred birds—were roosting and nesting in the temple. Many of them were very busy tearing up the sacred carpets to get material for their nests. A number of boys sat on the floor crooning out their lessons from the Koran in weird sounds that made a cold shiver steal up your back. Numbers of dirty, ragged Turks moved carpets to different places, unrolled them and fixed them for services we could not understand. In the midst of their work they wrestled, played leap frog and rode about on one another's backs, notwithstanding the place was very sacred and we poor Christian dogs had to wear their holy dirty slippers about the temple while they followed to see that our unhallowed heels touched not the sacred carpets.

Just to see what would happen I quietly slipped my foot from the slipper and went on without it, to be followed post haste by several outraged keepers of the temple who jabbered, sputtered, harangued and spit at me in great excitement, punctuating their deliverances with a multitude of gymnastic exercises as they told me how I had insulted the holy name of Mohammed. I quietly raised my foot for them to tie on another slipper and went on my way, through the midst of temple beggars and men prostrate in prayers, who, with one eye on Allah, kept the other treacherous, gleaming orb fixed on us in a way to make us feel how readily the Turks can mix religion and other things. Thus passed our first visit to a pagan house of worship. The feeling that sweeps down on your soul on such a visit your tongue can't tell. How far away from God religion so often is!

In the Royal Museum we saw many things of interest recently brought to light by British and German excavators. Among them was the skeleton of the king of Tyre (?) with a hole in his head made by the work of the murderous axe; bracelets, breast pins and many other articles of dress and ornament said to be 3,000 years B. C., a beautiful sculptured sarcophagus with many figures of weeping women, no two of them in the same position, an elegant sarcophagus of Alexander the Great. But the most interesting thing was a gold spoon the Sultan always takes with him on his annual pilgrimage to Mecca. As he comes in contact with the masses he is liable to find upon his body some of the multiplied millions of vermin that go with the worshippers. These insects being sacred animals even the Sultan is not allowed to remove them with his hands but must use this gold spoon for the purpose. What the common folks do who cannot afford gold spoons for such work, we were not told. Perhaps the Sultan passes the spoon around or more likely the masses consider a great honor to furnish hospitality to these sacred animals and go their way rejoicing with them. We were not so pious on this score nor did we confine ourselves to gold spoons in seeking relief.

Constantinople has thirty times been destroyed by fire and now it seems to be a perfect fire trap. There she sits full of the heathenism, ignorance, filth and shame—with all the odors of the world meeting in her streets. She occupies the greatest seat on the highway of nations waiting for civilized nations to redeem her people and give them a chance. Who can tell what the future of Constantinople will be when these war clouds roll away?

Some of our party grew poetic and expressed their feelings and impressions in verses. One after another submitted their productions. Some were grave some provoked a smile. I wish I had these poems to give, but none are available. They called on me for a poem. I have a poetic soul, but no poetic tongue or pen and have never been able to get any space with verse, but under the spell of the East I thought I might woo the muses sufficiently to make

some poetry since the others were so successful. So
I gave myself to the task. The result was the following lines, which I dedicated to my friend and
fellow-traveller, Rev. L. T. Williams, because he
longed so much for the things at home, and could
never relish old bread and goat meat.

> O Turkey, land of ease
> With all thy dogs and fleas,
>   Of thee I sing.
> Loud will thy donkeys bray,
> Because they need more hay
> And always in your way,
>   While Turkey's king.

> O Turkey, land of goats,
> (So bare of pigs and shoats)
>   And men so slow.
> I'll soon eat biscuits hot,
> And coffee from my pot,
> With ham I've not forgot
>   For now I go.

> O Turkey 'tis of thee,
> Thou land beside the sea,
>   Of thee I sing.
> Long will this awful glare
> Fall on thy hills so bare
> Of which thy people share,
>   While Turkey's king.

O Turkey, land of death,
Where freedom has no breath,
        To thee I bring.
A feeling of disgust
Because thy souls are thrust
Down in this filth and dust,
        While Turkey's king.

O Turkey, land of doom,
Where children have no room
        To live and sing.
Long will these shadows fall,
And all thy hearts enthrall.
God lift this heathan pall,
        And let Freedom ring.

CHAPTER VI.

THE MORAL AND RELIGIOUS CONDITION OF TURKEY.

(1914)

One of the most prominent points in him is his lack of progress. He is the original stand-patter, opposed to advance of every kind. He is too lazy to go forward, being the most slothful mortal you can find. He has never added anything to the world's constructive life but has destroyed all he could that others had constructed. As John R. Mott has well said, "If the Turk cannot find a desert he will make one." In his restful ease he bitterly resents all interference and delights to stand or rather sit where he has been for centuries. He uses the same implements he has always used, threshing out his wheat by driving his cattle around it, plowing with his same crude plows, carrying his commerce on his head, his back and the back of his donkey, never having looked with favor upon wheel vehicles. He has no factories for he'd rather do all his work with his hands as his fathers did.

He is also the dirtest mortal you can find. Filth is a part of his being. He is too lazy to be clean. To be clean is too much like a Christian dog or a hated Englishman; therefore filth is a virtue. Of course this is not the case with all of them but it is true with many.

And he is a fatalist of the deepest dye. It is ground into his blood and stamped upon his soul. Everything is worked out by an unchanging fate, and it is worse than useless to try to put yourself against it. Things are just as they were intended to be. His hills are full of oil and ore but he digs it not for if Allah had intended it to be on top of the ground it would be there and since it is under the ground Allah intended it to remain there and it would be the grossest insult to him to dig it up. This is the reason he resents every approach of western civilization that would change the old order of things. It is sacrilege to try to change the things fate has fixed.

He is also cursed by superstition. It haunts him, poisons him, possesses him to a degree seldom found anywhere. His religion and all his makeup is tangled with a web of superstition. He wears charms on himself and on his horses to keep off the "evil eye," believing there are people so in league with evil spirits that when they turn their eyes upon you they bring a train of evil with that look. Several times our horses chanced to lose these awful looking beads from their necks and everything had to wait until the lost ones could be found or new ones secured, for it would have been ruin to go on without them. A king would not be more distressed over the loss of the crown than was my driver over the loss of those beads and no king could say as many awful sounding things in the same length of time. They go on long pilgrimages to their holy cities, Jerusalem, Mecca, Modena and Hebron that they may touch the sacred spots and rid themselves of all ills to body and soul as well as secure a passport to Everlasting Blessedness. Rugs and robes are placed on these holy spots and carried back that their touch may impart a magic power and work

many wonders. We saw many of these pilgrims
who had gone through the worst denials and priva-
tions to save means enough to take these long and
arduous journeys and everywhere we went they
were our fellow travelers.

The Turk is absolutely unreliable and dishonest.
Nobody can beat him lying. He seems to prefer a
lie to the truth. They cannot trust one another.
The government has inspectors to such an extent
that everybody seems to be watching everybody
else. The government and the thieves are in league
or rather they are one and the same. If you don't
want the robbers to bother you you can pay the
government for protection and the government will
divide with the thieves. Everybody is open to bribes
and often this is the only passport that will get you
through. We were charged an entrance fee of two
dollars each as we entered Turkey; another sum to
get through the Balkan mountains; another to get
out of Constantinople; a medical fee to enter Alexandria, and a fumigation fee to get out of Beirut.
We would not have objected to paying the last if
they had fumigated themselves, but the rascals took
the fee and fumigated us. You can't trust them.
They will rise from their prayers and kill you if
they get a chance, and they will steal anything from
anybody.

The Mohammedan is on fire with hatred toward
all foreigners, especially Christians. His Bible en-
joins it upon him. His religion excites him to holy
wars to exterminate by the bloodiest methods all
who do not believe as he does. His country has run

with blood in many massacres and if they do not again flood their hills with foreign blood it will be because they fear England and America too much. Their missionary propaganda is one of bloodshed. It was the way their founder won his victories. It is their future hope, and woe to the foreigners who fall into their hands when the Holy War begins.

They are cruel and heartless despots to their own people. The burdens their state and church put on them is hard to realize. The government sells the tax-gathering privilege to the highest bidder. He pays the government whatever is agreed upon and grinds out of the people in the district he covers whatever he chooses, the people having no redress whatever. Often the people have to pay over fifty per cent. of what they make for tax. One day our train stopped and we saw a man with a flock of sheep and goats, about a dozen in all, about two hundred yards from the track. The trainmen who were officers of the law, the government owning the railroads, left the train and had an argument with the shepherd. They took the finest lamb from the flock and brought him bleating to the train. We learned from our guide that they had a law that whenever a shepherd let his flock get in a certain distance from the train (close enough for one of the rascals to steal a sheep I suppose) they took a lamb as a fine. This poor man was unable to pay the price of two mejidos ($1.60) to redeem his lamb and the trainmen carried it away for their dinner. This was another of their many methods of robbery. The fruit trees have been taxed until large sections once rich with fruitage are desolate. It is cheaper to have no trees at all than face the unmerciful tax of Turkey and the trees are cut down.

A very marked trait of the Mohammedan character is his attitude toward women. He professes great chivalry. He has veiled the faces of his women. Not even her own household can see her face. He has private quarters for the women of his house even though he lives in poor tents. And when she leaves her shoes at the tent door as a sign that she occupies her quarters, no man, no matter how near, by family ties, can go beyond those shoes. He has been given great credit for the way he honors women because of these things, but he deserves no credit at all. He has the most degraded opinion of women. His bible teaches him she has no soul, but is merely a piece of property below par with his sheep or his donkey. His religion allows him to trade her for anything he chooses when he tires of her, and his bible tells him when she does not please him to take her to the tent where the cattle stay, the place where she belongs, and beat her until he is satisfied.

This bible also tells him his allotted number of wives is four, but if he really desires more "God is merciful and kind." When a girl baby is born into a home he goes into a protracted spell of mourning; his friends stop speaking to him and often he divorces his wife or sells her, all because she has become the mother of a cursed girl instead of a boy. A poor little girl is born to a life that is a curse. We saw little girls from four (not fourteen) to twelve working in the brass factory hammering out with their little hands the fine brass ornaments we prize so highly. We saw girls hardly grown building the new Turkish railroad under guard of armed soldiers. We saw hundreds of girls and women carrying heavy pitchers of several gallons, each full of water, on their heads, many miles through the awful Syrian sun. Often we saw women walking, carrying children or other heavy burdens on long journeys, while their gallant husbands rode beside them.

What does the leaving the slippers at the tent door and the veiling of the face amount to in the face of these things? Poor woman! She is a brute and a beast of burden. She looks old and haggard before she is hardly grown. What can a people amount to who treat their women—the instruments of the best and the purest in the human race— that way? And after all, as much as Christ has done for men, how much more has He done for women! We feel this more in foreign lands than in our own. Our religion and civilization is the only one the world has known that has raised women to the place where she belongs.

The Turk is the most religious person on the earth and yet the most non religious. He prays five times a day and yet he does not pray at all. In Constantinople alone he has five hundred and fifty mosques or churches, with many others scattered over his vast domains. Five times a day the priest mounts the stairs to the minaret or belfry, comes out of a little door upon a little porch that extends all around the tower and sends out upon the world his weird call to prayer. He lifts up his voice in this call four times, each time standing with his face toward the four points of the compass. This is perhaps the most doleful sound that falls on the ear of the traveler in any land. At the sound the Mohammedan stops whatever he is doing and prostrates himself in prayer, first turning his face toward Mecca, his most holy city. He carefully spreads his rug, robe or kerchief upon the ground or floor wherever he is. Sometimes he is hindered for lack of room. He can't go through his performances very well in crowded quarters and often if he is on a train at the hour of prayer he will wait until the train reaches the next station and get on the ground beside the train where with one eye open on the conductor and the other closed on Allah, he prays. It takes him a long time to go through his prayer, and the different actions, motions, postures and prostrations he goes through would run Father O'Hooligan a close race when he grinds out pontifical mass over the incensed corpse of an arch bishop. One reason the Turk takes so much time to his prayers is because it gives his lazy nature a chance five times a day to stop whatever he is doing and loll out his sleepy devotions. He does not seem to say anything, it is all motions and at times he seems to be asleep. If you are near he watches you with one treacherous eye while he keeps the other closed to the world and when he finishes his prayers you better keep both eyes on him.

It is hard to realize how burdened the people are. There are practically no schools and the people live in an ignorance and degradation that is appalling. They haven't any home life and many of them have no homes. They live in the fields until winter comes and crowd in mud huts, dens in the ground or anywhere they can, like rats. Many of them do not get enough out of life to call it living. They can often be seen going to the shops with coins that look like tobacco tags they have begged from the travelers, stolen, worked for or gotten any way they can. Some of these coins are worth as little as one-tenth of a cent. They will pay one or two of these for a little piece of dirty bread, many months old sometimes, and a handful of pumpkin or melon seed and upon this make their meal.

Some one asks why do they not rebel and overthrow their accursed government? You might as well ask why does not a team of mules overloaded and abused, rebel against their master and set up a new government. What can people so completely crushed do against the government that oppresses them? They haven't strength, brain or spirit to do anything.

Thus southern Europe, much of it Asia, upper Africa, Palestine and the vast desert lands of Arabia, have for centuries been under the power of the Turk. He holds the most strategic part of the earth, unequalled in fertility, unbounded in commercial possibilty, great in historic value, and he curses it, while the civilized nations, desiring to carve the Turkey but in their jealous hunger for the biggest piece can not determine who should wield the knife. But the day of the Turk is nearly done. His crescent that has shone so long over this great part of the world in places rich and holy, is waning in the west. Faster and shorter grows the gasping breath of the sick man. Soon it will be hushed; he will be buried in the graveyard of Oblivion and upon his grave a better civilization will spring to bless the land he cursed so long.

In simple justice it should be said the Turk has one good trait. He will not drink strong drink. It is against his religion and his law. Many times we sat with him at meals in the midst of clinking glasses and flowing wine, but not once did we see him touch it.

One of the wonders of the human race is how an ignorant camel driver like Mohammed could arise with a perverted form of the Christian religion, mixed with the worse things of paganism, and gather about him such a powerful dominion that has blocked the march of civilization and held sway in a large part of the world for centuries until it includes one-seventh of the people of the earth.

Street Scene in Bethlehem.

The 1921 Party on a Donkey ride around the Walls of Jerusalem. George Jallouk, the dragoman, is standing in front. The author is on a white donkey (kings always ride white donkeys) on the extreme right. The black gentleman in waiting is Ahmed Ben Hassen, the author's donkey boy.

CHAPTER VII.

SOME INCIDENTS OF THE SECOND TOUR.

The best way to learn folks is to live with them. Traveling with them is the same thing as long as it lasts. When folks get down on the job of the pilgrim's path, they show their good and bad points better than when they ride their Supers out to hear the Elder, all dressed in their dandy duds. It is interesting to watch them getting acquainted. They are much like animals. When new dogs come into a kennel or new chickens in a yard everything halts until they finish acquaintance. It is a delicate dangerous time. If the strangers can be carefully guided over the rocks until they really know and understand one another, there will be no better friends, but one slip will precipitate a fight that will fill the kennel with fur, and the yard with feathers. When two strange dogs stand staring each other in the eye with tails erect and muscles rigid, you may hit one of them with a pebble and produce a conflict that will be heard in the next township. Tourists are the same way. Everything must halt until they have studied eccentricities, peculiarities, defects and short comings and finished talking about themselves and their folks. If while this is in progress, the party gets on the boat and seasickness comes the act of becoming acquainted is greatly hastened. There is nothing that establishes such a close point of contact and intimate acquaintance as to become sea sick together. When two strangers go through that they are friends forever after.

Rudyard Kipling says there is a rocky hill on the Road of Matrimony not far from the marriage altar. It is the time when two strangers must learn to fit into each others lives. Most divorce wrecks come then. If they can successfully pass this crisis, they nearly always live happily ever after. The lot of the traveler is somewhat akin to this.

Out of our party of sixteen, we had three lady bachelors, four men bachelors, two widowers and seven preachers. There is no "spoilt baby" in the class with a bachelor preacher, who has long had kind sisters studying all his whims and satisfying his every notion. He has had everybody to give in for him and he is never required to give in for others. He needs a bit of married life that meets him at the door and demands he remove his shoes before he comes in, and he should be required to spend a whole day shopping with a "lady boss" paying bills and carrying bundles, as he is told to do. Then he needs to have *her* sit up in the presence of two former school girl friends and review his peculiarities ala matrimony.

But back to the track—We met in New York two days before sailing to get all red tape trimmings on and meet our fellow pilgrims. Of course, you are interested in your room mate, will he snore on the Ford style or as per the saw mill route? To which one of the fifty-seven variety of assorted nuts will he belong? What kind of a hobby will he ride? Will he be a germ lunny? Or will he

have one young son at home who says smart things?
(Perish the thought). Will he loll in the shade of
his family tree, and chew the rag of his pedigree?
And worst of all, will he—Oh will he think he knows
some foreign language and try to use it on the
defenceless foreigners when he gets there?

My room mate was Rev. E. R. Welch, now pastor
of Chestnut Ave. Methodist Church, Asheville. And
here and now, let me say I tell tales only on folks
I like and love. The others I let coolly alone. I
have been offered $25.00 not to tell all I know on
Welch and even more to keep quiet on Williams,
but money can't bribe me. They are hereby permitted, empowered and authorized to release any
and all things they can remember discover or in-
vent on me, but I will not be bribed, blackmailed,
begged or entreated to keep quiet about them.

Welch is a distinguished scholar and preacher.
He has an inquiring mind and a genius for dis-
covery. Human interest and human nature run
strong in his make up, and he is ever hunting a
point of contact. He holds first International Prize
for gathering a wider assortment of curios than
any man whoever held a passport in his hand. His
collection ranged from a left hind foot of a graveyard rabbit killed by a wild Arab in the land of
Moab to the rib of a departed Monk, who went to
purgatory from the banks of the Tiber. He brought
back a jug of Jordan water, which somebody sat
on and squashed. I shall never, oh Gertrude! never
forget the night in the London hotel when he discovered that his jug was busted. I see him now

picking out 3748 pieces of glass from his embryonic museum and spreading his things over the room to dry (His case was waterproof and the water soaked in the things instead of running out). The Smithsonian Institute didn't have much on that room when his things were spread out. He had a cat fish head from the River Jordan, rocks from Lebanon, Switzerland and France, pebbles from the dead sea, sand from Sudan, a snake skin from Syria, a goat ear from Egypt and time would fail me to speak of pictures, scarfs, beads and many things not in the dictionary, the custom men draw on you in New York. If I had the money, I would have paid Welch $1,000. for the pure joy of watching the custom men nose in his conglomeration of curios.

My room mate is the first man to install a radio machine in his pulpit so he can preach to everybody absent as well as present. Perhaps before the publishers can raise the money to get this book off the press, he will have completed the radio mirrow by which the folks can also see him as he preaches, even tho they be a thousand miles away. I have been told he rubbed the Moab rabbit foot on Bishop Darlington and got his present appointment, and that the Bishop has not been the same man since.

He was also a pollyglot linquist. He never saw a soul he couldn't talk to in his native tongue. He made himself so widely known that he will be receiving foreign callers of the friends he made for the next ten years. We will hear from him some more as these pages run on.

We sailed on the Asia of the Faber Line. From New York to the other side of the Atlantic and across the Mediterranean we went on that boat, which was our home for three full weeks. It was glorious but it was hard on Hill billies who lived on land and not on the sea. Leaving New York, we steamed to Providence. Some policemen came on board and bribed the stewards to sell them some liquor. I got the number of their caps and if I am "pinched" in Providence, I shall "squeel on these cops.

One of the finest gentlemen among us was Rev. A. L. Stanford, pastor of one of the greatest churches in North Carolina. The church runs over Sundays and standing room is in demand. He has been a great success as an Evangelist and caused many to flee from the wrath to come and get ready for changing worlds. Imagine my surprise therefore when I went in his room and found stretched upon the floor, one of these water proof suits that looked like the skin of a sea demon. The agent was painting in glorious colors its excellence when the ship goes down. You spread it out so your right foot enters A, your left B, your right arm is put through C and then with your left hand you pull cord 4, and clamp Z. Then you button it up and as the boat sinks, you float out. No water can enter it and it can't sink. He rented it for $15.00 and carried it for 15,000 miles over desert sand and rocky wastes, from train to train and the last I saw of him in New York, he was taking it back to the office of the firm who owns it.

He asked me what I thought of it and I told him it was fine if he could induce the captain to keep the boat from sinking long enough for him to find a good place to read his instructions and put it on properly. Then when he was floating out, he would have to put up a sign to keep sharks and whales from biting off his foot and letting in water enough to sink him. But another thing that bothered me was he always demanded eggs boiled just three minutes, no more and no less and coffee a certain temperature. I feared he would have trouble getting served this way out there.

But another thing troubled me more. In this age even common sinners cry "woman and children first." It made me sad to think of the boat going down with all the women and children sinking and a bachelor Methodist preacher getting into a contraption like this and floating out to safety. He could not take any lady with him. Perhaps when the hour came, he would have placed a certain lady snugly in this contraption and followed her the best he could. But he proved himself a first class traveler and brought more home than many others do.

It is a sad and solemn time when the boat sails out. I went to the office for my mail as she settled down to her speed and found a pile of mail that friends had sent to me to the steamer. I had thirty-five letters, cards and telegrams and two boxes of chocolate candy from two young ladies. Among these messages a friend sent this little poem, which helped me all along the way—

MY STAFF.

I have a staff to prop my way
As I plod onward thru the day
And if by stormy paths I fare,
I lean on it—the staff of prayer.

And so I must toil and scale
The heights that frown above the vale
It aids my longing foot steps there
It buoys my heart—the staff of prayer.

It is my comrade and my friend
And so shall be unto the end
Of every mortal toil and care,
Staff of my soul, the staff of prayer.

CHAPTER VIII.

For several days, we had a rough voyage and our folks began to look puny. Their actions were not all that could be desired. As it grew worse, and one by one they looked pale and sick and sad, my sympathy turned to them. They were a sad and hopeless lot of tourists, lolling about with faces pale, eyes watering and lips trembling. But I couldn't do anything for them. I was like a woman who went to the ship doctor saying, "Doctor, please do something for my husband." "Madam" said the sea dog, "just let him alone, he will do something for himself presently."

I shall ever remember a bridle couple. The bride looked so pale, pathetic and sick; she seemed to be almost ready to give up the grip on life. She leaned her throbbing head on the groom's shoulder, turned her sick watery eyes toward his and in a feeble voice said,

"Sugar pie, do you really love your honey lump?" He nodded his aching head, and answered in the affirmative while a hot fluid filled his mouth. She grew quiet a moment and then turning toward him with a sicker look than before said,

"Honey I thought that would make me feel better but it didn't."

While they were at their worst, I penned the following lines, which I read to them when they grew strong enough. The poetic merit is not much, but the description is accurate.

I took a trip one time across the briny deep
For of the big old world, I longed to have a peep.
I had my bag and baggage and a passport in my
    hand,
As I turned my back that day upon my native land.
I sure was feeling bully as I stood upon the deck,
And saw the tug boat take that steamer by the neck
My face was looking outward to lands that lie afar
As I dreamed of scenes resplendent beneath the East-
    ern Star.

She turned her prow outward toward the rising sun
And I pranced upon that deck, ready to have some
    fun.
But the sea was getting angry, and the billows roll-
    ing high
And my nogging it was aching as the waves went
    dashing by.
My stomach felt just like the land of the Russian
    Red,
And it seemed to me ten demons were dancing in
    my head.

The sky was looking awful and the world was turn-
    ing round,
The sea looked like perdition and the winds made
    fiendish sound
Then a slimy, creeping serpent crawled right up
    into my throat,
And I knew right then the ocean would surely get
    my goat.

My mouth was tasting bitter with a devilish awful
    taste
As I took me to my stateroom in the greatest pos-
    sible haste.
Then—I longed for *tera firma* with a sad, pa-
    thetic wish
As I hung upon the railing—looking at the fish.

It is interesting to study the characters on board.
Here are two old Jews—man and wife—journeying
back to Jerusalem in their old age to stand on holy
ground and let their dust mingle with the soil of
the Holy City when their hearts stand still. Every
day they spend much time reading their Hebrew
Bible and praying to the God of Israel. They are
very attentive to each other. Both are old and not
long for earth's Pilgrim Path. What is more pathetic than devout Jews of God's chosen race, who
will not accept God's Saviour?

Here are two sweet and bright little Portugese
girls, who were born in America, eleven and thirteen. Their mother is dead and an aunt is taking
them to Lisbon to put them in a convent. They are
nice and full of life. We talked with them a great
deal. What a strange idea of religion to take children like these and confine them to gloomy prisons!

There are many of the better class of Syrians returning to their native land. Some have been in
America several years and with their usual thrift
and economy, have saved money to take home for
investments. Some are going back to look for loved
ones, they have not seen or heard from since the

war. They are thoroughly Americanized. Here is one from Macon, Ga. He has two little tots by the name of Joe Brown Maroon and Hoke Smith Maroon, showing that he caught the spirit of Georgia politics and honored two of that State's Governors. He begged us to go home with him to the Lebanons and visit him for several days. He meant it and would have given us all styles of Eastern hospitality.

NADIA ABRAHAM.

No character on board was more charming to me than Abraham. One day with a cheery smile, a soft voice and a gleam of his brown kindly eye, he bade me "good morning." I was much with him after that and the more I saw him, the more the charm of his heroic soul uplifted me. Gradually I got his story from him. His people were christians in Mesopotamia. His good mother and father died a few years ago and he and his brother went to America, leaving two brothers and two sisters behind them. One brother, who was a missionary, was slaughtered by the Turks. The other brother, also a minister, remained at his post, but had to send his family to Egypt for safety. He has not been able to see them for years.

Abraham saved his money and was in the steerage of this boat, sleeping in a place no better than a stable and eating food hardly fit for pigs, to save his money to send himself and nephew to school, while preparing for the ministry. A letter from him a few days ago, says he is in the University in

Beyrout. He loved a sweet Armenian lass and one day, she was to be his but when the brutal Turks drove the women and children out like cattle on the long road of deportation to death and horrors far worse, they laid rough hands on Abraham's sweetheart and he has never heard from her since.

He took us thru the steerage, and we held services for the folks. It was a strange service on the deck of the boat as we sailed right on into the rising sun. I preached once and the other preachers helped. Abraham acted as interpreter. At the conclusion, a Mohammedan, a Greek Catholic and a Roman Catholic also took part, and Abraham said they were speaking words of appreciation for our interest in them and for the messages we brought as well as paying high tribute to the ideals and christianity of America.

When I reached Egypt, a handsome and courteous young man called for me one night at the hotel. He was Abraham's nephew. He had been advised of our coming and was there to offer his services as a guide. He also brought invitations from his mother for us to visit their home and take tea. Rev. C. M. Pickens and myself went. As we received their christian hospitality and gracious manners, we felt we were in the presence of God's noblemen. I have not met finer or more heroic lads than Abraham and this boy Gilbert. I wish some mail would bring me money to help them in school. What a great investment!

THE SINGING SYRIAN.

He is singing his song tonight—weird, trembly, soft, quivering, like Orientals sing. The moon runs low and the breeze of the Mediterranean is soft and dreamy, while the bright stars shine on us. There he stands, up toward the prow where he sleeps on deck at night. He pours from his lips—his soulful song. I was taking a stroll on deck with Abraham before I slept and I paused to ask what song this youth was singing. His song was not a lamentable wail of Jeremiah or an outward howl of inward pain. His food was the kind poor dogs—not rich dogs eat—but he was glad to get it. His bed was blanket on the hard deck but he was happy while some in the First Class with the best they could buy, were growling all the time.

I wasn't much struck on his music but it was better than I have heard choirs deliver with the anthem wiggle wobble and the tenor toe dance as they do the chromatic scale like a monkey on a ladder. But I wanted to know the song he sang. It was, of course,—I might have known—a love song. He was nearing his native hills and his heart was throbbing. He was singing to his Syrian lassie up near the Lebanon cedars as the boat, plowing thru the blue waters, brought him nearer home. He shut his eyes and sang and dreamed. What was a hard bed and harder bread to him when his soul was sailing in Loveland and Dreamland? Let him sing. If I had known the tune, I would have joined in.

JOE JABER, THE DRUSE.

He is a bright and inteligent son of the Hauran hills where Abraham lived. He is going home after nine years to see the country and find his mother. His people are Druses—a peculiar faith with a mixture of christianity and some heathen religion, but Joe is a christian. He is thoroughly American and had great admiration for our country.

He begged me to go home with him and be "A religion man" to his people. If I would live with them, they would take me as one of their tribe and all my wants would be supplied. Hospitality rules them. They do not sell to one another. All is gifts. I am sure I would have found it even so. Then Joe said with his charming broken speech.

"Me no like our religion man. He tells us God hates other people, and we must hate them. But me like American religion man. He tells us God is love and we must love one another. Me go to church in Ohio. Religion man tell people to give money to send food and clothes and doll babies to little girls in Syria. American girls have these but ours not. I cry and say that the religion man for me."

What a telling beautiful tribute! And what a fine example of a Macedonian call! I left Joe in Beyrout but one night he walked in the hotel at Damascus. He had found us and we received him as a guest of honor. He gave Bro. Welch and myself each a beautiful Damascus brass vase for our wives. He had a curious looking Kimona clad dignitary with him, who looked like he might be a

Druse Presiding Elder, and as he and Joe departed for the Hauron, I had a lingering suspicion there might be a wedding brewing. Oh! how I wish I could have been best man.

EATING—THE EUROPEAN PLAN.

There are three kinds of eating—The American plan, which is pay for it before you get it; European, pay for it both before and after you get it; The Ethiopian, get it any way you can. All of them have merits and demerits.

It is not polite to kick about food away from home. It is a sure sign we haven't much at home and then it accompishes nothing but hurts your toes like most kicking. European fare on the whole is good. If there was some way to eliminate 97½ percent of the style and take the starch out of the Bourbons and Dukes who are called waiters, it would help. The biggest trouble is, you get no breakfast save a cup of coffee and a hard roll, and at luncheon and dinner, it takes three hours to eat the ceremony and the food. They have a mania for changing plates and washing dishes. They will lug in plates big enough for a roast turkey and implements sufficient for a barbecue and all the food that comes with that course, will be a piece of cheese as big as a domino with a smell as big as abattoir. Macaroni herbs and long tail coats are much in evidence. There are fifty-seven variety of cheese. Some are dead and some very much alive. There is one kind that is said to be confined in an air tight iron cage between meals and tied on the table at meal time. To like it is a cultivated taste but you are liable to lose all your friends and all respect for yourself during the process of cultivation. It is best to use a gas mask when you attack it.

It is said no waiter is admitted to the waiter's union until he can stand in one postion for seven minutes without showing signs of intelligence. And the chief waiter—Oh boy, he has more dignity than the Arch Bishop of Cranberry and the Duke of Spaghetti combined. I am writing particularly of Italy.

An illustration. In one city, we saw the head waiter at night, and told him we would breakfast at 7, and would like so many cups of coffee and so many of tea. When we entered the dining room, they looked at us as much surprised as if we were pre-historic animals. They all stood stiff at attention with an air that we were intruders not welcomed. We sat down and they retired in orderly form. After a conference, the head waiter advanced, bowed stiffly and asked our business. We told him we wanted breakfast, which consisted only of a certain number of cups of coffee and tea with bread and butter which was ordered the night before. He went to the kitchen and was gone long enough to parch coffee and brew tea. When at last he returned from his vacation, some one asked him for a scrambled egg. He said they were extra and they did not know how to scramble them. He was ordered to bring three boiled eggs. Then all of them stopped to figure the cost of three boiled eggs, made

JERICO - Fontaine d'Elisée.
Elisas's fountain.
Elisaquelle.

Elisas' Fountain.

Our Party in the Garden of Gethsemene.

out the bill and presented it before the egg was boiled while all the others waited. Then someone called for a drink of water. This waiter reported the breach of manners to the chief, who advanced like a cardinal and asked what the confusion was about. He went back to the kitchen, was gone four minutes and returned with a menu with fifty-seven variety of strong drink. We begged, we lost patience but never got water that morning. They cannot understand why folks want water.

In Belgium, I went all day under a burning sun unable to get a drink of water. I went to a lass in front of a home and asked of her a cup of water. She offered me whiskey, wine, beer, milk, tea. When I refused and asked water, she threw back her head, gave a peculiar laugh and said, "Water"? "No water."

This Italian hotel is one of the finest in all Europe as is proven by the fact that the Carusoes were there when we were and Lady Astor was expected the next week. Perhaps this is why they were going so strong on stiff stuff and then perhaps we Democratic Americans appeared so green and lacking in the exalted atmosphere of peers and nobles, that we just shocked them beyond recovery. They were keen, however, after tips and I handed out this one complimentary from the party.

Here's to the waiters of the Palace Hotel
With their long tail coats, they cut quite a swell.
Like dukes and nuts and Royal rakes,
They look you over while maccaroni bakes.

They stand at the table three times a day
With their long tail duds getting in the way
You may be hungry and want a piece of bread,
But no such idea ever enters his head.

You long for water and ask for a drink,
He looks at you blank, unable to think.
He has booze and beer, and all kinds of wine
But never heard of water when folks come to dine.

He stands like a shadow of a ghostly witch
With never a move, save a coat tail switch,
This wonderful Lord of this beautifull Bay,
The tourists must face when they dine each day.

You get some coffee, but cold and strong
After you have waited and waited long.
You can't drink with your fingers and ask for a
    spoon
He looks at you queer, like he thinks you a loon.

They are waiters because they wait and they wait,
And you wait, and you wait and you wait and
    you wait,
As you sit at the table by the beautiful Bay
And beg for your rations three times a day.

There is no auger, no matter the bore,
That could put in an idea not there before.
Boob McNutt is a star of the first magnitude
Compared to you in your dress prelude.

I know what you ask with your speechless lips,
Your only thought is thinking of tips,
And there is one good tip I long to bestow
On you knights of the soup bowl before I go.

But all hotels and all service of our tour was not like this. Service in Switzerland, France and especially in England far surpassed this. But to me the service and the food was enjoyed far more in Palestine and Egypt than in these other countries. The hotel proprietors were more cordial and the waiters more human and considerate. From the time we landed in Syria until we closed the journey of this section and embarked in Egypt, I had no fault to find with our food and our service. They too believe in ceremony, courses and dish washing but they are not as stiff and dehumanized as some other European public servants.

The food and service this year, was far better than in 1914, due to western notions that reached them during the war as well as to the fact that they have long been without tourists and are glad to see them. As far as you see in the markets and hotels, the war has done little hurt to things. Food is high but native products everywhere are cheaper than at home. American products are high of course.

A great ghost that haunts the tourist is the vicious tipping system. And yet I must register my experience in this matter was not as disagreeable beyond the ocean as in New York. I was threatened cursed and ridiculed at the pier there for not delivering heavy tips after I had paid all that was agreed upon for transportation and this by the man with whom I dealt. He did not get it. Now all your regular tipping is provided for by an arrangement that always adds 10 per cent. to your bill for tips. But even then, there is enough tipping demanded to make it interesting. This does not include the steamer service for then some require so much more attention than others, that it is best to leave this with the individual.

The stewards and servants are to be pitied. They receive small pay and have a hard time and we found them appreciative and satisfied with a every little sum. I must again say that Italy did not measure up to the others in these matters.

CHAPTER IX.

SOME OTHER INCIDENTS—MY LOST CHEESE.

I own up to a lot of natural and unnatural depravity. Like most people, I admit some low and depraved tastes. One of these is a strong liking for all the cheeses of the Old World. The greater claim that cheese can make to antiquity and the dark ages, the better I like it. I have no patience with over fastidious folk, who refuse to sit at a table with a cake of Limberger after its whiskers are gray or frown on Comembert and Roqueford because of the streaks of yellow and green running through them.

A friend in Jerusalem, knowing my taste in this direction, did a gallant and courteous thing. He brought me a ten pound cake of his home made cheese that was old enough to talk. In fact that was what it was doing. It was strong enough to force Henry Cabbot Lodge out of the Senate and put the quietus on George Harvey. He put this cheese in a strong metal bucket, sealed it so it would be air tight, then placed it in a strong basket and tied it with a rope. When he gave it to me. I heard a sloshing noise and he informed me as near as I could understand that this was the embalming fluid to "keep" it. But it didn't keep it. Later on, I had occasion to remember his caution, not to let any air get in it or any of the odor get out.

I carried the basket from Jerusalem down to Egypt, via Beersheba and Gaza. I guarded it like it was a precious treasure, and often dreamed of supping coffee as I ate it at my home far away. When we reached Kantara, the Egyptian border on the Suez, we had to go thru the Customs House. That is always fun and it was more so this time for the officer was a typical Englishman of the Duke of Lancaster pattern with up curled mustache like the Earle of Essex wears. He couldn't see a joke if you would slap him in the face with it. He examined all of us as we passed and when my peculiar shaped basket, tied with a rope passed in full review under his official eye, he asked in a voice like it came from the tower of London,

"What ave you in ere? Hany hexplosives or hintoxicants?"

"Yes sir!" I meekly replied, "Both."

"Let me 'ave hit."

I passed it to him and he examined it, thumping the basket. He then asked me again what it was. I told him that it was Arabic Cheese. He took one step backward and motioned me forward without a word. As I moved on, I thought how well I could smuggle in a million dollars worth of diamonds by putting them in a bucket of cheese.

I carried my basket two thousand miles up to Milan, Italy, where the present Pope was at that time Presiding Elder. As I slept, I had it by my bed and as I toured on, it went by my side. I did not let my fellow travelers know what it was, for touching this cheese, people are divided into two classes, those who like it and those who do not. And the feeling is very intense, conviction strong and lines of division marked. I didn't want any division or argument in the party. Rev. E. R. Welch did know but he was better to me than I would have been to him in not telling it.

But at Milan, my cheese came to grief, almost disrupted the party and was in a fair way of raising international questions that could not have been settled at the Hague Conference. Smaller things than that, have caused wars.

The waiters at the Milan hotel were typical spiked tailed, dining room dudes. They stood about like the statute of Lord Nelson in Trafalger Square. Dignity stood out like horns on their faces. It was impossible to get one to see or do anything out of the routine. It was beyond all their ken to understand how anyone would want a drink of water when he could get Milan Gin. They stood, stared and thought but most of it was just standing and staring. A craving passion for vengeance seized me and I wanted to do something to them that would shock them. I am sure I did it. I am only sorry I was not there to see what they did when it began to dawn on them there was something rotten in Denmark and Milan.

As we started for the train, I discovered my cheese box was leaking, and I have already said, air must not get to it. I think some enemy did a dirty deed and punctured the bucket while I slept. I have offered $100.00, for his capture and if I find him, I am sure when the Bishop calls my name and asks, "Is there anything against him," my Presiding Elder will arise and answer, "There is."

I well knew this cheese would not be tolerated in a semi-civilized country twelve hours after it got out of that bucket. I had to do something and do it quick. If necessity is the mother of invention, the old lady mothered me. While the Dukes of Macaroni were rubbing their palms for tips, I stole back into a dark pantry room deposited my leaking cheese, covered it with some bags and hurried for the waiting carriages.

I grieved over my lost cheese but the loss was somewhat lightened when I tried to picture the scene at that hotel as the odors from that pantry floated out on the breezes of sunny Italia, and smote these dignified dukes in the face. I wonder—Oh I wonder—what that head waiter said, what he did and how he jesticulated? I wonder what the tourists thought. Perhaps the health officers and the police came in to investigate. I have almost become reconciled to the loss in drawing this picture. And as I have thought it over, I decided perhaps no one punctured the can.

Perhaps it just stunk the bottom out of the basket.

CHEESE A LA TURK.

I shall never forget the time and place when I was introduced to real Turkish cheese. It was far in the interior of the Old World. The morning was very early and sleep had been poor and short. Many nerve racking things had brought us to the point where it would be hard to live with our in-laws and out-laws. A yellow streak was running through our constitution and by laws and our mouths had a taste like we had been eating mud.

A spiked tail coat worn by the Knight of the hash bowl sat me down in a corner of the room and went off as stiff as if he had a golf stick down his back with his nose pointing toward Greenwich. He brought in an English lady and sat her at my table. She had her husband with her. She seemed to take him wherever she went. The Duke then went off and remained long enough to make several pastoral calls for in these hotels, they serve you while you wait. He returned with a box of real Turkish cheese. I had never met it before nor have I met it since. It has overtaken me a few times but not met me. But unlike some other folks I have met, I have not forgotten it. It had a pointed and pungent impression on me. It is served as an appetizer before breakfast. It also cuts down food consumption among tourists and adds to the savings of the hotel proprietor.

When he opened the coffin, I was sorry he didn't have the burial without it. The lady put her handkerchief to her nose and told her husband to get some fresh air. Like all well raised husbands, he obeys his wife and he hurries off to get some. I knew he would not find any for they do not have it in that part of the world. As he returned without it, I took the cheese box and dipping out a big spoonful placed it in my plate. The lady looked sicker than ever and feebly asked,

"What are you going to do with it?"

"Eat it Madam," I replied, "Do you think I am going to wear it on my coat for a bouquet?" When

I finished, she said in a faltering voice, "How does it taste?"

"Just like it smells Madam," I answered, "Will you have some?"

Then I made the following little speech to my comrades. "You folks do not seem to realize where you are. We enter Turkey presently. It is the most unsanitary country in the world. The air is literally laden with germs of deadly disease. Bubonic Plague and Yellow Fever lade the air and germs of Small Pox and Typhus run rampant everywhere. The only thing that Science has ever discovered that can cope with the deadly germs of the many maladies is this cheese. Therefore the Government requires you to eat it. If you have its odor on your breath and come in contact with an epidemic of plague or fever, the germs break their necks falling over one another getting out of the way and appendictis and hook worm can't turn a peg when you are trying to digest this stuff." When I finished my eloquent speech, she said if that was the case to pass it over and she would try some of it but when she got a close whiff she pushed it back saying almost in tears, "I will catch anything before I will eat that stuff."

THE PRISONER OF PIREUS.

As our boat stood in the harbor of Athens, we noted two boats loaded with prisoners from the Turkish army. Greece and Turkey were then at war and the battle was raging. The boats were not far from ours and some of our Syrian friends conversed with some of the prisoners. Several gave their names and homes and begged us to notify their families they were still alive if we reached Syria. Some of them had not communicated with their loved ones for over five years. Our hearts were moved for these poor fellows and we longed to help them. What horrors they must have suffered forced against their will into the Turkish army with its awful life, as well as a prison ship that was little better. We heard a splash in the water and strokes of a swimmer. One of them unable to resist the temptation to try to reach our boat that was sailing to his home and loved ones, had leaped into the water and was swimming toward us. Some of his fellow countrymen let down a rope and after hauling him in placed him in the hold of the ship. But his liberty was short for an officer discovering his escape came on our boat and carried him back to prison. We tried to start a move that would give them their liberty and hope it was not long until they walked again their native hills and mingled with their loved ones.

SNAP SHOTS ON THE BOAT.

The return trip on the Rochembeau was full of interest. She is one of the most popular boats afloat and all her rooms were full. They came from every class and style, from Francisson monks to professors, who believed their fathers were monkeys. We had French girls coming to America to enter school, bent on bringing French culture of the smoking, drinking variety and also a head of the department of French in Blank University, who was returning from a vacation in France. He explained his conduct by saying he had a very trying year and was relaxing, and the old boy was well up on the French style of relaxation.

The sea is ugly and the storm is raging, so we must go inside. We will keep our minds off of other troubles by studying the passengers. We are in the writing room. It is full of folks writing and reading. Every morning a musician, who thinks folks are charmed with his gas and jazz, takes the stool at the piano, presses the accelerator and opens wide the exhaust pipe. It was horrible. He went from one side of the key board to the other with his gyrations, his coat tail keeping time to gymnastic steps over the chromatic scale. He did it like a leghorn rooster, scratching in straw. There would have been no difficulty in organizing a mob to throw him overboard and make fish food out of him. We just lacked a leader.

Early one morning while I was waiting for the Monk Presiding Elder to come into the room to hold quarterly conference, which he did at 6:30, I found myself alone. I had time for meditation and action and I did both. I filled the piano with paper, carefully packing all the keys back in the internals of the machine. At the appointed time the performer bore down upon us with music rolls, port folios, and a silly self conscious look of self exaltation. He bowed and got ready. He screwed the stool to the proper pose, pulled up his trousers, fixed his coat, winked his eyes and slammed his fingers down on the keys, hoping to make a noise that would drown a thunder storm. But instead, he heard only a dull and heavy thud. Again and again he tried, raising all the keys, opening the throttle, turning on the magnetor and everything. As he thumped, he turned his head sideways and listened like he was listening for his master's voice. He then opened the machine and spent about an hour removing a waste basket full of paper from the lungs and liver of the instrument. He said some things in French which were never translated to me.

PROF. A. MONKEY.

There he sits. He teaches in some Eastern University. He wears side whiskers, big automobile tire glasses, and a know it all look. He has ten hens about him. He, rooster like, is scratching for bugs. When he finds one he holds it up before the hens, they chuckle over it and when they try to peck it, he swallows it while he struts off muttering, "Don't you think I am a smart fellow."

This morning they sat near me as I wrote and I heard and saw. I found delight in watching this rooster scratch and hearing the hens cackle over the bugs he found. It is fine fun to watch a man make a fool of himself if he is not your husband. He scratched in the field of Literature, Music and Politics. Then he hopped up on the fence, crowed loudly to the hens and jumped into the field of Religion. A know it all always heads there. He knows more about Religion than all the folks who have had it or the God who made it.

He was dead sure the Bible was man made and inspiration a myth. Man was not created, he evoluted from some atom. We were all once monkeys. I had never been tempted to believe that until then. As I looked at him, more and more the features and actions of a baboon stood out. He smacked his mouth like a monkey, and had that strange look you see in the eyes of the inmates of the Zoo. He certainly had not evoluted very far in the matter of looking silly.

Then he said he believed all of us have existed in some other state quite a number of times. As I listened I had a prehistoric impression I had known him somewhere. It struck me I might have been an ant eater in South America a long time ago which accounts for poking my nose in other people's business. I used to range along a tropic river where an old gray monkey roosted on a tree, scratching cooties and blinking in the sun. I recognized the professor. One of the women there was then a parrot in the hollow tree.

Then the Doctor said the soul was just animated emotion. Religion is the physic urge after some higher brain cell. All of which reminds us of the Scott, who spoke to the student who would not believe a thing he could not see and understand, "Young man, have you ever seen your brains? Do you believe you have any?" Then he added—"You and I know everything. You know ivey thing but what a fool you are, and I know that."

THE MANNISH WOMAN.

She eats in front of me. She gives me the creeps. The shivers run over me and ice bugs make a skating rink out of my spine when I get close to her. She is the woman who tries to look like a man, talk like a man and dress like a man. Her hair is short and her tongue is so long, I don't see what she does with it when she is not using it. Her voice is like a bishop at conference. She stands with her hands on her hips with that "dog gone it" pose and smokes. Her face is florid from drink. If the court is ready to pass sentence on me, Your Honor please send me to live with hounds or hogs or exile me to the jungle of Africa where the cooties crawl, the hyenas bawl and the stinging serpents look at me with fiery eyes out of the dark as they wait for me to sleep so they can suck my breath. Do anything to me Judge, but deliver me from a thing like that.

THE OLD BIRDS.

She eats at the next table. She is a gray haired American woman. She spends all her time in the saloon and smoking room, drinking and smoking. Her specialty is to coach young women and men in this French Culture in which she is a specialist. She has not been sober since she boarded the ship and maybe a long time before. Her eyes are bleared and she wears a sinful luring look. She looks for coarse things and laughs loudly at them while she drinks and gambles. A fallen man is a sad sight but a fallen woman must make angels weep.

There was another group of American girls. They were college girls, touring France to get some culture, and they got it. They had marks of nice sweet girls once—but the marks were fading fast. They took one grand plunge in drinking, carousing and smoking. At the end of the journey, they looked like hags—faded, haggard—old. With them was a young French lady—gayest of all. She was vivacious and pretty. She married an American officer in the war and was returning to him from her summer in France. She drank continually, danced and led the rough house day and night, like a wild thing who had thrown all modesty and restraints to the winds. But the day before we reached New York, she got herself together, made up her face and met her mother-in-law with a gracious smile. The lady seemed to be a nice cultured woman, and putting her arms about her sweet daughter, placed her in the auto and buzzed out into the city.

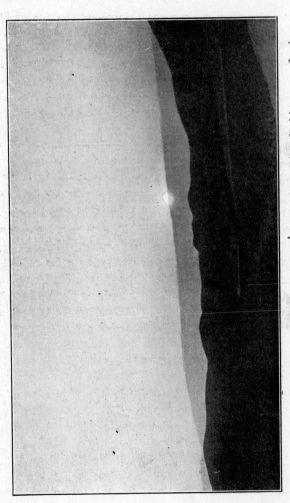

Mount Nebo. Taken from the Hills of Palestine at Sun Rise, looking over Jordan.

The Governor's Mansion on the Mount of Olives. It was built by the one-time German Kaiser for one of his sons when the German Empire conquered the world. The British Cemetery is in the foreground.

CHAPTER X.

HITTING THE HIGH PLACES.

(1922)

Little space will be given to the tour of Continental Europe since the purpose of these pages has been to linger longer on those spots more closely associated with our Christianity.

We struck a storm coming from Egypt to Italy. It took some of the spunk out of the folks and made us several days late reaching Brendizee. We were to reach this port at late afternoon but we were 2:30 A. M. getting there. To transfer a party from a steamer thru the Customs House, get rest and sleep for them, as well as breakfast, and then transfer bag and baggage across town to the seven o'clock train for Naples all in four hours was a lively time.

After leaving Rome, we proceeded north to Florence. The northern section of Italy is very beautiful. Florence is called the "Lily of the Arno," and this fair city does bloom as a lily on the banks of the river Arno. It holds some of earth's most precious treasurers of art as well as the history of many of the world's greatest artists. Elizabeth Barrett Browning lived and died here and her body rests in a quiet cemetery in the town. The tomb of the great Michael Angelo, who designed St. Peter's Cathedral is in the beautiful Cathedral of Florence. The dust of Galileo likewise found its resting place near by.

But Florence is noted above all things because it was the home of the great preacher Savonorola. Here he lived and here he hurled with the fire of John the Baptist his judgment fires against the rulers of the House of Medici, the rulers of that Kingdom. In burning messages, as bold as Nathan before David, and John before Herod, he hurled the truth of repentance and right living into the face of sinful rulers. No man ever set himself more against the sins of his day, and like John again, his head was the price of the sermons he preached.

We stood with bared heads in the monastery where this mighty man of God lived, and looked on his books, his vestments and the place where he prayed. Then we went to the tower where he was imprisoned, and then to the gallows where he died and the spot where in a rage they burned his body after which they cast his ashes on the waters of the Arno. The river bore the ashes to the seas and the tides have swept them on thru the years all the while singing songs of the blessings such heroes bring the world, and the flames that enrapt his body have shown around the world and by this light, a groping race has seen the way to the cross.

Then we went in the chapel of the Medici where in gorgeous state that outshines kings, the vile rulers, who sinned out their days and killed the prophet of God, were laid away in state. There are no tombs, mausoleums and monuments in all the world that show greater wealth and art. They

were canonized while Savonorola was ostracised.
They were worshipped while he was burned. They
had him killed because they had the power and they
chafed under his condemnation. But the death
angel called for the House of Medici to stand before the Throne while their proud forms were en-
cased in perfumes and treasurers where as the
years go on, men behold their gorgeous glory. But
brighter than the light that shines about their
tomb, shines the light of the Truth from the soul
of Savonorola as thru the years his spirit goes
marching on.

From Florence we went to Venice. Most cities
have many things in common but they also have
something distinctive that puts each one in a class
by itself. Venice is in a class all alone. She has
no auto, no horse, no street car. Instead of board-
ing an auto or car to go down town, you step from
the door into a boat and glide over the water. We
went from the train to the gondolas near by and
passed down the grand canal by famous houses of
noted artists, glided under the Bridge of sighs
and arrived at the Royal Danielli hotel which was
our home while here. Any effort to picture Venice
as she is—"Queen of the Adriatic"—would be doomed to failure. All I had read of Venice had not
pictured it as it is. The Venetians are handsome
and finely dressed. The ravages of war seem not
to have hurt them in these matters. I do not know
how so many of them get enough of the root of all
evil to cut such a swell. Perhaps their main trade
is skinning tourists. They seem to spend the most
of their time dressing, sporting and drinking.

The Rialto in Venice s a noted spot made famous by Shakespeare in "The Merchant of Venice." Then you must see the home of Robert Burns as well as the Palace of the Doges, who were ancient rulers of Venice. Here you will be overfed on art and history, and will declare with Mrs. Sheba, you didn't realize fifty per cent of it all. But you will soon come to St. Mark's, one of the greatest cathedrals of the world, where you will feed the pigeons and admire the wonders of this great building. St. Mark's ranks with St. Peter's in Rome, St. Paul's in London and the cathedrals of Florence and Milan, which are the greatest church buildings in the world. You will have admiration for a people who build such temples to the worship of their God even if you do think that worship staged and stilted.

OVER THE ALPS TO SWITZERLAND.

It is a never to be forgotten trip to travel from Milan, Italy to Lucerne, Switzerland. We left Milan early in the morning and reached Switzerland on the lake by lunch. I am sure all our folks will long remember that splendid dinner served by those nice and courteous Swiss girls. This meal was served in true home style and was more in that class of the cooking Mother used to do. For often in these lands do you eat things like Mother and Grandmother did not make.

After lunch, we boarded the boat for Lucerne, steaming on that beautiful lake among lofty mountains clad with snow rising out of the waters of this magic lake. I have seen much of mountain secenery and know we are likely to go in rapture over the last thing we have seen, but in all calm, cool judgment, I register my opinion that there is no mountain scenery in all this world quite as charming and beautiful as the Alpine scenery about the lakes in Switzerland. As we sat upon the deck of that boat an aeroplane rose and soared above us up and out around the snow clad mountains. The heavy timbered mountains green with life and charm ran down into the very waters, while high above, the perpetual snow lay heavy on the summits of the lofty peaks. It is a picture unlike any other we had seen or could see.

We reached the charming city of Lucerne on the banks of the lake in the late afternoon and found our home in one of the best hotels we had seen anywhere. Everything seemed quiet, beautiful and far removed from the sinful rabble and squabble of the world. It is a delightful place to go and stay awhile when you are tired and threadbare and want to find your way back to nature and nature's God.

It seems people who live in this Swiss country ought to be noble people above the sordid things of a sinful life. And the Swiss are a hardy rugged people of clean life and strong character. They are the best type of Continental Europe. It is a wonderful thing in the Swiss history that when all the rest of the world went mad with the hydrophobia of war and came so near tearing down the pillars of civilization on its head, the Swiss nation was the only country that did not go crazy. In the midst of all the mad ravages of war, they kept out of it and attended to their own business at home. They have no navy and a very small army only for police duties. This is the most powerful example favorable to disarmament and peace.

In leaving Switzerland, we passed thru some more beautiful country, out of Switzerland into Alsace, which was one of the bones of contention and which country was won back to France after being held by the Germans since 1870.

We reached Paris late at night, and found our way to the St. James hotel. We spent several days in Paris keeping busy, seeing al the wonders of this great old city. To remember and record all the wonders seen in Paris would overtax the descriptive powers of the Queen of Sheba.

I climbed to the top of the Eiffel Tower, one thousand feet into the air and from this lofty height looked down on the great city, stretching along the banks of the River Seine. The builder of this great tower was told he could not build such a thing but he did it and for a time lived in the top of it.

We went to the wonderful art gallery of the Louvre and saw many of the great products of this noted collection. We saw the car in which the armistice was signed which was a very interesting relic of the great conflict. We saw the wonderful war picture painted by great painters to reproduce and save the history in a great picture running on a great canvas all around a large ampitheater. Almost everyone of the leading characters are preserved in life size natural form on that canvas. Whatever glory the ancient artist may deserve for the great masterpieces they have produced, there is nothing that surpasses or even equals this great war picture.

We saw the grave and tomb of the great Napoleon. His war trophies and many conquered war flags and banners are hanging about his gorgeous tomb to tell the tale of the mighty deeds of the little Corporal when he was marching triumphant over nations and bringing the world cowering at his feet. But the time came when the conqueror was conquered. No matter how great and powerful the conquering monarch may be, the time will come when he will be conquered. There is a last great foe who leads the conqueror off to prison and defeat. There are solemn lessons of life and death, pomp and power that comes to you as you stand beside the tomb of the mighty Napoleon.

We also visited the great palaces of the Louis and Marie Antoinette at Versailles near Paris. It was interesting to stand in the midst of all this splendor and review the tides and storms of the French revolution. You see where poor Marie slept her last night in the Palace before she was carried out to death and you see some wonderful furnishings and products of art. Here Louis XVI and Marie bankrupted France and brought on the destruction of the revolution on their own heads. To go thru all the wonders of this gorgeous life of theirs makes you feel that Solomon and all his glory was surely second place compared to Louis and Marie. They put themselves above God and claimed to own and operate the State. In reality they were themselves the State. Everything, Royal robes, royal chariots, crowns, and gold, glitter and glamour, finery and splendor of millions and millions of dollars expended to enable pampered Royalties to entertain their whims is a staggering tale to tell.

But the end of all the gorgeous and extravagant glory came. They pulled down the pillars of this temple of splendour on their own proud heads and at the same time, they almost destroyed the whole fabric of the nation's life.

As we stood here in the gardens of Marie, we looked upon a strip of woods a few miles away where the German army was in their charge on Paris. This brought home to us in a stern vivid reality how near the Huns came of over-powering Paris.

IN BELGIUM.

Leaving Paris we caught the express to Brussels and in a short time we were going thru the war zone. On all sides, we saw the ravages of the brutal Huns. The bleak ghostly skeletons of ruined houses told the tale of the guns that wrought ruin on this fair country.

It did not take us long after lunch to reach Brussels. The capital of the Belgians is a large and beautiful city. It is now full of life and the streets are crowded with well dressed prosperous folks. Whatever havoc the war wrought in Brussels, there is no sign of it now to the passing view.

We visited the King's Palace, Churches and other public buildings built by King Leopold and others and we rode out to the barracks and stood on the spot where the barbarous Germans murdered Edith Cavil for doing deeds of mercy. Reverently we stood on the spot where they shot her to death by order of the German brutes. Here also they murdered many more Belgians, who were gulity of no other crimes than that of being patriots.

We took one day for an auto drive thru Flanders and the Belgium battlefields. The ruin of war is awful and indescribable. It is easy to see why the boys who went thru it have so little to say about it as you travel along and picture the horror of the campaign.

Everywhere you look is ruin. All the trees for miles are dead, shot down by shell fire, blown up by bombs or killed by gas. Miles and miles the land is in trenches, dug outs and barb wire.

We passed one hill where after the battle 260,000 dead bodies were found. In a radius of forty miles there are twenty-six cemetries. In one small strip of woods, 16,400 Germans were killed and in another place, we saw a cemetery where 7,500 German bodies were buried.

We ate lunch in Ypres. To describe the ruin of this town would not be possible. It was before the war a prosperous city of 38,000. Not one house was left standing. The church was shelled and demolished while the people were at worship and three hundred and ten people were killed in the wreckage.

All about us as we rested here at lunch, was ruin and debris and the skeletons of buildings.

We also visited the big gun placed by the Germans to shell Dunkirk twenty-four miles away. This gun is still standing. It cost about $7,000,000.00 to build this gun and $20,000.00 each time it was fired. This big gun along with Big Bertha was intended to cause panic among the people and knock the spirit out of them. People can never rise above their spirit. When you have knocked the spirit out of folks, you have conquered them. These big guns throwing powerful shells many miles away might not do much military damage but they might play havoc with the morale and the spirit of the people. But herein the Germans misjudged. The Belgiums, French and English were not as easily frightened as the Huns thought they were. Such efforts only put new vim and life into the allies to fight a greater fight.

The thing that impressed me most was the wonderful ability the people have in coming back. The progress that is being made in redeeming the section devastated by war is far more rapid than one would think. Already much of the war salvage has disappeared and the country is being speedily restored to its normal condition. In another year the destruction wrought will almost disappear under the heroic efforts of these brave people to rebuild their stricken land.

It seems such a blow would be too much for a people to overcome. To have your homes destroyed, your lands ruined and many of your friends and loved ones killed until all your land was a grave yard would seem to be too great a blow for a people to overcome but not so with these people. With a marvelous courage and faith they have thrown all their souls into the rebuilding of their land. We saw many men and women, who were employed by the Government in the public work of clearing away the ruin of war and restoring the public buildings. For a small wage, they thus work for the nation all day and going to their homes, they work far into the night and are there soon in the morning clearing away the ruins and building up their own homes. Thus out of the ruin of their own country, they are rapidly building a better and a greater country.

Many of the people were living in small metal houses furnished by the Belgian and the American Governments.

All the people were working—men, women, children and the dogs—they were all working with a vim and a cheerfulness in restoring their land. All along the country roads and the towns and village streets, we met dog carts pulling loads and burdens and thus contributing their part to the rebuilding of Belgium. One dog was trotting along pulling a cart in which was a man, a boy and seven chicken crates and he was a dog of ordinary size.

In Ypres amid all her ruins, there was a stir, a buzz and a rush as everybody worked to restore the city. Temporary shops had gone up selling refreshments, souvenirs of the war and post cards. A people with a courage like this and such a heart of hopefulness cannot be kept down, but soon will cause to bloom in the ruins of their stricken country, a greater and more beautiful country than ever.

In the midst of the wreck and ruin of Ypres, I saw a baby in his carriage. He was cooing his baby coo and laughing his baby laugh and as I looked on him in his strange surroundings I was impressed with the lesson. He represents the spirit of Belgium, the spirit of life—the spirit which will win. He is happy in the midst of wreck and woe. He knows and cares nothng about the wreck. He is looking forward and not backward. So the world will look on and forget. The hurts will be healed. Babies will be born, who will know naught of that awful woe and the vitality of the race will make this awful curse a stepping stone to higher and better things.

IN ENGLAND

We went from Brussels to Bruges and took the boat across the channel to Old England. It was good to look on the white chalk cliffs of Dover and inspiring to take that interesting ride from Dover to London, thru that beautiful section of England.

We felt more at home in England than any place we had been because we were among our kith and kin and these Britishers were our real cousins. From these historic slopes a few centuries ago, my sires sailed the rolling sea, landing in Virginia and South Carolina, thus making me a product of the New World and not the Old.

I have always admired the mother country and her mighty civilization, which has been the greatest government of the world if we measure the help it has been to other nations. The English have their faults plenty of them if we go fault hunting and the same may be said of us. As individuals and as a nation, they make blunders, but granting all this, the English Government and her wonderful colonization has been a great blessing to the world. She has had a genius and passion for building up and civilizing the world. One of the most important thing among nations is a friendship and bond between our own country and the English. Any man in either nation, who is doing anything to cause a breach between us, is a menance to the world's peace and a blot on his own country. The English races must hold the world together and save it if it is saved and the greatest calamity that could come to our two nations as well as to the rest of the world is for a breach to come between us.

I am giving my own impressions formed from my visit and years of study and observation. They may or may not be accepted. As usual they are simple, plain and frank. I confess there are some things about my British cousins that strike me as funny. Of course, they are slow to see a joke and do not laugh very much. It may be they haven't anything to laugh at. It is said they see nothing funny in our movie comedies of knocking a man in the head with a mallet until he looks like a fool and throwing custard pies in the face of innocent bystanders. When they first saw these things that make Americans scream with hysterics, it is said the London folks looked sad and were sorry for the nut, who was knocked silly and the fellow who had the pie thrown in his face. This may be to the credit of the English and not to us. They still glory in literature and great things while in America now a real artist would starve while the biggest fool became a multimillionaire.

It is also true that much of the talk the English have is not English. It is about as hard to talk to some folks in London as it is in Cairo. They seem to chew it up and swallow it instead of spitting it out like we do. You will not recognize your mother tongue in many places when you go out to buy some trifle and are told the price is "tippance" or "thripence" you will have to get someone to tell you they mean two pennies and three pennies.

It is also true, they are over-loaded with dignity. A cab driver in London and a hotel porter and waiter can put on more dog than a cabinet member in Washington or a Governor at his inauguration. The clerks in many of the stores are required to wear high collars and long tailed coats while on duty. The plain shirt sleeve Democratic ways and spirit of America shocks them beyond measure. They need some how to be shaken out of their dignity. There is nothing on the earth more dignified than a London policeman unless it is the men who guard the King's Palace. I don't know whether these officers unlimber in a riot or not. The curse of the country is their craze for drink. They are drinking themselves to death—far too many of them. The custom of having girls as bar maids to dispense rum and lure men to ruin is a disgrace on

Great Britain. Multitudes swarm the saloons and beer houses, even women and children. Let us hope the day is not far distant when a better day will dawn and Old England will redeem herself on this point.

Now having said some things in the way of criticism about the mother country, let me speak a bit to her praise. There are many strong and great points in English life that are worth noting. I was impressed with the uniform courtesy and politeness of the people everywhere. The police with all their stiffness were the most courteous fellows and the most willing to help you. Clerks, porters, waiters, and all the folks I came in contact with showed the same type of kindness and good breeding that was worthy of note. This brings us right down to the rock bottom truth we must recognize. That is the English blood is good blood and the English training is good training.

I did not hear of the complaint that everywhere folks were trying to skin you and take advantage of you as was the case in other countries. London is a busy rushing city but there is a great strong principle and character in the people.

They are looking back to the great things in her illustrious past and they are bringing the spirit of that past into her present. There is a strong religious principle in the English race. The city of London was on Sunday the most shut up and Sabbath observing city I have ever seen. There is certainly a great strength in a nation that can close up a city on the Sabbath that way. And the people

are church people. They are religious—I believe
more religious than America. Much of their religion is the English Episcopal. I heard them preach
a good many times and while I always had to take
more ceremony than I wanted, I always heard a
good practical sermon and I always found a large
company of worshippers. I believe the church life
of England is freer from rationalism and destructive foolishness than the church life of America.
I have profound respect for the religious life, training and teaching of Great Britain and I believe
this largely accounts for the greatness as a people.

It was our privilege to drive many miles out
into the country sections of England and study the
land of the people as well as the big Metropolis.
The farms and country sections of England are
wonderful in their beauty and well kept state. It
was a great privilege to see the fine farms, nice
farmhouses, splendid villages and towns and everywhere everything spoke of a very high order and
of a prosperous, tasty, thrifty people.

We ate lunch one day at the quaint and charming
town of Warwick and found a high type of cultured
people, who treated us in the kindliest manner.
We visited the ruins of Kenilworth Castle made
famous from the novels of Walter Scott and Warwick castle linked with the famous Duke of Warwick so noted in the career of Queen Bess.

We also visited Stratford on the Avon, the home
of the greatest of all English authors, Wm. Shakespeare. We went to his grave in the church, read
the original record of his baptism and his marriage

The Surrender of Jerusalem to the British. The Turkish Mayor of the city is the man with the cane. The white flag was raised, and the British lads advanced to escort the Mayor and his party to General Allenby. This is the first picture of this event to appear in America.

In the Ruins of Ahab's Palace in Samaria.

to Ann Hathaway and then we visited the birth places of Shakespeare and his wife, the home where they lived and inspected many things that were in the home as it was in their day. These homes are now owned and managed by the Government and are preserved as National Museums. They gave us some very interesting examples of English home life habits and customs in the days of our ancestors. Over one hundred thousand people visited these homes last year and the day we were there, the crowd was very large, which shows all the world has not gone mad over fools but some still appreciate artists.

We took another trip seven miles across the Thames to Windsor Castle and Hampton Court. The first is the present country home of the King and Queen, and is one of the greatest mansions of the world. It was built by William the Conqueror in 1068 and is a stately castle in a beautiful setting. Hampton Court was the home of Henry VIII, the much married and sinful monarch of England. He took this mansion from Cardinal Woosley by force before he had him killed and occupied it himself. Anne Bolyne, one of the wives of King Henry, lived here and it is said her ghost still remains here.

We passed Runnimede Meadows on the Thames where King John signed the Magna Charta in the eleventh century giving the world the great constitution of Freedom and Liberty.

I shall not be foolish enough to try to describe Saint Paul's or Westminster. These are two of the greatest institutions of English life. St. Paul's is a great cathedral of the Episcopal church and is second to St. Peter's—among the large cathedrals of the world.   In this church are the tombs of many of England's most noted men and women, among them, the Duke of Wellington, King Charles the First and King Charles the Second, Queen Elizabeth, Queen Mary, General Gordon, known as Chinese Gordon.   It was he who discovered the real calvary where Jesus was crucified and the real tomb where his body was buried.   The body of Sir Christophe Wrenn also rests in this noted place. He was the architect and designer of the cathedral and the inscription that is on his tomb is as follows:

"If you would behold his monument look around you."

Westminster Abby is a great monument in the form of a cathedral but used rather as the resting place of notables than a place of worship.

These two great memorials keep constantly before the british the greatness of their illustrious dead.   There is something impressive and ennobling about having the great ones of a nation's life buried where all their tombs may be easily seen and the greatness of their lives kept constantly before you rather than having them buried in unknown places scattered far and wide.   And yet there comes to you often a feeling that you are too much among the tombs and too much looking back.   An old country with a long and glorious past may be in danger of living too much in that past.

In taking our country ride to Oxford and Stratford, I was impressed with the strange names of

some of the country and village taverns we passed.
A few of the names were as follows—"White
Horse", "Red Horse", "The Dog", "The Dog and
Gun", "Red Bull", "Fat Pig", "Star and Garter",
"Three Sisters", "Black Boy," "The Temperance
Tavern," "The Quiet Woman". Just why they
have such odd names for their taverns and whether
or not there was real significance in the names,
I did not learn.

THE ECCUMENICAL CONFERENCE

At the time of our visit the Great Eccumenical
Conference of Methodists was in session in London. Several members of our party were dele-
gates to the conference and others planned to
attend. This was a great meeting of all the
Methodist bodies of the world. At one session a
German delegate made a rousing speech pleading
for the world to forget and forgive Germany. When
he finished his speech, he turned to an American
negro and hugged him while a southern bishop
led the singing of the song, "Blest Be The Tie That
Binds."

CHAPTER XI.

A VISIT TO SMYRNA

An eighteen-hour ride on the Aegean Sea, by islands that were old before our country had written a line of history, brought us through the Dardanelles from Constantinople to the bay of Smyrna. The boat was rough, the odor bad, the food smacked too much of goat and there were too many Turks along; but above all this were the soft blue skies, below us the blue waters, and all about us that wonderful heavenly night with the moonlight upon the waters.

I shared my little room with a Methodist preacher, a Baptist preacher and a Mohammedan cat. The Baptist and the cat were very sea-sick and kept us from sleeping well. My place at the table was between two Turks, whose main diet was a big bowl of spaghetti cooked with an abundance of goat grease. There didn't seem to be any beginning or ending to the snaky looking dough. They ate it by suction. Getting their mouths near enough to the dish they guide it with a spoon and keep a perfect stream of the greasy stuff going to their mouths like cotton in the cotton mills running through the spinners, while the goat grease goes where it may. I was reminded of the Southern belle of dusky color who informed her beau at supper that she did not like to eat watermelons. When, with great astonishment, he asked the reason why, she said, "Cause I don't like to git de juice in mah years." Try our best, we could not eat spaghetti like the Turks. It is a distinct privilege, however, to sit between two and see them eat it, especially when you have seen the spaghetti hanging up in the back yards to dry where it is made, and the goat meat that is cooked with it, hanging in their markets. This was not the first nor the last time we had to eat what was set before us and ask no questions for conscience's sake and other reasons.

Our boat cast anchor in the beautiful harbor of Smyrna, and we prepared to go ashore. Several boats from different nations were hung up at the dock and we had to stop several yards from the shore and be transferred by little row boats. It seemed that from every quarter these little boats came—about two hundred of them—with the skill and speed of birds to our boatside, while their owners set up an awful howl and jabber as they quarreled with one another for the best positions and called to us at the top of their voices for our patronage. All of this in a general mixture of broken English—badly broken—French and German at the rate of about ten per cent., with the rest in Arabic, all made emphatic with jerks and gestures astonishing to see. A crowd of hungry geese at feeding time would not have set up a more lively scramble and their talk would have been as much understood. We were soon landed on the main street that runs along the water front, where a little car, drawn by donkeys, seemed determined to run over us. The street was crowded with camels from afar, bringing figs, rugs and other native products to the sea to exchange for other things needed. Nearby was the fish market which needed no sign to advertise itself; also the packing places for the celebrated Smyrna figs, and a short distance up the street the bazaars.

One of the greatest things in the East is the bazaars. No tongue or pen could justly describe the wonderful sight produced by this great mixture of men with the still greater mixture of native products, all blended in endless confusion of styles, costumes and colors, while the black men and still blacker men (for now and then among the other hues you run upon a Kafir, Nubian, or a Sudanese. black enough to make a common negro look pale), brown men and yellow men, all clattering, jabbering, sputtering, gurgling sounds at you which vary in sound from the roar of a lion to the mixing of a Seidlitz powder. To go through the bazaars of Smyrna, Constantinople and Cairo, to be pulled and jerked, sputtered and hissed at with an endless array of goods, of every color of the rainbow and several that have never been hung up in the sky, with hundreds of figures of every countenance and costume known to man, on exhibit in the little half-lighted booths, with as many odors as they have colors, has the effect upon the subconsciousness something akin to the jim jams, but more pleasant. In these famous trading places you can buy the finest products of the East at almost your own price.

Smyrna is of great interest to the traveler because it has long been the second great city of the Turkish Empire. It has a fine location and from any point of view produces a most pleasing impression. Before it lies one of the greatest harbors of the earth and on beyond the blue waters of the Aegean Sea. The city sits upon the side of a commanding hill, while behind it are great and imposing mountains, among whch old Mt. Pagus raises his lofty head, speaking of the distant time when about him the proud old city surged, while upon his crest rested the crown of Roman life and glory. Smyrna claims an unbroken history of three thousand five hundred years, and is now one of the greatest cities of the country, pouring from the regions beyond into her harbor a wonderful stream of commerce. Another great honor claimed by Smyrna is, being one of the seven cities in which Homer was born.

But the point of greatest interest to the Christian is that Smyrna was the home of one of the Seven Churches of Asia to which God, through Saint John on the Isle of Patmos, not far away, sent those messages which were to come with light and life to all churches for all time. This is the only one of the seven cities in which those early churches were located that is great and prosperous, the others long ago having gone to dust through the wear of the ages and the vandalism of man. The church at Smyrna claimed another distinction in that it and the church at Philadelphia were the only two of the seven that received only words of praise in those letters. In all the others when the good points had been recounted the Almighty voice spoke to the Revelator these awful words: "Nevertheless I have somewhat against thee." How many churches and how many souls our Lord will thus address when he writes our record it is sad to contemplate. When God spoke the good deeds of the church at Smyrna there was no "nevertheless."

You surely feel linked to the past in Smyrna. The missionary links in the chain of the years gone and the Dark Ages glow with heaven's light. You are at the site of the church of Smyrna with the second chapter of Revelations before you, and the history of Irenaeus, who was bishop at the close of the second century. He was the pupil of Polycarp, bishop of the church at Smyrna, and has written things about him that have come down through the years to us. Polycarp was the disciple of Saint John and John was the disciple of Jesus. So that morning as we stood in Smyrna we felt our hands were holding the unbroken chain of history back to Jesus, which gave us strange feelings as we looked at the links—Irenaeus, Polycarp, John, Jesus.

It was here in the market place of the city one Saturday afternoon that the great and good old Polycarp was fed to the flames when the devil and his angles tried so hard to destroy the faith of the early Christians by burning their bodies. Little did they think those martyr fires were starting a light that would outshine the stars, and that by the aid of that light that shone on the world of sin and darkness so many souls would be able to see the face of Christ. They wrought more for the Lord in their death than they could possibly have done in their lives. Truly does the Scripture speak of all such "Of whom the world was not worthy." Polycarp was offered freedom if he would deny his Lord. The old saint's answer was, "Eighty and six years have I served Him and He has done me no ill; how, then, can I blaspheme my King who has saved me?" He fed the soldiers who came to take him and requested of them an hour for prayer. As they saw him praying a strange awe came over them and they repented they had arrested him, but led him to the Roman Court, which sentenced him to death. They burned him, and his friends gathered up the old man's ashes and buried them, overlooking the beautiful bay. Heathen Turks tramp the sacred spot, crying, "Polycarp toomba' backsheesh" (all they know of English), little knowing what that spot means to the Christian's heart.

The church of Smyrna is gone. The congregation is gone. The Turks hold forth where the glorious light of this spotless church shone long ago. But the faith they had is not dead. The flowers they planted have not withered, nor is the vine they planted by the wall of that church blighted. Across many seas and into many lands the fragrance and the fruit of that early religion has gone and lives to the glory of God. Standing in these ruins where heathenism has followed Christianity, some ask, "Isn't religion a failure?" Because the sun goes down does it go out? It goes beyond our vision to shine on the other lands, and so the Sun of Righteousness went beyond the view of some of those people who would not open their eyes to His saving light but the light of that sun did not go out. On those people who open their eyes to His light He is shining with ever-increasing splendor, and there is healing in His light.

One of my favorite texts to preach from has long been Rev. 2:10, "Be thou faithful unto death and I will give thee a crown of life." My visit to the Bible lands opened many texts in ways I never dreamed of, and this was one of them. This text was to the church at Smyrna. All the commercial and social glory that crowned Mt. Pagus in the height of her Roman splendor made Smyrna appear as the queen of the world sitting on her throne above the sea. So the ancients regarded her. They referred to her crown of life and glory. If the Roman life of that city could be called a crown, what a crown the life to come would be to those in the church at Smyrna who, in the persecutions to follow, were faithful unto death! How that life— pure, endlless, sinless, painless—compares with the life of Rome at her highest! What an exchange, death for life; Smyrna for heaven! But I will just mention the fact and not preach the sermon.

Being very anxious to visit all the scenes of this sacred history in and beyond the city, we soon had a dozen carriages in line, driven by as many treacherous looking Turks, and drawn by horses small and ugly, but tough and fast. It is amazing how much hard driving and rough treatment these little horses will stand. The Turks—in fact nearly all the drivers we saw—have a recklessness and speed

in their driving that would make Jehu take a back
seat. Numbers of times we held our breath and
closed our eyes as we furiously drove through narrow streets crowded with venders, camels, donkeys,
people and dogs, and through the whole summer,
with many hairbreadth misses, we had only two
minor accidents. In Athens we upset a fruit
peddler with no damages save a few spilt apples and
lingual explosion that sounded like a pot full of
Heroditus, Livy and Modern Eloquence boiling over.
The other was in Damascus, in the street called
Straight, where through the crowded market and
hundreds of dogs, we made schedule time with no
mishap save running over the left hind leg of one
of the Sultan's Fidos. It should be remembered
that these European carriages are almost the only
wheeled vehicles found in Turkey and Palestine.

Up the narrow, crowded street of Smyrna our
carriages went for Mt. Pagus. The streets are
only a few feet wide and are full of venders, basket-
makers, shoemakers, coppersmiths, etc., the most
of whom sit flat upon the ground. Our horses
dashed along, sometimes brushing against them,
but they seemed too busy or too lazy to notice us.
Streams of dirty beggars of every age followed us
with the cry of "backsheesh," which is ever in your
ears.

Deep in thought and meditation of the sacred
history born here, we almost forgot the degradation about us. Higher we climbed until we had a
wonderful view of the city below with the ships
of many nations swinging on their anchors at her

quay and the waters of the Aegean Sea stretching
on until they touched the blue Mediterranean. To
our left herds of goats browsed about the base of
the old Roman bridge, over which the splendor of
the empire went in the days of Jesus. Up ahead of
us was the site of the church of Smyrna and still
beyond the tomb of Polycarp. Our little horses
settled down to their up-hill pull while we settled
still deeper into meditation. The beautiful morning, and the sacred scenes made a day seldom
equalled in a lifetime. But how soon were we to
be served with one of those sudden changes these
folks thrust upon you as they sweep you through
centuries of time from the things that used to be
to the things that now are.

In the midst of our deepest and most profitable
meditations some of the horses balked—how many
I don't know. Really I am not sure that any balked
at all—anyway that or something else caused us
to presently be served free of charge with one of
the greatest shows which in all my life I have ever
seen or heard. I would give a good price if I had
the power to produce with word or pen or motion
picture what followed. I hesitate to try, for I know
I will fall so far short of doing it justice. I am
sure no member of our party can ever forget it,
but all will ever consider it one of the richest experiences that was ours—something that was not
on the regular program and for which there was no
extra charge whatever.

Our carriages all came to a standstill, and the
Turkey drivers began to gobble at one another and

make signs. At first it was mild and slow, but soon the grindings and the gratings that came from their throats grew faster and louder, while gesticulations, gyrations and contortions became more 'violent, increasing every second in rapidity and force. They let go their lines and stood up that they might be freer to practice their bodily and guttural performances, all of which increased in volume and movement like a gasoline engine getting under way. Presently they all went down upon the ground where they could have still more room and get at one another better. They met face to face, and growled at one another until their eyes, aflame with Satanic fire, seemed to bulge from their heads. Their faces were so contorted that their noses, eyes, ears and mouths seemed to rapidly change places like the letters of an electric sign on the street in the night. They trembled, stamped their feet, rubbed their fists in one another's faces. They stood straight up, with their hands and faces lifted high toward heaven, calling upon their God with more vehemence than the prophets of Baal on Mt. Carmel. Then they went down upon the earth and prostrated themselves with their faces near the earth and the palms of their hands upon the ground, and prayed. Then they arose and swore.

It will help to picture this scene when you think of the pants these Turks wear. It seems they can't be mean enough in their nature and conduct, but must add to it by these abominable clothes. Their pants are full in the hips, with legs dwindling down on the mutton-leg plan, until they are tight at

the ankles with a seat that bags down about two
feet. It is the most grotesque costume ever designed by the children of men. The actions of these
fellows in those breeches was something not soon
forgotten. This went on until every condition
known to the body had been gone through with,
while all the time a noise as loud as lungs and
throats could make it rolled from their throats with
a swiftness that would make an auctioneer or a
lady at a tea party green with envy. This stuff
could not have been talk. They could not have understood one another. A cat serenade in the back
yard at midnight was Shakespearean rhetoric compared to this. Mark Twain said, when he heard
cats fighting at night, it wasn't the fuss that
bothered him, but the fact that "they used such
miserable bad grammar." If catawailing is bad
grammar, I don't know what this was. It varied in
sound from the boiling of mush to the grinding of
glass, with constant explosions from their internal
regions as though they had swallowed several packs
of firecrackers each and they were going off.

Why they were thus giving their attention to
one another and not to the horses, if they had
balked, was strange, and led us to think the horses
had not balked. And yet, if that was not the case,
I don't know what it was. The whole thing will
remain a mystery. Some thought it was a little
side show they were serving to us with the hope
of some extra backsheesh. Others thought it was
a plot to get us out of the city in this lonely place
and rob us, and they were merely debating how

they should proceed and how they would divide us up. When this theory was advanced, some of our men became alarmed and our ladies began to cry. As for me, I did not think of danger. I forgot all about the sacred spot and its history. I almost forgot who I was and where I was. I could not even be a knight to the hysterical ladies. I sat back in that carriage, looking upon the greatest circus I had ever seen, and it was not costing me a cent.

After awhile, about the tomb of Polycarp, I tried to brush all these things away and enter into the spirit I expected to find up there. I often close my eyes and stand there again. I see Mt. Pagus and the city below, the boats in the harbor and the blue sea beyond. I see the teeming life of Rome in the height of her glory surging about that proud old city. I see Polycarp going to the flames. I see the messengers coming from Patmos with John's letter to the church at Smyrna. I see the angel coming down from heaven with the crown of life to put upon the heads of those who, in the midst of trials we can never realize, were faithful unto death.

At other times in other moods I close my eyes to things about me and see that circus again, and I cannot keep from wishing I could, by tongue or pen or artist's brush, put it in a living picture. When the performance was at its height our horses started to run with all their might, without any drivers to stop them. I had listened to some strange thing they often said to the horses, and, realizing something had to be said and done, I yelled at the horses as nearly as I could that thing I had heard them say. I don't know how near I came to it. I don't know whether I was swearing or not, or whether I was praying to Mohammed, but it answered the purpose, the horses stopped, and we got the lines and held them until the performance was over.

When we reached the boat our ladies fixed their hair and otherwise adjusted their disordered looks as they almost cried again for joy, while the men smiled and sighed for the same reason. Some lady said to our guide: "Oh, wasn't it awful? Did you ever see anything like it?" The guide looked at her with a smile and said, "Madam I have been going through that every day for twenty years."

CHAPTER XII.

ON MARS' HILL.

Leaving Smyrna our boat turned her nose across the Mediterranean to the land of Egypt. That cruise on that wonderful body of water so rich in history, those glorious days, and soft summer nights, will never be forgotten.

We spent a day in Athens, landing in the harbor five miles away and took the car for that city—great in the days that are gone. We were struck with the difference in things here and in Turkey. We saw about us more thrift, intelligence and decency, also more kindliness and friendliness toward foreigners.

We took carriages from modern Athens up the hill to the site of the Athens that used to be, and it was truly an upward way. On top of these commanding hills stands the ruins of this great city of culture and learning. Even a feeble imagination can paint a thrilling picture of those people and those days as one looks from this big hill that rises above its fellows, giving a fine view of the sea and the hills behind, while all around are ruins, some crumbling back to earth while others stand, and when a multitude of generations still have come and gone will still be standing the dash of the winds and the roar of the storms. To look upon these massive, majestic ruins makes you feel that the worldly culture of this age is hardly standing on the same platform with those days. The

Acropolis, the Stadium, the Theatre of Dionysius, the Temple of Zenus, and the Parthenon, standing here when centuries have past, are still marvelous monuments of the boldness and skill of Pericles, the builder, aided by the genius of Phideas, the sculptor, and Ictinis and Mnesicles, the architects. The ruins and the museum full of relics of the greatness of those days are so overpowering that I feel powerless to describe them, and shall not undertake the task. We looked upon the finest sculpture of the world and emblems of life thousands of years old that looked as modern as anything the world can show to-day. The dress and the ornaments of the ladies, as far as design and art goes, looked like they were just from a modern shop.

My mind and heart soon found their way through all the ruins of Grecian glory to two spots that have always stood out as the two most important places in these great ruins. One was the grave of Socrates. It makes the heart leap faster to look through the bars to the grave of that old philosopher who drank the hemlock and left this world, because long before the man of Galilee had walked the hills of earth on His mission of Gospel and Life, this enquiring mind and hungry heart had grasped, even though faintly, the life that gleamed beyond the hills he walked upon, and, single-handed, in that old market place, fought for his new faith, and when they had overwhelmed him, refused to renounce the new light he had seen and gave his life to pay the price of his faith. Perhaps the life of Athens dropped at once into its usual channels and moved on unhindered, glad that the silly Socrates was gone; but how much greater was that idea to grow than all those philosophers had ever dreamed!

The next place my heart turned to was Mars Hill, and climbing to its crest as nearly as can be determined, where Paul stood when he made his speech to the Athenians—one of the greatest speeches the world ever listened to—with my Bible in my hand I read the seventeenth chapter of Acts. Clearly rose the picture before us. There was the market place where the gentlemen of proud Athens gathered to discuss the issues of their minds and propound questions one to another, since they had no papers and magazines to write for and to read. (This custom still exists in many places and it has some good features.) They were ever after some new thing, and every new thing in religion or anything else they could find they brought it as a trophy and added it to their collection. They had introduced all the gods they could find and had erected altars to them.

One day a little man, buffeted and storm-tossed, was conducted by some kind friends into this great city. The world had served him rough. He received no welcome on land or sea, for the waves tried to swallow him and the hills engulf him. He was a little weather-beaten, wiry, unattractive looking man. No, there was something so odd, unnatural and strange about him that it made him wonderfully attractive. He was accused of turning the world upside down, but he didn't look like

he could do it. His hands were swarthy and tough
looking, but they didn't look like they could turn
a tent upside down, much less the world. But he
was like old Socrates whose body went to dust just
across the way, he had an idea and it was this idea
that was turning the world and regions under the
world upside down. It is ideas and not hands that
turn the world upside down now and then. Ideas
were in great demand in the market place in
Athens. These gentlemen of Athens spread them
out like traders do their wares and looked them
over. They turned them over in their hands,
mashed them to see if they were sound, smelled
them and scrutinided all their fibres.

They ran constantly to their bargain counters,
bringing and taking away some new thing. They
were afflicted with that disease that crept in Eden
and has never left us. It is "Newitis," a burning
fever for some new thing. Eve caught it and turned
her face from the Tree of Life to the Tree of Knowledge, because already, though she had been there
such a little while, the Tree of Life was getting
stale, and the Tree of Knowledge, which the devil
had just called her attention to, was new. The
child is born with this disease, and as fast as his
baby hands can catch things he throws them down
because they are old, and reaches up for more because they are new. So before breakfast is ready
on Christmas morning all the invention of Santa
Claus for a year has grown stale to him. Ladies
have "Newitis," so they must have new clothes. No
matter how good a dress and a hat may be, if they

have been worn a few times and the eyes of the
saints have seen them, they are old, and new ones
are very much desired. If you throw pigs a thousand ears of corn they will bite each one once and
hasten on the next one in search of something new.
Not that I intended to put the ladies and the pigs
in the same class, but that I was only illustrating
the disease.

So one morning an Athenian, climbing up the
shining way to the Acropolis with the fevers of
"Newitis" burning in his blood, chanced to see a
crowd about the Jewish synagogue, and thinking
here was something to feed the hunger he had and
give him a choice morsel of gossip to carry to the
market place, he turned aside. He heard Paul
preaching to the Jews about one named Jesus who
was crucified in Jerusalem and arose again from
the dead, thereby proclaiming to those who followed
him that they should do the same. The Athenian
threw back his head and laughed. His heart beat
faster, his eyes shone, he quickened his pace up the
shining way along the sculptured path to the place
where ideas were exchanged, for he had one that
was new, and he was anxious to get there with it
before all others. When he broke into the circle
of idea venders they saw from his looks and his
movements he had been out on a hunt, and had
made a new catch. So they gave way for him. He
at once spread before them the idea he had found,
and a number of them ran down the sculptured
marble way on the hunt for Paul like a crowd of
boys go out for the man with a monkey. They

got him, and as the gathering crowd grew larger
they pushed him along until they reached the
Areopagus, and here in this out-door court where
Greece heard and passed judgment on all things,
the apostle of the Gentiles got upon, perhaps, this
very knoll where I stood, with his speech in my
hand. The heavenly fire of Paul and the marble
philosophy of Athens had met, and throughout
history, when heavenly fire and marble philosophy
have come together, the marble has been left in
ruin and the fire has gone on.

The great speech was made. No time was lost
in elaborate preliminaries or silk-spun flowery introductions. Paul went to the point. He never
had time for long introductions and conclusions.
He never spends any time getting ready or closing
up. "Ye men of Athens," he said, "in all things I
perceive that ye are very religious. For as I passed
along and observed the objects of your worship I
found also an altar with this inscription: ' To the
Unknown God' (How that dart of irony and sar-
casm went home!)   (Acts 17:22-31.)

How that speech must have fallen upon their
proud ears! What a mighty thrust it was at all their
traditions, superstitions and philosophies! Here
were new ideas for them. They had something to
chew over now. They could herald the new faith
of this man far and wide. But strange to say they
got mad. The world has always been so. When
Divine Truth sweeps the foundations from devils
and men they get mad. There is nothing else to do.
When logic fails, wisdom answers not and the pride

of the world parts not its lips, it is time to get
mad. Sometimes a sage cannot answer a question,
but any two penny fool can get mad about it.
No matter how cool and quiet Divine Truth is,
when it comes into the presence of the devil the
devil gets mad. Jesus never did an unkind, unjust
or unmanly thing. He was as gentle as a lady, as
free from ill as an angel, but He made the devil's
angels so mad they killed Him. The drowning of
the hogs, the healing of the sick, raising of the
dead, and, worst of all, forgiving sins and preaching a resurrection, made the devils so mad that the
volcanoes of perdition belched forth their age-long
accumulations of vileness. So Athens got mad with
Paul.

While the greatness of the world goes down the
light of the Gospel goes on. The old Athens has
passed away, its glory is dimmed, and its sun is set.
These great ruins stand as the lasting monument of
the great minds of a great race, but all these things
exist only as shadows. At great labor and expense
they wrought to build their monuments, but they
are gone. How few souls on earth to-day know of
Pericles, the builder? And when you name Phidias,
the sculptor, and Ictinis and Mnesicles, the architects of Athens, not one man in a hundred, long out
of college, can tell you who they were without running to the Encyclopedia or the Greek Professor.

But who doesn't know the Apostle Paul? He built
no Acropolis, or Parthenon. He only built tents; but
the heart of the world beats over the work of Paul,
the builder of tents, more than it does over Pericles,

the builder of marble Parthenons? Paul had no money. He hired his own house and paid the rent when he sold a tent. Pericles had a mighty nation behind him and the money and wisdom of the world at his call. He built marble temples where Athenian ideas would shine. Paul built tents, but looked beyond the place they were pitched to "the city which hath foundations whose builder and maker is God," as he set in motion the idea that has sent countless souls rejoicing through the shadows to the Heavenly light and everlasting life. Which has blessed the world more, Pericles, the empire builder, Phidias, the sculptor, Ictinis and Mnesicles, the architects, or Paul, the servant of Jesus Christ? Verily the work of man goes down but the work of God goes on.

As we steamed out of the bay over historic waters, our faces set toward Egypt, the sun was going down and throwing the glorious light of the closing day upon the hill, upon the white marble ruins of Athens, and across the quiet waters came the thought that while the light of the earth goes out the light of the Lord shines on.

CHAPTER XIII.

OVER THE SEAS TO EGYPT.

Great was the journey down to Egypt. Wonderful seas, historic shores, historic memories, balmy days, soft summer nights with liquid stars and low hung moon. These things will not be forgotten. Our path had passed ancient Troy and crossed the line of Paul's historic missionary journeys.

Sitting upon the deck, with the breeze blowing softly and the sun shining peacefully upon the far flung line of the sea, we read from Acts Paul's account of his experiences there in the years gone by. How different was his experience and ours! We were with friends. We had above us the flag of a great Christian country to protect us. We carried passports from our government guaranteeing us proper treatment. We had the fair skies, gentle breezes. But how storm-swept Paul's journey was! "And when neither sun nor stars shone for many days, and no small tempest lay on us, all hope that we should be saved was taken away." It is hard for us to realize what these strong words of the Apostle mean. But God had not lost sight of his child in the teeth of the storm for "There stood by me this night an angle of God whose I am and whom I serve, saying 'Fear not, Paul. Thou must stand before Caesar, and lo, God hath granted thee all them that sail with thee.' wherefore, sirs, be of good cheer for I believe God that it shall be even as He hath said." Thank God for a faith like that!

Thank God for such heavenly visitations in the time of life's worst storms.

The 27th chapter of Acts gives a thrill at any time that cannot be surpassed by any literature of the earth, but, reading it here gives feelings that are indescribable. Here was the very spot where the heroic Apostle to the Gentiles—weak, frail and half dead, with all the world against him as he was on his way to the court of a brutal Caesar, on what he knew was a hopeless appeal, took charge of that boat and its crew in that awful storm and guided it safely ashore, while he made the darkened heavens shine with a mighty faith. He was cast up upon yonder island, where he shook the viper in the fire and preached the power of Christ to save and deliver. Oh, to have Paul's faith, so that in all the storms of life we can feel our Pilot at our side, and, looking through the storm clouds, behold the shore to which he is sure to lead us.

We had a mingled, mixed, and motley company aboard our boat. There were Christian travelers, tourists and missionaries from England and America on their way to Egypt and Palestine. There were merchants from Athens, Smyrna and Constantinople going to Cairo and Alexandria on tours of trade. There were Egyptians going home from those cities from like missions. There was an Austrian count and countess, with attendants and a lazy, greasy, bench-legged pug dog—their only child, who had to be walked by the maid every day. There were Turkish officers and gentlemen, and a good sprinkling of Italians along with some coal-black Soudanese and Kafir negroes to add color to the parade. But the most numerous and most conspicuous part of the company was the steerage, full of Mohammedan pilgrims en route to holy cities. There were several hundreds of these of every age and kind. There were old men, white of beard and brow; old women, bent and wrinkled; strong men and women in their best days; lads and lasses, full of wonder; little ones and ones still smaller, crying, sleeping, crawling. These were packed on two decks like chickens in a coop, with hardly room to eat, sleep and go through their prayers. Such an array of rags, filth, colors and odors would be hard to find. They ate their stale, dirty bread, pumpkin seeds, dates and whatever they had in their dirty, ragged bags, and drank from their dirty water bottles they had along, while those who had nothing to eat did not seem to greatly mind it, perhaps being accustomed to it. Some seemed so near starved and so lazy that they couldn't develop energy enough to get hungry. They didn't talk much. They ate, yawned, prayed, stared and slept. Many of them had been making hard sacrifices for a long time to get the means to take these pilgrimages. There was no denial too hard for such a trip. Now they were about to realize a life-long dream and visit their sacred shrines from whence they could go back to their fellows with the triumphant bands upon their caps and with the assurance that whatever came and whatever went, they were sure to reach Mohammed in heaven, because of where they had gone. One of the most

interesting things in Eastern travel is these bands
of pilgrims. We moved among them but were cau-
tious on account of germs and fanaticism. No wonder the English government enforces examinations
and quarantine regulations in these waters, and
in spite of all, plague and other disease often break
out. We narrowly missed quarantine twice on account of plague among the pilgrims.

One of the most interesting characters on this
part of the journey was an Egyptian judge who had
been over to Athens on a legal mission of some kind
and was en route home to the land of Pharoah, to
assume his judicial duties. Not being able to exactly understand his name, we called him Judge
Bathrobe, for the reason that he came to breakfast
just as he got up, wearing a dirty night-shirt, with
barefeet, his face unwashed and his hair uncombed.
If it didn't suit his honor he didn't change his costume all day, and as I remember it didn't suit him
until he was ready to leave the boat. The judge was
very friendly and tried hard to cultivate the friendship of the Americans. He was very talkative to
the men and exceedingly courteous to the ladies.

The fourth of July found us on this sea journey,
so when the day was done and the stars came out
in the soft blue sky, we took ourselves to the outer
deck where we could have room to let off steam,
and entered into a regular American patriotic celebration. It was indeed a striking ceremony, as far
away from our native land, surrounded by staring
auditors of many nations, afloat on the Mediterranean, we sang our native songs in our native

tongue and paid tribute to our homeland so many miles away. I wondered what impression this service and our religious services made upon those children of the East. Doubtless it was all as strange and comical to them as some of their movements were to us. Anyway, we seemed to hold the attention of the people. The Turks, the Jews, the Italians, the Greeks, the Egyptians, the Austrians, the Germans, the English, the Arabians and some others so hard to classify that they would best be put on the remnant counter came near to look and listen. Even the tired, lazy pilgrims got a little life in them and took a little interest in what was going on. Some laughed, some talked about it in strange sounds, some turned away disgusted, but the most of them looked on silently, with wide eyes and open mouths.

One of our most ardent listeners was His Honor Judge Bathrobe. He seemed to fully catch the spirit of American independence. He clapped his hands in true American style and proposed something that looked and sounded like a toast to the Red, White and Blue. Having the fires of his patriotism so well stirred he got a good supply of strong wine to help him celebrate, and long after we retired His Honor kept up the exercises by prancing up and down the deck in his night shirt, making the night alive with his patriotic speeches, or maybe they were speeches of anarchy, how could we tell? And like many an American judge he misjudged the capacity of the court, over-charged the jury with a preponderance of evidence, and being unable to prove an alibi his friends had to resort to habeas corpus proceedings to get him to bed at 4 A. M., July 5th. (If this is not legal language it gives the idea.)

We touched the interesting city of Alexandria, named for Alexander the Great, sailed under the shadow of Pompey's pillar, and went ashore to take our first look at Egypt and supply ourselves with cork hats and thin clothes suited for the heat and the travels that lay ahead of us. We found this great city both ancient and modern. There is in its streets, shops and buildings much to speak of England—much of real elegance, and there is much, very much to speak of the East, the old East, and the dusty ancient days of Egypt.

We resumed our journey to Port Said at the mouth of the Suez Canal. This canal is under the control of the British government, which several years ago purchased a controlling interest from the Khedive of Egypt, the sum being twenty million dollars. It has revolutionized Eastern travel, opening a shorter way around the world and pours in and out an immense amount of commerce. More than four thousand boats each year, carrying more than half a million souls and ten million tons of freight, touch at this custom house, and for the privilege of this waterway pay a toll of twenty million dollars. So great is the traffic through this canal that often a boat is delayed two or three days in getting her clearance papers. This canal gives England a tremendous prestige in commerce and military power, and along with Gibraltar makes John Bull's power hard to shake on this part of this terrestrial ball.

Among the army of venders that poured on our boat was a very intelligent Mohammedan who pressed us with his wares. We told him it was our Holy Day and on that day we neither bought nor sold. He at once, with evident respect, made ready to move on to other buyers, saying as he did, that Friday was his Sabbath and that nothing could induce him to trade on that day. Whether he spoke the truth or not I do not know, but one thing was evident time and again, the Jews and the Mohammedans better regarded their sabbaths than many Christians we chanced to meet.

One thing of special interest at Port Said was the Egyptians coaling the big ships. They carried the coal in little baskets on their heads and in a little while a crowd of them put six hundred tons on the ship. They moved like clock work, singing a droning song, all their movements keeping time to the music, like our old cotton-field negroes used to do. What a difference in this method of coaling ships and our method here in our ports. The big crane picks up a car in a minute, lifts it clear of the track, dumps the load of fifty tons and puts the car back on the track with as much ease as you would put a shovel full of coal on the grate and put up the shovel. But one thing we learned over and over again was that human flesh is cheaper than machinery in the East.

After supper we had our Sabbath service in the dining room, and after committing ourselves to our Father's keeping, we fell asleep, thinking of the sacred ground upon which our feet so soon should walk.

CHAPTER XIV.

IN THE LAND OF THE PHARAOHS.

The shades of evening were falling over the Land of the Pharaohs when we emerged from the Custom House and boarded the train for Cairo. Our faces were toward the Land of Goshen, whither the children of Jacob journeyed with their aged father after the famine had driven them from their native hills into the arms of their long lost brother in whose hands a providential God had put corn to feed them in their hunger.

How strange and wonderful are the ways of God in the lives of men! Who would think Heaven's Guardian Angel would follow a stripling lad like that. Sold as a slave he was guided into a strange land among strange people, saved from all the dangers of a slave's life, guarded among those who sought his ruin, brought into the leadership of the world's greatest nation where he was made the savior of those who plotted his ruin. Thus ran our thoughts that evening as we went through the land where Joseph was so great and God was so good. The rays of an Eastern moon, that turned on its light when the sun went out, but added to the charm of the pictures that rose before us as the train sped on. In the soft and liquid light of the moon falling on that land so rich in yielding corn, but richer still in its harvest of history (nowhere does the moon shine like it does in this land), we could almost see the sights of the centuries coming up before us.

Mt. Zion, where David Lived.

Grave of Lazarus. Jesus was buried
in such a tomb hewn out of solid rock.

The Breach in the Wall made for the Kaiser in 1898.

We could almost hear the groans of Israel and the fall of the task-master's lash as he drove them on to make brick without straw. We could almost see the shadows of the plagues falling across the court of Pharaoh, and it started a creeping chill to think we were where all those horrors took place. Large loomed the majestic figure of the stalwart Moses coming down from the sands of Midian to lead his people, and clear and strong rose the hand of God as over yonder in the surging waters of the Red Sea He showed that with all the greatness of Egypt God was greater still. We wondered if we crossed the path our Savior came, as his parents brought him down here to hide from the bloody hand of Herod? That must have been a tiresome trip for the mother and the Little Child as over the burning sands they came! Christ fleeing from a wicked man! And yet, he did it more than once to show the plan of His Father's love to save the world.

Sometimes these old bodies get so tired that even in the midst of the world's greatest glories they sleep on as if they were at home. We were back in the common scenes of home as if we expected to stay there a long time, when called from our slumbers by the loud cawing of the sacred birds of Egypt. Our room opened out on a little porch onto a court full of trees and flowers, and to get full benefit of the breezes we left the door open. At day light these sacred birds came to the door to greet us and bid us welcome to the Land of the Nile, or maybe they came to protest at the intrusion of foreigners into their old and sacred shrines. Whether a welcome or protest, it was loud and enthusiastic. The land is full of these birds and so sacred have they been held by Egypt through her long centuries, that their lives have been protected and people have lost their own lives for killing them. These are the birds that according to the Old Religion of Egypt, bore the soul on their swift wings to the court of Osiris, the chief god of Egypt, where it was judged after it left the body. They were honored and protected that they might carry on this sacred and important work. Whether they had come to our room that morning to offer their services to us in this capacity, I know not, but from their mean looks I would fear if we fell into their hands they might carry us to the bad place, for they looked like birds of ill-omen to me. Like Poe's raven, they sat about our door crying, "Evermore" or "Nevermore," I know not which, but they evermore squaked.

We had breakfast—coffee, bread and butter—the Continental breakfast as it is called, because it has been adopted as the universal breakfast over the continent of Europe. It is all you get, and many times, as you long for an old southern breakfast, you feel it has the right name, for, compared to the breakfast a preacher gets in the South it is not worth a continental. The first time I was introduced to it, was in a fine hotel in Germany. From the fine appearance of things I set the notches of my appetite up for one of the finest breakfasts I had ever seen. Presently the waiter brought me two little rolls, a little piece of butter and some coffee. I sat there a few minutes waiting for steaks, ham and eggs, fruits, fish and an array of savory dishes with hard names, but they didn't come. Others started on what they had, and so did I, thinking they had just given us this to amuse ourselves with while they were getting breakfast ready, Surely such a fine hotel would have a fine breakfast. After a while the others got a toothpick and left and so did I. This was our breakfast in Cairo and everywhere else except on the ocean going boats and in England. There is no limit to their fare.

Soon after breakfast, as our custom was, we met in front of the hotel to begin our sight seeing, and no sight seeing was more interesting or helpful than those days in Egypt. There is a great deal to see in Cairo. Its charm is both ancient and modern. It is a great city of nearly a million souls, being the center of the life and activities of all Egypt and that part of the world. The European section will compare favorably with any city, in its streets, business houses and the business that is done. It has a distinctly English air, every where you go you see the touch of England's hand; her troops keep order, her money and men control business and her rulers dictate the policy of Egypt. The better element of the Egyptians have a section of the city which is rich and attractive. Many of these people are wealthy and live in great pomp and splendor. Some of them, both men and women, are very handsome. In addition to these two elements there is a very large class of the poor that make up the rest

of the city's life. These are made up of many
classes but are chiefly Arabs, Egyptians, Nubians
and Soudanese. From all parts of Upper Africa
and other surrounding countries they pour into
Cairo in streams. The business of Cairo in its traffic in native products of Egypt and North Africa,
and its stream of outgoing and incoming commerce is immense.

While Cairo is one of the most interesting cities
of the earth in its present day life, in its ancient
life there is a still greater charm, for in it and about
it was written much of the history of Egypt's
ancient glory. One of the chief places of interest in the city is the great museum. This was
one of the first places we visited. In the East, there
is much that is mere legend and the traveler must
keep busy separating the real from the unreal.
Much that is shown you is mere tradition like the
wonderful parable in the negro preacher's sermon,
"got up fur de purpose ob finances." This is partly
due, however, to the fact that in the passing of so
many people and their deeds, no record was made
that would stand the wear of the years and the
hands of vandalism. Egypt, however, has done
otherwise. Not only has she left abundant evidence
in the abundance of carvings and hieroglyphics in
her tombs and buildings but she built with such
strength and skill that her works endure and speak
for themselves beyond all doubt. So when you see
the wonders of Cairo's museum you need not think
they are the inventions of yesterday. They are
the real relics of the fargone yesterdays. When

you look upon the face of Pharaoh (Rameses II), who oppressed Israel and contended with Moses, don't look skeptical. It is beyond all doubt the old fellow. It gave us the creeps to look on his strong but tyranical looking face.

Not only did we see the mummies of those distant days but many other mummyfied objects of ages long gone, some of them over five thousand years old. Many of these objects had been preserved in such a perfect manner that it was truly wonderful to behold them, and they looked so modern that it seemed you were gazing in the shops of yesterday. Knives, beads, jewelry, chairs, swords, axes, hats and clothes, very much like ours, safety pins, baked potatoes, apples, rolls, roast fowl and many other objects in great abundance, made us wonder how much like our own day those distant ages really were. Imagine how a Methodist preacher feels looking on a cooked chicken over five thousand years old.

Another very interesting object to be seen in the museum of Cairo is the renowned "Village Chief." It is a huge stature made of wood, representing the landlord of the old days. When the natives first beheld him, they named him at once "The Village Chief." This stature is made of wood and is nearly five thousand years old. It is one of the oldest and most wonderful relics of long-gone ages. You can but wonder how any kind of wood could be preserved so long. It is in perfect condition, showing no signs of decay from the wear of so many centuries. The features and the form are very strik-

ing, no stronger or more perfect human face has
ever been produced by art. It really seems to be
alive and looks out at you with eyes bright and
piercing. The balls of these eyes are made of white
quartz, the pupils of silver nails and the eyebrows
of bronze. They stare at you where ever you go and
those lips, though made of wood, seem trying hard
to tell you about the distant day and wonderful land
from whence they came.

We looked upon some of the mummies of the
sacred bulls. They also came from that fargone
age and represent the wonderful skill of Egypt's
hands and the magnitude of some of her schemes
as well as the strangeness of her religion. These
bulls were Egypt's gods. They were believed to be
deified and were the living form of their greatest
and most honored duties. They were kept in temples surrounded with all the luxury and gorgeous
wealth the richness of Egypt could bring before
them. To the temples of these beasts the people
came to worship and sacrifice while they lived, and
when one died he was embalmed with all the art and
ceremony Egypt could muster and buried with pomp
and splendor seldom given a king. It is said, the
cost of the funeral of one of these bulls was nearly
one hundred thousand dollars in our money, which
in that day would have been indeed a fortune. To
the tomb of the bull's mummy the people flocked
with their worship and their offerings. When a
bull died the priests were given the task of traveling through Egypt seeking for his successor. He
was selected something like our prize calves are

selected at our agricultural fairs. When one was found whose marks and qualifications satisfied the priests, he was elevated to the divine throne and taken to the sacred temple where he spent the rest of his days in circumstances becoming his position.

The religious ideas of that fargone day were indeed strange and seem harsh and shocking to us, and yet there is something about it all that had a fascination for the people of those days, and in the study of that religion, like the study of all religions of heathen and semi-heathen people, we were struck with the fact that the heart always has had upreachings for something Eternal. Egypt spent all her energy, resources and marvelous wisdom and skill in her effort to lay her hand on something Eternal, and herein lies the chief charm of all her greatness and the wonderful works she has left the world. There is something touching and pathetic about how she spent herself to do these things. She believed in the Eternal with all her soul, though her ideas were vague and clouded with the superstition of her age. She longed for the Eternal and spent all her powers to lay her hands upon it. All the pyramids, sphinx, temples and statues were built at an expenditure of time and strength that staggers the swiftest mind. The idea in their building was to have something that would last, something that the storms of future years could not blow away, something that would be eternal. There is something in the heart that can but honor those who build that way.

They brought all the skill of their fine arts,
now unknown, to bear, that they might so embalm
their bodies that all coming years could not crum-
ble them away, for they believed the soul was eternal and when it left the body it went through a
series of preparations getting ready for the better
world. If it was unworthy of that better world, it
was sent into some animal that it might be dis-
ciplined and punished. Thus, through a continued
journey of animal existence it made its way upward or downward until called for to enter its eter-
nat state. The body must be made eternal for the
soul to occupy, so the body was embalmed. If the
body was not thus preserved, the soul would have
no eternal dwelling place, but must wander homeless through the ages to come. Food was placed in
the tomb for the body and also for the soul when
it came to visit the body. This food was embalmed
for the body, but many offerings of food were
placed in the tomb near the body for the soul on
its regular visits. The loved ones and friends looked
after this and were encouraged in their faith when
on future visits to these tombs they found their offerings gone, never wondering which beat in the
race for that dinner, the soul or the priest. Thus
before the days of the Pope, did the priests feed
themselves fat on the stupidity of their worshipers.
There were many more things of interest in this
great museum which have been brought to light by
the long and faithful efforts of the explorers of
America, England and France, but we must pass
from them.

We next visited the old Citadel which is now known as the "Tomb of the Mamelukes." This will always bring keen and cruel visions to the student of Egyptian history. The "Mamelukes" or "White-slaves," were the lieutenants of Mohammed Ali, the great ruler and maker of the present Egypt. What Diaz was to the Mexico of the past generation, Mohammed Ali was to the Egypt of the past generation. The Egyptian was even more cruel and despotic than the Mexican, but like him, did some great constructive work in the government of his people. The Egyptian's work was greater and when he passed away the hand of England reached out to conserve and carry on the work to higher and better achievements and not let it all be lost by rebellions and strife.

Mohammed Ali in building up his kingdom selected some trusted men to help him. These men were true to their leader and wrought well to bring him to the zenith of power and glory. When Mohammed Ali had Egypt in his iron grip, he grew jealous and uneasy for fear the Mamelukes who had brought him into power might turn their hands against his to take that power from him, so he devised a scheme to rid himself of them, which in its diabolical conception and bloody execution would suit the taste of a Nero and gladden the soul of the Archfiend who delights to see blood flow. He invited four hundred and eighty of these, trusted lieutenants, to feast in the citadel, and when the festivities were at their highest, his soldiers, who had been concealed by him in the building, at a given signal, opened fire upon them. Mohammed Ali listened quietly to the dying groans of those who had made him king of Egypt and saw them lying in their blood. When the bloody deed was over he quietly remarked that nothing now was between him and the undisputed sovereignty of Egypt. One of the Mamelukes escaped by mounting his horse and forcing him to leap the walls of the citadel, and in spite of the rain of fire, made good his escape to the Mokattam hills. A little over a half century ago, he could be seen on the streets of Cairo, an old man with white whiskers, quietly going on his way.

One of the deeds of Mohammed Ali was the building of the Mahmaadiah canal from the Nile to the city of Alexandria. This canal irrigated the surrounding country and made possible the rebuilding by Mohammed Ali of the modern city of Alexandria. This canal, before the railroad was constructed from Alexandria to Cairo, connected the two cities, with a medium of traffic, bringing from Cairo, the inland city, the commerce of the Nile and taking from Alexandria to Cairo the commerce of the seas. This was one of the greatest things that could have been done for Egypt at the time, in opening up the trade for Egypt's cotton and other products. The canal is forty miles long. Twenty-five thousand natives, many of them men, women and children, worked on this task, digging the mud and dirt with their hands under the fierce rays of Egypt's burning sun and the still fiercer lash of the overseer's whip. From fever, dug up in the mud, and exposure and cruelty, nearly three thousand died before the work was done.

We also visited Shooba palace, where Mohammed Ali spent the closing years of his old age, surrounded by wealth and luxury becoming the mighty monarch he believed himself to be. Here, he lived at peace and in ease, notwithstanding the stormy life that lay behind him, so full of blood and horrors. His favorite pastime was sitting on his gorgeous cushions smoking his long Turkish pipe and ordering his servants to take the ladies of his harem out upon his lake in little boats and at his order, upset the boat and give them a good ducking. As the old fellow beheld them floundering in the water and screaming in their fright, he would laugh until the tears ran down his cheeks. It is strange how the heart of a criminal can amuse itself and stranger still the things bloody hands will take for their playthings.

Egypt's greatest blessing is the Nile. It is Egypt's life. Without the Nile there would be no Egypt. Unless the life-giving waters flow down upon Egypt's fertile lands they will be like the barren deserts on each side. On one side are the Libyan mountains and the limitless sands of the deserts, while on the other side the Arabian desert with its unknown sea of sand running from the Nile to the Red Sea and southward through the great Sahara to Central Africa. Here, in this world of sand, lies Egypt. Wherever the waters of the Nile go Egypt goes, and where the water stops, Egypt stops. The line that divides Egypt from the desert is as plain as the line dividing the land from the sea. Through all the slow-going centuries it has been a fight be-

tween life and death, between the waters of the Nile
and the sands of the deserts. When the lack of rain
has kept back the waters the desert has closed in
on Egypt, and when fall rains have again overflown
the Nile, Egypt has pushed the desert back, thus
preaching a mighty sermon on "Everything shall
live where the river cometh," Ezk. 47:9 Wherever
the river does not come, nothing can live. Thus it
is with the River of Life that flows from the Hills
of God. It is a fight in the lives of men between
that river and the Desert of Sin. Wherever the
river goes, the sands of sin turn to an oasis of
heavenly life, and when the waters of the river are
kept back, the deserts of death and sin close in on
the soul, producing famine and death just like a
drought will do for Egypt. Many times famine and
death have come because the waters of the Nile have
not come. The seven years of plenty in the days of
Pharaoh were seven years of the Nile's full waters
going out into all Egypt's borders to make the harvest come. The seven years of famine were seven
years the Nile waters did not come down, and the
deserts closed in to take Egypt's life away. So, in
all our lives the years of plenty are the years when
the River of God runs full and free through our
souls and the years of famine are the years when
we let the desert's sand bear down upon us and the
River of Life cannot come to bless us.

The Nile is the longest river of the earth, being
over three thousand miles in length. For many centuries only half of this distance—up to the first
cataract had been explored—it remained for Henry

M. Stanley, who found the body of David Living-
ston and opened dark Africa to the world, to find the
sourcces of the Nile many hundreds of miles further
in the interior of the great unknown wilderness.
The ancients, not knowing from whence the Nile
came, believed its source and origin were from divine sources. They thought it bubbled up in the
fields of Paradise and at its source the angels drank
and bathed and then the waters ran on to bless the
race. They naturally deified the river and worshipped it. So when Moses, by God's order, turned
the waters of the Nile into blood, causing it to yield
death instead of life, it was a humiliating and
deadly thrust at their god.

Through the spring rains in the Nile basin it rises
for several weeks, gathering in its long journey,
rich deposits which it takes down to Egypt as well
as its moisture. One truly remarkable thing about
this great river is that for the last fifteen hundred
miles of its journey it has no tributary. The burning sun pours down upon its waters to dry them up,
and seldom does a drop of rain fall to pay back the
debt. The deserts on each side run down to take
up its waters and all that long distance it is the
only source of life for the multitude of people and
living things, and the population of more than
twelve million souls, and yet it is not exhausted.

For centuries in art and literature the Nile has
been honored by the earth as well as by the people
who depend upon it for life. In the Vatican in
Rome, there is a stature of Father Nile, the father
of Egypt, leaning on the Sphinx, with sixteen pyg-

mies playing over him. They represent the sixteen cubits' rise of the Nile as it flows by the Sphinx, which will give life and plenty to Egypt. If the sixteen pygmies climb on the old fellow as he leans on the Sphinx it means blessings to the people.

The richness of the Nile Valley is almost beyond conception. The harvests it produces is unequalled by any spot on the earth; corn grows like a wilderness and its height and thickness looks black in its richness. Cotton and sugar cane likewise flourish in a way that is astonishing to see. Everywhere we went we saw the half naked inhabitants lounging about or taking their siesta in the shade, if it was the middle of the day. Sometimes they were working in a lazy way, plowing their buffalo oxen or driving them around their irrigating machine which is constructed something like our cane mills The beast goes round, turning a big wheel on which are buckets of some kind which go down into the water and fill themselves and as the wheel revolves, rise to the top to dump their water into the ditch from which it runs out into the fields. Sometimes these buckets are nothing but old pumpkin shells. The men then get out in their bare feet, in the dirt and mud where the water runs, open a little channel with their toes for the water to run from each row to each plant. It is not a very clean or healthy looking task. When I looked on this scene I called to mind the words of Moses in Deut. 11:10 "For the Land whither thou goest in to possess it, is not the land of Egypt from whence ye come out, where thou sowest thy seed and waterest it with thy foot, as a garden of herbs." Whatever theologians and commentators had said about this text, the picture was there before me to speak for itself. Many times the Israelites had done this filthy and unhealthy work, for it was all the way Egypt had to get a harvest. But God was leading them out of this land that thus depended upon life for its crops, to a land He Himself would water from the skies.

We saw many of the water buffaloes working at their task of irrigation and cultivation or lying in the water covered with mud to keep them cool and save them from the flies and fleas. Many times we saw them coming up out of the Nile where they had buried themselves, all but their faces, like Pharaoh saw in his dream. All we saw were fat and not lean, for Egypt was not in a famine then and they could find plenty to eat. We saw many date trees full of dates. These trees grow up with a long trunk, bushy at the top, containing several bunches of dates often so large that a single bunch will make a bushel. These dates are a popular and very useful fruit throughout the East. They are delicious and very wholesome.

In Egypt as well as throughout all the Eastern lands the middle of the day is very hot. From about eleven o'clock until three the sun is so hot that nobody but the natives who are hardened to it can endure it, while in the shade you can keep very comfortable. The people are in the habit of sleeping or taking their siesta as they call it. The stores and business places close and if you go out shopping you can hardly find a place to buy anything.

A few of the poorer natives go on at their tasks, but the most of them forget their troubles in sleep. It is at first a strange and amusing scene to see people everywhere you go, taking this long nap. The "well-to-do" lie in their homes upon their beds or rugs, or perhaps the men close their shops and lie down at the door or in the shade near by. The poor can be seen in great numbers sleeping in the dirt in the streets or in dirty houses where dogs, donkeys, goats and folks in one tangled mass forget their burdens in "nature's sweet restorer." I laughed at these people for what seemed at first to be their laziness, and the first morning we came in from sight seeing I decided to strike out down town to see what I could find, but before I got back my brain was almost cooked in the hottest sun I ever felt, and I concluded they knew better than I did. I did not sleep for I could never do much of that in the day but I was content to seek a shady spot and stay there until the rising breezes and the receding sun brought in a better hour. About three o'clock the air changes, a breeze begins to blow and from then on it is very comfortable. I found only three or four nights too warm for comfort and suffered far more from heat after I returned to Virginia than I did in Egypt and Palestine. The greatest difference is in the burning sun of the East; sometimes instead of a sea breeze the breeze will blow in from the desert. It is called a Sirocco and makes life almost unbearable, we encountered one, of which I will speak later on.

One night in Cairo we attended the Feast of Ramadan, the greatest feast of the Mohammedan Church. They celebrate it after a long fast, and, like some folks higher up in the scale of culture, they seem to make their feasting more strenuous than their fasting. I had never seen anything like that event and never expect to behold its like again. It was held in a big park in the city, which was enclosed, and all who entered had to go in at the gate and present a ticket to the keeper. As we desired to behold Mohammedanism at its best as well as at its worst, we secured tickets and went. I wish I had the power to describe that event but it is impossible. There was no end to the people; it seemed that half the world was there; the multitude was made up of all classes, from the Governor and his Company to the waifs and outcasts, but the great and the gay seemed to predominate. It would be hard to find decorations and display to equal it, while the costumes worn were staggering to the senses. Some of the people were indeed fine looking. We saw some of the prettiest women we saw on the entire trip and some of the finest looking men. One man, a commander-in-chief of the event, I think was the handsomest man I ever saw. In many different places celebrations of various kinds were in progress with crowds entering into them with great interest and enthusiasm. The crowd that seemed to have no end, moved on in song and celebration; old Egypt seemed to be awake, she seemed to be coming up from the dust-covered cemetery of the centuries in pomp and

splendor to sit upon her throne again even though
that throne was that of Mohammed. The old country was on fire and she was on dress parade. The
spendor, dazzle and glitter of that celebration in
its wierd mixture of ancient Egypt, the Prophet of
Mecca and modern things can never be forgotten.
The Feast of Ramadan must be seen, however, to
be understood; no man can describe it.

But we must bid you good-bye, O Egypt, and make
our way toward Rome. Our days within your borders
have been full of interest and into our tomorrows
we will carry with us the charm of your yesterdays.
Great hast thou been, O Egypt! Wonderful upon the
page of human history; tracing back thy beginning
over the sands of the centuries until thy tracks are
lost in the sands of dim and distant days. Thou
art the mother of all the civilizations the earth has
known! You were white with age when the foundations of Rome were laid! You were looking back
over the sands of your long-gone yesterdays when
Solomon dedicated the Temple of the Lord in the
City of Jerusalem. Long before the glories of Greece
surged about the parthenon you were wearing the
white of the centuries on your head; O Land of
Magic and wonders so full of buried glory and richness in things that are gone! Land of Cleopatra and
Anthony! Land of the Pharaohs and their mighty
deeds! Land of Israel's redemption from famine,
oppression in tyranny and deliverance from bondage! Land of the mighty Joseph and birth place of
the Law Giver of God! Long will the work of thy
hands still stand to dazzle the gaze of those who

walk beside thy wondrous river that flows on as
it has since the world was young, to bless thy people until its journey ended, its work done, it pours
itself from its seven mouths, out upon the sea!
Before thy greatness is gone and thy glory buried,
may there come out of the storms that sweep the
earth, a better day for thee, and may some hand
lift thee up to a better place among the people of
the earth! Yea, may the Christ thou dids't shelter
from old Herod, who sought his death, come to thee
like Moses from over Midian sands and lead thee
out from the dust-covered centuries to a greatness
more lasting than thy pyramids!

CHAPTER XV.

CLIMBING THE GREAT PYRAMID

An experience to which I had looked forward with keen interest was that of climbing the pyramid of Cheops. While it is a hard and dangerous undertaking, I had firmly made up my mind, if I was permitted to get there, I would not leave until I had stood on top of this great wonder of the world and looked out over the land of Egypt.

The race of man has never left a greater wonder on the sands of time than these pyramids of Egypt of which Cheops, or the Great Pyramid, is the most famous. No description or array of figures and fancies can give a clear impression of this mighty monster sitting through the slow-going centuries on the sands of the desert. When you stand beside it and look up its enormous sides, or put forth your strength to reach its top, climbing over its massive stones so high up in the air, you almost feel like the old fellow who visited his first circus. The elephant engaged his special attention. He walked around the great beast several times gazing in wonder at his wonderful, giant form. He looked at his tail and then at his snout and head; he watched him take his food in his snout and put it back in his mouth. Unable to endure the sight any longer he walked away in disgust, exclaiming, "There ain't no such animal no how!"

The base of this pyramid covers thirteen acres of land—a small farm, and contains eighty-five million

cubic feet of solid masonry. Many of the stones
from top to bottom measure from four to six feet
in their height, length and thickness, and look as
large as two pianos put together. How these great
stones were ever put in place with such scientific
exactness, I haven't time to explain. The heighth
is nearly five hundred feet. It has masonry enough
in it to build a rock wall ten feet high and a foot
and a half thick around the states of North Carolina, South Carolina, Georgia, Virginia, Tennessee,
Florida, Alabama, Mississippi and Louisiana, and
have nearly five thousand miles of wall left over.
It is built in the form of great stairs, and while the
wearing weather of centuries and the still more destructive hand of man have made the stones crum-
ble somewhat, unless some earth-quake destroys it
it will perish only when Eternity's storms bear all
things away on their winds. The outer surface was
finished with hard cement but this is gone, leaving
the stones rough, which makes it safer to climb.
It must have been a sight of unequalled beauty and
wonder when thus complete, it stood out on the
sands with the sun shining on its sides.

Many strange, weird theories have been advanced
as to the plan and purpose of this pyramid in the
Divine Plan and final destiny of things. These ideas
have been discussed with such length and learning
as to stagger ordinary minds. It has been shown
that the building is perfect in its mathematical and
scientific construction, sitting to the four points
of the compass with no stone varying a hair's
breadth in its position. Strange and extensive re-

cesses within, with many symbols and measurements, have been understood to point out all the eras and events of the world's history and from them the learned have figured with a final nicety, not only the past, but the future of the world's history, even to the day of its passing away. Such theories are wise and deep and profound but miss widely the meaning of this mystery of stone. Whatever the Almighty had to do with its building He did not mean this.

The question rises, what is this strange thing, and why would any set of men spend so much labor and expense to build such a structure? The answer is simple: It is a monument built by an Egyptian king for himself, while he was living. The recesses were for his body and those of his family. The Egyptians believed much in eternal things, but their eternal was built out of stone. A king had a desire to build for himself a monument that would end only with the world, and he was willing to spare no expense or labor in the undertaking. It must be admitted, his success is wonderful, and yet I could not but think of the eternal monument built down in Egypt by Joseph and Moses and not of stone. Their monuments will stand. Millions of children know who they were and how they built, but the wisest doctors have disagreed on the man whose brain thought out and hand put up this monument of stone.

Then the question comes. How did they build it? There is no quarry near. How did they get these stones? Where did they come from? How many men worked on the job? How did they put them in place? How long did it take? It is not good form to answer all questions. Some must be left for the students to find, and besides, the day is too hot to do this subject justice, so I will hasten on to what I set out to tell—how I got up and down the Great Pyramid.

We went on cars out of Cairo toward the pyramids. At the end of the car line we transferred to donkeys and camels, and turned our faces toward the wide stretches of Sahara sands. Thinking a camel more in keeping with such a journey I selected mine. As I looked him over I became more and more impressed with his ancient mien and stately dignity. He seemed to have the manners of the Pharaohs and the odor of those dim centuries of the past. Had his owners told me he was gotten out of the pyramids and was ridden by Pharaoh when he pursued Israel to the Red Sea I should have raised no question. He looked it. While I have read elsewhere Pharaoh rode in a chariot, that might have been a misused word, for chariot and camel in the language of Egypt, sound very much alike. But when I looked my beast in the face my feeling of wonder, ecstasy and reverence knew no bounds. It seemed that all the tragedy of the centuries and the woe of the world was stamped upon his face. I never knew before just how solemn, sad, serene pathetic tragic a camel could look. His lips were hanging down in woe and disgust; his head was poised high and still. Out upon the far-off line of the desert his eyes were gazing at nothing in particular unless they were trying to rest upon the beginning line of Egypt's history. At the sign from his driver the camel lay down with precision and care. I mounted to the saddle and at a punch from the driver he groaned and complained as though he bore on his back the woe of the world. But he began to get up. He started to get up behind as all cud-chewing beasts should, and he kept on getting up behind before he started to get up in front, until I was afraid he would get up all the way behind before he got up at all in front. When he had gotten up behind until he seemed to be on a line with the top of the pyramid, he started to get up in front and I thought he would get up in front beyond where he had got up behind. At length he stopped getting up and I suppose he was all up, but when I looked at him in front he looked higher than he did behind and when I looked at him behind he looked higher than he did in front.

At length we started for the pyramid, some on camels and some on donkeys. When I tried to guide my beast or induce him to go faster he rolled his eyes up at me, dropped his lower lip still lower, lolled out his tongue, humped up his back and bellowed out in a way that made me entirely agree with what he said. Every camel and donkey had a driver with a large number thrown in for good measure. They were along to entertain us and make the journey seem short by crying out for backsheesh, begging to tell our fortunes rubbing our feet with their uncanny hands and other innocent pastimes. My driver Mohammed, soon managed to get my beast out of line with the others and at my question as to the meaning of it he informed me there was something very interesting behind a near-by sand dune that he wanted me to see as it would take only a few minutes. I stormed at him like I meant to feed his flesh to the eagles, post haste, and ordered him back in line under all the penalties I could remember, chief of which, not a coin would he get unless he went, and he went.

When we reached the great wonder of the desert we prepared to gaze up its age-long sides, lost in admiration, but it was not to be so, at least, not just then. Rather, we forgot the greatness of Egypt's past as we faced the greediness of Egypt's present. It seemed that they rose from the sands or fell down from the sky like a flock of big white birds. They bore down upon us, a mighty company of eagles that gather about the pyramid to feed upon the tourists. These guides are Egyptians who wear white garments and go bare-foot. In the evening shadows, in their robes, under the great pyramid, they seemed spirits of a dead age and we seemed in the cemetery of dead dynasties. The whole atmosphere seemed so mixed with the supernatural and the satanic, the dead and the living, the past and the future, that a hypnotic trance seemed to come down upon us and fixed us so these fellows could play us in their hands. Nobody can describe the atmosphere about the pyramids and how these fellows carry on their business. I doubt if the world could produce a set of men who can skin you with better skill and send you away happy, like they do. You go away penniless but charmed, and in the chambers of your soul, where you keep your acquaintances, you give them the front seats. They are wonderful fellows.

The British government requires two of these guides to accompany each tourist. One is to hold while the other skins. You feel you can make the journey without help but it isn't long until you are glad you have two and you would be glad for another one. I selected two of the oldest and steadiest looking ones I saw. They were both Egyptian doctors, Dr. Macboon, the more charming of the two, was indeed an interesting gentleman. (I enquired of my old friend on my recent visit and learned he died of the ravages of war.) He informed us he was the man who carried Mark Twain up, and whom Mark offered a hundred dollars to jump off and break his neck. However I met about twenty others who also claimed the honor. They certainly do know Mark Twain around the pyramids. The doctor also told me he carried the late King Edward of England up to the top when he was Prince of Wales and in proof of the fact showed me where the prince carved his royal name and the date. One of the medicine men took me by one arm and the other by the other arm and I started sky-ward with the feeling that I was either going to an executive chair or an electric chair. When we came to two paths up the rocks where feet for centuries had climbed, one of them would go one way with part of me and the other the other way with the rest of me, and when they went to lift me from one of the high ledges to the other, one would go up with part of me and the

other would lag behind with the other part. When
it seemed we had gone almost to the front door of
the moon, Dr. Macboon asked if I wanted to rest.
I tried to nod my head. We sat down on a ledge of
rock somewhere between heaven and earth and he
asked me to look down at the view. I had lost most
of my sense but I had enough not to look down. One
sat on each side of me as close as they could get,
holding my hand and looking with all their power
into my soul, like two snakes charming a bird to his
doom. They pressed my hands and rubbed them in
a way that made creeping chills in spite of the heat,
run through my blood. Their sharp black eyes
seemed saintly and satanic. Their face so close to
mine wore a dusky veil from buried centuries. Their
voices were soft and low and sweet and calm, and
yet fiendish in their insidious penetration. They
seemed to link the dead and dusty past with the
dim and distant future. Before me stretched the
wide expanse of Sahara's sands with mighty waves,
all still as though the hand of God had struck an
ocean dead. A caravan of camels—ships of the desert—far out on the horizon, like a fleet, moved slowly, bringing spices down to Egypt. The sun was
going down across the desert, where a sea of sand
merged into a sea of fire. The light was shining
on the sides of this old rock mountain, built when
the world was young, and it was shining on the
ghostly forms holding my hands and whispering in
my ear. They asked if they were satisfying me, I
said they were; they then wanted me to satisfy
them, and then and there pay them the first instal-

ment of what money I had, feeling sure they would get it all before they told me good-bye. Did I get scared and hand over my money as most tourists do? No; as strange as it may seem I was charmed, half dazed with the feat before me, intoxicated with the atmosphere about me, I felt my blood throb for adventure. I was ready to go or come. There was a game before me and in my dazed condition I longed to play it. So I resolved to hold my nerve, for with them, once your nerve is gone, you are gone. I refused to pay by installment but told them to take me up and down safely and I would treat them right.

Dr. Macboon then wanted to tell my fortune. I told him I did not care to have my fortune told, I was trying to forget the past and didn't want him digging that up and just at that time I thought it unwise to nose into the future. I didn't think that was any time or place for such performances. He then put his hand back in his belt or sash and began to bring out things for my inspection. The first was a little mummy-like Pharaoh he had gotten out of the pyramid and he wanted to sell it to me. I told him I had not expected to go in the undertaking business and did not care to have a corpse on my hands, ascending the pyramid, but if the corpse was alright and he would carry it down for me, I would take it. He wanted pay then but I told him I would not pay him until we reached the end of our journey, then I would pay him what I thought it was worth. He next brought out some sacred bugs. These I likewise bargained for as I did other things. His belt was a regular museum.

When rested, we resumed our journey and after a few repetitions of our first rest spell, found ourselves on the top of the great pyramid looking out on the sands. Dr. Macboon told me I was faint and needed something to revive me. I readily agreed to this but asked him what I could get up there. He turned around behind to an Egyptian sitting on his feet beside some burning charcoals and handed me a cup of the best coffee I have ever tasted,.for which I paid him five cents. I told the doctor that prescription cost less and did more good than was sometimes the case in America. Several of our folks were almost exhausted when they reached the top. It was a wonderful sight. The area on top is thirty feet square, composed of huge stones.

After a period of rest and meditation we descended. At the bottom our parting came. It is a matter of getting away from them any way yau can. I offered Dr. Macboon a sum for his trinkets, which I knew he would not take. He gave me an Egyptian water pitcher which I greatly appreciated and carried through all the rest of the journey and brought home. It sets on the table before me as I write. In the Oriental style I gave him a gift of some money in return (not buying but exchanging presents) I then paid them thirty cents each for their services and went my way. Some were out many times this. In values as they are there, this was more than they were worth, but I was very much surprised to get off so easy. That climb was a very violent experience. My clothes were torn to pieces and I was sore for a week.

The Sphinx—another wonder of the world—stands near the great pyramid. It was a heathen temple used by the Egyptians for funeral services and other religious rites. The Sphinx stands in front of the temple itself which is almost buried with the sands, which must constantly be cleaned away to prevent the winds from covering it up deeper. It is a great stone monster with the head of a human and the body of a lion which represents a union of intelligence and strength. It measures in height sixty-four feet. It seems to stand here on the edge of the sea of sand and on the edge of the centuries guarding ancient Egypt's buried treasures. That motionless face gazes out on the sands and the centuries. The stare upon its face is strange, mystic, painful. It seems to fix its gaze beyond the things that are to be. Certainly its gaze is fixed on things far off and not on us. It has thus been looking on things while the slow moving centuries have moved over its heads and storms that no man can number have dashed their rain, wind and sands in its face. Those set eyes were gazing as they are now before a single living nation was born. They have looked on kingdoms' flourish and fall. They beheld Rome in her glory and Rome in her gloom. They looked on Greece in her sun shine and Greece in her shadows. They were looking on before there was an England or an English race. They saw the Nile roll on before Abraham came down to Egypt and they saw Israel go out on their hunt for the Promised Land. This object is supposed to be the oldest remaining work of man's hands. The head is per-

fectly formed and the features in the main have
stood the weather of the centuries without being
destroyed. The head is carved from one huge piece
of stone and is a hundred and two feet around. The
time, labor and skill in producing this mammoth
figure with all its perfect features and workman-
ship history does not say and man does not know.
It has no beauty to be admired but there comes a
strange charm, as, looking in its face you see how
lonely, how still, how changeless it has been through
the centuries. The face has not moved, the eyes
have not closed, the lips have not spoken and yet,
as you look, those eyes seem to see, that head seems
to hold countless secrets in a throbbing brain and
those lips seem about to tell you many things.

"O Voiceless Sphinx
Thy solemn lips are dumb,
Time's awful secrets holdest thou in thy breast,
Age follows age—revering pilgrims come
From every clime to urge the same request
That thou woulds't speak. Poor creatures of a day,
In calm disdain thou seest them die away.
O Voiceless Sphinx."

MY FORTUNE IS TOLD ON THE PYRAMID

I have never believed in fortune tellers. I was
raised to believe they were servants of the devil.
On my first visit to Egypt, I maintained my integ-
rity on this point. I went and came without allowing the snaky eyes of an Egyptian mystic to gaze
in my hand. But the last visit, when I reached the

Pyramids, I backslid. I made the tours without drinking strong drink, or murdering any European waiters and pirates which is a commendable record. I did not cut loose from my moral moorings like some tourists, who are high up at home but low down away from home, but when I reached the heights of the Pyramid of Cheops, I fell. This is a good place to fall in more ways than one. Stately Presbyterian Elders, who have kept in the middle of the road of the perseverence of saints, have slipped up here and said things and done things under these provocations, that they had never done before and will never do again. Orthodox Episcopal Vestrymen and Rectors have caused their robes to trail in the dust of Egypt's dead dynasties when they met the temptations of the Pyramids, and long after they reach home they sadly say, "We have done many things, we ought not to have done and left undone many things we ought to have done." And Baptists and Methodists with their weakness and bent to sinning, stand no more chance of getting out without backsliding than a mouse going thru a cattery.

As before, we rode our camels over the sandy path to the base of this mountain of rock. As soon as we crossed the line of safety, they bore down upon us. There was a small army of these guides, venders, fortune tellers, beggars, doctors, sheiks, sentinals, quack performers, advisors, photographers, donkey boys, camel boys, and several others I do not classify. It was a hungry horde of hideous hounds, and every second the mass grew larger, drawing recruits in a mysterious way from nobody knows

Threshing Wheat in Cona.

Riding Camels to the Pyramids.

where. They seemed to drop out of the sky, crawl out of the ground and appear by magic. One would be whispering in your ear, with his hot breath on your cheek, and you didn't know where he came from. They begged, teased, pled, talked, danced, sang and pressed their case in such varied and persistent ways, that you were soon like a bird in a snake cage. You declined, threatened, yelled, roared, pawed and said emphatic things while they sweetly smiled and came back unabashed.

I remembered what was said about Moses not far from here, when he saw some of these fellows pestering a fellow Hebrew. He looked this way and that, and when he saw no one was looking he slew the Egyptian and buried him in the sand. Time after time I tried this but others were always looking.

One poor brother had been bedraggled, pestered and tormented until his money was gone as well as his patience, with his hair standing up and his eyes shining like a madman he yelled.

"I aint going to give you narry nother cent. You didn't do what you promised. I will take your picture and report you to the police."

And Frank McKinney of Petersburg—he who was always so gentle, kind and quiet with such good manners—when all his patience ran thru that sand and fire flashed in his eyes, I covered my face and stopped my ears to shut out the tragedy.

And Dr. Squires, the Presbyterian—he looked and acted like another man. I am sure he needed a Methodist revival after it was all over. I shall never forget the faces of Mrs. Jarrett and Miss

Warlick, as the camels began to bellow and get up in sections.

But never, no never can I forget my comrade Welch. This is where all his reason took the wings of the morning and flew up the Nile over the Mokattem hills. His eyes had that look that makes you feel like calling for the fire department, the police and an alienist. He got on a camel, yelled something that almost made the Sphinx break her long silence, and hitting that camel on the back with his kodak, fled out on the wide wastes of burning sands toward Sahara's stretches and Sudan's fastness. I don't know where he went. The last time I saw him he disappeared behind a sand hill, his coattail flying as the camel with his wonderful waltz made thirty-seven miles an hour, his tail straight out behind (of course) and his head poised straight out in front (of course) while about forty of these wolves and pirates went with all speed after their victim.

I never expected to see him again. I was planning to take charge of his museum and become his executor. But he did turn up. He steered his brute in a semicircle, keeping out of the way of his pursuers until he beat them back to British territory and landed at the feet of an officer.

The ascent of the Pyramid and the Pyramid itself is described elsewhere and I will only mention now the fortune telling on the top. There is not in all the world, a place more weird, romantic, spooky, fascinating, mystic than the top of Egypt's Pyramid, as you set there gazing on the delta. With the Nile

and Cairo, Memphis, the Mokattem hills and rich
fields in one direction and the eternal wastes of sand
stretching out in the other direction. There is something strange that seems to rise up in your face and
sweep you under its intoxicating spell. It was while
thus sitting on the summit of Cheops, that the fortune teller took my hand and said he would read my
future for 40 cents. Then I fell—I backslid right
then and there and let him do it.

He poured out a bag of magic sand and smoothed
it out on the rock. All the time he was looking into
the sun, muttering strange things, while with his
hands he made still stranger signs and motions. He
drew figures in the sand, put his face down close
to the sand pile and did more weird spooky
mutterings. He then took my hand, read the
line a second, looked in the sand a second, and
muttered something which was explained to me by
his assistant. My fortune as he told it was this—

I would never be more than moderately rich. I
am sure he was safe on that. I was to be successful.
I was energetic and had a good disposition. Something was on my mind, which was true. Everybody
has something on his mind save Boob McNutt and
Happy Hooligan. He said I would soon get two
important letters, which turned out to be true. Most
letters are important and most folks now and then
get letters. One came three days later from my
wife, telling me to be sure and keep my face clean
when I went to London, and another came from a
Texas Oil Co., offering to make me a millionaire if

I would buy a share of stock at ten dollars down and the same at each full moon until the cows came home.

He then rolled the white of his eyes over toward the Mokattem hills, looked closer in my hand and said my greatest success was ahead of me. I would change my position as well as my residence in a short time and enter something entirely new. Next year I would be happier than I had ever been. Of course this has turned out to be exactly true. I was to my surprise elected Editor of the Richmond Christian Advocate and ought to be happy. Then he told me if I would place eighteen more piasters in his itching palm, he would tell me a much better fortune. I told him this one was entirely satisfactory and if he told me one any better, I would be so overcome, he would have to carry me down from the Pyramid.

THE SHEIK AND THE SHRIEK

While we were at the Pyramid, a rare character drove up. He was a distinguished looking oriental, adorned in striking regalia with a great display of many colors. He looked like a cross between the High Priest of the Potentates of Potolemy and a plain faker. He rode in a chariot that was a relic of the dark ages of the past and the moontide of the present. It had big iron wheels of the threshing machine variety and a body on the Cleopatra type It was drawn by a flee bitten mouse colored ass. We were told he was the Sheik of these tribes and had made a personal visit here to see that we were properly treated. For this favor and protection all tourists were expected to make his Sheikship a present. I never knew just what protection he gave us.

Then came the Shriek. We call him this because of his voice. He was a duck legged little Egyptian with a shrieking voice like his radiator was leaking. His eyes were snappy as a snake's. He offered to run to the top of the Pyramid and back in twelve minutes if we would give him two piasters (8¢) each. He came bowing before me as if I was the Governor and asked my permission to go. I told him he could go but I would not be responsible for the pay, nor the support of his family after he committed suicide. My words were lost on the desert sands. He was off like a streak. Piasters to these pirates had been scarce and he would do the daring deed and get the backsheesh later if he could. I knew we would have a big fuss about it, but it was well enough. We had to have a fuss about something and it just as well be this as anything else.

He made the trip back in less than twelve minutes. Some folks expected him to fall dead from the heat and exertion but he did not. He looked like a wild man. His hair was standing up, his eyes red and protruding, his mouth open, his nostrills distended and he was gasping for breath like a wind broken horse in a fire race. But he was after collecting his piasters. He shrieked, cried, yelled, fell down, moaned and did like a mad man. He tried to force me to pay him for everybody and I almost had to club him to keep him off of me. He kept on until he collected from almost all, and he earned every piaster he got. Of all the fool things I ever saw a fool do for money, that was the limit.

CAIRO UNIVERSITY

It was my pleasure and privilege while abroad to register as a student in Cairo University which has the largest enrollment of any institution of learning in the world. I was duly awarded a regular degree from this University. It was given me in due form by the Dean, and is kept as a treasure. It has an enrollment of over fourteen thousand students. I had heard of its wonders but like Miss Sheba, they didn't tell me fifty percent of the whole. Barnum was an armateur at burlesque compared to the faculty of Cairo University. Instead of a great building, we found a dirty old mosque well filled with beggars, dogs and cooties. All these are perhaps enrolled as students. It is in the dirtiest section of Cairo and that is saying a good deal. Beggars, babies and dogs slept on the floor and women were drying their wash in one end of the mosque. Several classes sat in groups on the floor on their feet and moaned and drawled thru their noses as they kept time by weaving their bodies back and forth as the teacher directed. They used pieces of tin and marked on them with black paint. All who enter the grounds are counted as students. A number of donkeys stood in the court too lazy to switch off the flies. As I looked at my degree, I saw D. D. on it. I had been honored in the East by Cairo University. The greatest institution on earth had conferred upon me the degree of donkey driver.

THE BEAD BOY OF CAIRO

He had all the charm of the East. His manner was gentle and gracious, his voice soft and musical, his smile winning, is movements like a spirit and his whole personality mystic. His name was Mohammed and his name told his faith. But he was not like most Mohammedans—distant, repulsive, distrustful. He seemed never so happy as when he could noiselessly, mysteriously appear beside an American and talk to him. He never seemed to be an intruder, and no matter when he approached you, you never felt he was out of place.

Other venders were kept out of the hotel but Mohammed had right of way on the inside. The patrons wanted him about. He didn't seem to be selling beads. His whole business seemed to be to help by giving information of all kinds to those about the hotel. But he was selling beads all the same. Morning, noon and night he sold them. He was dressed in Oriental style, and many strings of beads hung from his neck. He attracted attention to his beads without letting you know it and soon you were interested in them. If you saw a shining string and wanted them. he quickly advised you as a friend not to buy them, showing you their defect and comparing them with the genuine. You felt he had saved you from a foolish deal and you bought the other beads. If he found a certain bead was popular, he appeared later with more like them. If you asked for any kind that he did not have, the next thing you knew he stood by your side as if he rose from the floor

with his sunny smile, holding those beads in his
hands. There was nothing you wanted or wanted to
know that Mohammed didn't bring to you on short
order. In all our homes, the ladies are wearing beads
bought from him and we will not soon forget him.
If Mohammed could come to America and become
a salesman, he would soon be in the firm of some big
establishment. He is a master artist in opening the
combination door of your heart, so he can walk in,
sit down and sell you his wares.

THE MODERN MAGICIANS OF EGYPT

I asked Mohammed if he could find a magician and
send him to the hotel that night. He said he had a
boy friend, who knew the art, and he would send
him around. After supper as I read near the hotel
window that opened on the street, I heard a sound
in the window—"Br-br-urh-rrh"—and looking up,
I saw a big white rabbit sitting on the window looking at me. Guessing correctly the meaning of it, I
looked out in the street and saw Mohammed and a
youth, who claimed to be a lineal descendant of the
Master Craft of Egyptian magicians. And he proved
himself well able to establish his claim. We got
permission to use the hotel drawing room and took
him and our party there for one of the most interesting demonstrations they ever witnessed. It would
be impossible for me to even poorly describe all he
did but a few things will be mentioned.

He pulled several eggs out of the rabbit's nose for
in some mystic way, everything seemed to depend

on the rabbit. Then he told two of us to hold the ends of a cane, which we did with great care. He took a lady's ring put it in his handerchief and then wrapped the handerchief about the cane, jerked it off and behold the ring was on the cane and how he ever got the cane thru the ring with each of us holding an end, is a mystery, I can't solve. The ring then disappeartd and he located it in a brass cup. He had a set of ten cups within one another and the lids fastened. The ring was inside of the last cup and you could hear it before he even touched the cups. The ring got away from him again and a man found it inside of his coat pocket, and so far as I could see, he did not get closer than eight feet to that man. He pulled many strange things out of his ears, eyes and nose, and did other stunts too numerous to relate. He closed by blowing fire and smoke out of his mouth and nose while thru the flames, he drew out bunting containing all the flags of the Allies—all out of his mouth. He was not over eighteen but he was a genius of the A grade and would make his mark as well as money in America.

CHAPTER XVI.

AMONG THE TRADERS AND BEGGARS OF THE EAST.

One of the most interesting things in our travels in the East was trading with the people and contending with the beggars, for the most prolific crop these countries raise is traders and beggars. They block your way in almost every path and street; they follow on your trail in hot and hungry hordes; they come upon you streaming out of alleys, huts and holes; they swarm from the earth like armies of locusts to devour every living thing; they clamor about the windows of your hotels like hungry wolves waiting to tear you to pieces as soon as you get outside. They press their claims; they ply their trades; they thrust their wares upon you, each one pressing the other and all squalling as they recommend their goods and try to make a sale.

And beggars, beggars, beggars! Like vultures and eagles that darken the sky; like reptiles that crawl the earth at your feet, they waylay you, besiege you and follow you. Old and young men and women, girls and children, halt and maimed, deaf and dumb, cripple and blind (many just afflicted for your benefit) ragged and dirty bundles of germs and filth, they are waiting for you when you come, stick to you while you are there and see you depart for home. From the time you cross the line of Turkey's domains until you leave it, multitudes of dirty hands are held out to you and a ceaseless roar of voices is crying in your ears the shrieking, moaning, jabbering call, "Backsheesh, backsheesh."

There is nothing like it anywhere. With these things still in your mind when asked what these people live on we have not ceased to say "Tourists."

While the traders were extremely annoying to me at first, they soon became a source of increasing fascination and entertainment and day by day to meet them in their bickerings and barter away some pennies was one of the keenest pleasures I could find.

The first thing in trading in a foreign country of course, is to have some knowledge of the money; so it is best when you come to a strange country and want to do some trading to go to your hotel clerk, or to some leading store or to the office of Thomas Cook & Co. where English is always spoken. Be sure not to fall in the hands of the professional money changers for they will fleece you and load you down with worthless money. When you receive money from checks or gold, stay by until you have a fair knowledge of the coins they have given you. Fix in your mind as you look at these coins the American coin that comes the nearest to them in value. French and English gold is good anywhere, but your money will be more convenient and much safer to be carried in travelers' checks fixed before you leave home. For fifty cents on a hundred dollars your bank will issue these checks payable anywhere in the world. The cashier signs them in your presence and you sign them in his. When you want them cashed you countersign in the presence of the one who gives you the money. If you lose these checks or some one steals them they are worthless to the one who gets them and the bank will pay you the money.

If you have $5.00 converted into small change in Turkey or Egypt (the moneys of these countries are similar but entirely different) you better take a basket or a satchel to get your change or see to it that your pockets are large and your pants buttons well sewed on, for you will get enough change to start a bank, with that gold piece. I changed a four-dollar French gold-piece into Turkish coin in Constantinople, bought two towels and three cakes of soap, a big supply of post cards and stamps to mail them, an assortment of fruit, attended a concert and had my pockets full of money when I got to the hotel. I gave a man a piaster (five cents) and asked him to give me small change for it. He gave me a handful of change containing five distinct coins of different denominations and kept a commission for his trouble. The more we traded the more money we had. Some of these coins look like tobacco tags and are worth one-tenth of a cent.

In Egypt, Palestine, Syria and Turkey they have their own money but English and French coins will pass. A trick of the traders is to learn what money you have and then quote prices in a money they think you do not understand. You will soon learn never to give a man any money and expect any change back, for he will surely lose all his knowledge and suddenly become so thickheaded he cannot understand what you mean and he will move on for more victims. You will learn to have in your hands the coins you think the article is worth and offer it to him. If he wants more he will say so—if you want to give more you can give it. He will surely mount his prices high—several times above what he thinks you will give and what he knows they are worth, and expect you to jew him down. Herein lies the joy of traffic in the East. To meet a strange man with a strange tongue, sometimes hardly a word which you can understand, and bicker with him over prices, the most of it in signs and exclamations, each one watching that he be not cheated— this is a pastime more exciting than golf.

In Cairo en route to our hotel one day a Soudanese bore down on me. He was black as the coat of the Bishop of Canterbury. He hailed from the Soudan and he looked as though his near ancestors had more than once made lunch on a fat Englishman. Indeed he looked as though he might enjoy for dinner some fresh tourist who did not chew tobacco and was roasted to his taste. His face was horny and from his eyes the dim ages gone, seemed to look straight down on me. I learned his business was not to eat me but to sell me a cane. It was indeed a beautiful cane, made of African ebony highly polished and skillfully inlaid with one hundred and thirty pieces of ivory from the tusk of an African elephant. Not wanting to cheat the man I got the eye of the guide and asked what price I ought to pay. He informed me two shillings (fifty cents) would buy plenty of them. Making signs to him I learned he wanted twelve shillings (three dollors). Besides the sentimental value as a souvenir it would be worth much more than that here, but if two shillings was a fair price I had it in mind to buy it for that, so I held up two fingers. He

made signs at me and sputtered as though some of
his inside draw strings had broken loose, and lifting his head in disgust went down the street leav-
ng me to wonder just what the "cuss" words were
he had employed against me.

Presently he came back and overtook me as
I walked on pretending not to notice him. He
caught me by the arm and put his black horny
face so close to mine I thought he intended to bite
a piece out of my ear to see what kind of a lunch I
would make. He hissed something in my ear that
went all through my blood like a hypodermic in-
jection of undiluted contemptuousness, and held up
ten fingers. I don't know what the awful thing was
that he squirted into my ear, but by the ten fingers I
knew I had him on the retreat and he had fallen back
two shillings. With my American blood for venture
rising, I turned on him, hissed at him like a goose
and again held up two fingers. He again sputtered,
gathered up his wares and throwing his head high in
the air hurried off as though in pure contempt he
would go to the Soudan before he halted.

For a moment I feared my cane was gone, but it
was for only a moment. After suddenly stopping and
gazing at the ground as if it had done something
awful to him he snapped his fingers and muttered
savage ejaculations. He quickly turned and overtook me as I walked leisurely along. This time he
hissed louder and faster and held my arm tighter.
Whether he was trying to intimidate me or not I do
not know. The last two fingers on his left hand
were down. I had brought him down to eight shill-

ings. My courage rose and in the excitement of the
game I shook my head, made many sounds and held
high two fingers. He stamped his foot, rumbled deep
down in his internals like the foreboding of a volcano and showing his utter disgust in every way he
could, he went off as if by all counts I would see him
no more in the flesh. My friends who had been
looking on with keen interest and much amusement
said he was certainly gone this time. Making his
gyrations still more emphatic he soon returned with
the extreme air of finality which seemed to say that
though the heavens fell, the sea dried up, and Egypt
again be visitd by all of Pharaoh's plagues he would
see me dead and eaten by the Sultan's dogs before he
would recede another inch, and seeing the hotel
was near he dropped all but four fingers. I
also assumed a pose of finality, shook my head and
began to beckon to other traders. He suddenly
changed. The clouds left his face, he smiled until
his teeth shone, handed me the cane, and taking his
fifty cents went his way. As I write I see sitting
in the corner yonder that cane. I am keeping it as
a memento of my long-drawn-out trade with the
black oriental, neither of us speaking a word the
other could understand.

So pleased were several members of the party
with my cane that they desired one like it. My good
Baptist friend, Dr. W. R. Cullom of Wake Forest
College greatly desired one, but being unable to
suddenly come from the dignity of the class room
to such feats of street traffic, he offered me a very
large commission if I would buy him one, and that

night on one of Cairo's main streets I went the ground all over with another vender of canes and greatly pleased the heart of my good brother, so pleasant and brotherly in all our travels, by calling him from bed to deliver to him the trophy of that trade. His cane, however, cost him fifty-five cents —and in that extra nickel there lies another tale. Not that I was guilty of charging it for commission. That nickel taught me one of the most interesting lessons of Eastern trading. As I was going through the necessary preliminaries to the purchase of Dr. Cullom's cane a tall, sharp-eyed Egyptian came up and stepping at once between us he took the cane in his hand and asked me what I would give for it. I might have asked him what he meant by such rude interruption, but I did not. Rather, I stood there to learn what it meant. I told him I would pay two shillings and no more. I did not care to cheat the man nor persuade him to sell if he did not care to, but that was all I would give. He then talked to the man in his own tongue. The man protested and shook his head vigorously. I was informed he wanted more. To this I shook my head and turned to go. He handed me the cane and taking the money from me thrust it into the man's hand and pushing him said "Yallah impshi," which was interpreted by our guide to mean something not quite as elegant as "Get on out of the way you black rascal."

The man then came to me and informed me what his actions meant. He was what we would call a "go-between". This third party is really necessary

The Hole in our Ship, taken after the Collision.

ROMA - Piazza S Pietro

St. Peter's Cathedral in Rome. This is the Capitol of the Catholic Religion. The Vatican, home of the Pope, is to the reader's right.

to make any trade legally binding. When there is a difference of agreement between traders the third party who is self-appointed, comes in to consummate the bargain. Many times later on we saw this illustrated. If you buy something and it does not prove equal to the seller's claim you have no redress unless the third party was in the trade. Whatever he says settles it. It somewhat complicates matters, however, when you learn that this "go-between" dignitary will decide with the party who pays him the biggest tip. Of course he expects a fee for his services—usually from both the seller and the buyer. So I paid my man five cents. It is said to be a very lucrative business. I wondered how that system would work in this country. How would you like every time you tried to make a trade to have some man "butt in" and conclude it, then charge you a fee and tell you to "go to Guinea"?

We bought many articles of native products for trifling sums—beautiful beads, lace fancy work, mats, rugs, brass and other things—for almost nothing. Beautiful ostrich plumes in Cairo, sold for about one-tenth their value here. We saw many tourists, however, pay many times that because they took them at their first price. A lady in our party paid a dollar and a half each for two Turkey fezs to take home to her brothers, while a number of us who went together to the bazaars got ours for a quarter. And in the buying of those little red caps lies another tale. We thought a fez was a fez and there was no difference in them. So we got

them and adorning our heads like some pasha we
went through the hotel lobby with the other gentlemen on our way to supper. We didn't think anything was the matter with our harness. As we
gazed in the mirror we thought we were handsome
and we were wondering why those red caps were
not introduced in our country. But in the lobby
we met murmurs and unkind looks. It was explained when we learned there were two kinds of
fezs and while they were very much alike they were
very much unlike. One was the customary head-
gear of the people. The other was not quite so
high, darker in color and had a shorter tassel. It
was the badge of the insurrectionists and meant,
"Down with the Sultan." Some of us were wearing it. While we would not have spent much time
mourning if the old fellow should have gone down,
we had not come for the purpose of putting him
down, and we concluded if this cap branded us as
his enemy the other might class us as his
friends, and we put the little red skull caps away for
young Americans who would not be bothered over
such scruples and we crowned our pates with American toggery.

Numbers of times we were surrounded and our
way was blocked by the traders and beggars who
crowded us. Several times some of us used a borrowed plan that helped some. As they crowded us,
chattering away in words (if they could be called
words) we could not understand and gesticulating
with all their might, we looked them straight in the
face, gesturing violently and speaking loudly and

with great emphasis recited to them "Mary had a little lamb," "The boy stood on a burning deck," "Tom, Tom, the piper's son," and such other productions from childhood as we could recall and thought they would appreciate. It was always successful. They would look at us in a very peculiar way and move on. Whether they thought us crazy or whether they thought the proposition we submitted to them outweighed the one they proposed to us I was never able to learn. At other times we got ahead of those who came to us with outstretched hands begging for "backsheesh" by meeting them with open hands, crying loudly, "Backsheesh." Likewise we would meet traders and try to sell them things we had. These tricks usually nonpulsed them, but not always.

These Eastern traders are ahead of those of our own land in zeal and scheme and plan. They don't wait for you to come to their stores—they bring their stores to you. To the boats, hotels, streets, public places, everywhere they come with their goods. You have to watch them, but if you keep your eyes open you can make a dollar go further than you ever saw it go before and bring home things that make a lady happy for many moons to come.

CHAPTER XVII.

IN SUNNY ITALY.

From Egypt we turned our faces across the seas to Italy, having in us a desire to walk upon its sun-lit slopes as well as answer to the call that arose within, saying, "I must see Rome." The weather was good but some of our party insisted on getting sick, due perhaps to their surroundings and a small boat more than to the roughness of the seas; and then there was a little too much mutton grease or more properly goat grease in the cooking for some of our people. A very large per cent of the meat of these countries is mutton. It seemed to me sometimes about ninety-nine and a half per cent., and nearly all the mutton is goat. Of course, in a party of four dozen people it is quite natural to find a few unreasonable and fastidious people who are hard to please and insist on having some kind of meat besides mutton. Brother Williams, my fellow traveler and room mate, belonged to this class. He vigorously objected to having all his food cooked in goat greese. One day at dinner, as we took our seats at the table, he smiled at the stack of dishes before us. It looked from the big outfit in front of each one that we might expect something fine.

"We'll certainly get something besides mutton in all these courses" said Brother Williams. The first course came. It was mutton and potatoes. The dishes were removed and the second course came. It was mutton and peas. The dishes were cleared away and the third course was brought, it was mutton and squashes. The dishes were again removed and the fourth course came, it was mutton and macaroni. The next course was fruit, then coffee and cheese. Brother Williams came in on the last. A large per cent of the milk and butter in these countries is also the products of goats. Some of our ladies often said that when the rest of the fare did not suit them they could fall back on the milk and butter, for everywhere we went these two articles were good. This is true, for goat's milk and butter is richer and better than that that comes from cows, if you will banish your prejudice. Those who knew did not tell the ladies the kind of milk and butter it was and they came back from their trip commending these articles of diet.

The dairy business of Italy and these other countries is interesting and odd to Americans. In the early morning hours your attention is attracted by a bell ringing, which sounds like an oldtime bell on a home-coming cow. It is on the neck of the leader of a flock of milk goats. They are driven to the front door or shop of the customer who brings out a pitcher, and the dairyman proceeds then and there to milk as much as is needed while the goats proceed to clean up the yard of all trash and other things which come in the realm of a goat's appetite. When a customer lives upstairs, the traveling dairy mounts the stairway with ease and grace, cleaning up rubbish and serving milk to all who call for it. There are several advantages in this method of dairying: you are always sure to get fresh milk and the milkman has no chance to add water to it, and besides this, you get your

garbage, trash, papers, etc., consumed free. This
business so impressed me that when the war started
and it seemed we could not get home for months to
come I made a proposition to Williams to put the
few dollars we had left into the purchase of a few
goats. I thought between us we could carry on a
small dairy business and make an honest living
until we could get home. It must be very profitable
to have a dairy that will convert all the trash of a
town into milk and butter. The town ought to pay
for the cleaning up of the premises and the feed for
the milk producers would cost nothing.

The natural charm and beauty of Naples and the
surrounding country from this elevation cannot be
described by tongue or pen. Looking down upon the
city that clusters about the mountain like a necklace of pearls on the throat of a queen, with the
mellow light of the Italian skies shining down upon
it all, makes the heart throb faster but thickens the
tongue so that it can frame no words and stiffens
the fingers so they can write no lines to tell what
the soul is seeing and feeling. And at night when
the sun went on beyond those historic hills and the
moon came up across the bay to let down upon the
waters and the hills her silvery mantle of liquid
light, and the stars quiet and full of peace, looked
down from a cloudless sky upon the teeming life
and flickering lights of the city, while old Vesuvius
from her strange infernal-like funnel sent up her
flash of fire against the sky as though at any hour
she meant to cover the fairest scene of earth with
burning death, I put up my pencil and note-book,
unable to write, and looked and looked and looked for

"My soul today
Was far away
Sailing the blue Vesuvian Bay;
With watchful eyes
My spirit flies
Under the walls of Paradise."

Below me lay a great city full of misery, shame and poverty, for with all its glory nowhere on the earth is there more wretchedness than in Naples, but I saw none of these things. The dirty alleys, ragged beggars, half starved souls, hovels of misery and dens of shame came not to my view, for a glorious light seemed to transform all the defects of earth and humanity into a picture of unearthly beauty. To and fro went boats with the commerce of the world. Near by arose the rocks of Amalfi, Sorenta and Capri, and the Islands of Ishia besides many other points full of charm to those who take interest in the history of their fellow men.

Not only is this section full of interest because of its natural beauty but hardly a spot on the globe is richer in the history it has written. In the highest days of Roman grandeur and greatness, this, next to Rome, was the spot they loved the most, and here they lavished all the wealth they had, to make, with nature's help, a land to equal heaven. Down from Rome along the Apian way came a mighty thoroughfare, one of those well built Roman roads whose work still stands enough to show how great it was. Along this highway by the hills of Campagnia teemed the stream of Rome's richest and greatest life, coming and going to and from the Eternal City and Naples, the City of the Sea. Chariots rich and gaudy, drawn by the finest horses with lace and gold, bearing Caesar's retinue, litters of luxury in which reclined Rome's fair and well perfumed ladies carried by their slaves; caravans on missions of merchandise; battalions of soldiers with the Imperial uniform and the Roman eagle, went in ceaseless stream along this road. It must have been a wonderful sight to those who looked upon it.

In and about Naples many mighty Romans of those olden days when Rome ruled the world came here where they had mansions and villas. This was the home of Horace and Hadrian, and Cicero and Virgil. This great old Latin poet loved these hills with all the love of a poet's great soul, and on one of these hills today his tomb is found where, in compliance with his dying wish, his body was brought to rest on this wave-washed shore, where so often the old poet had dreamed the dreams he wove into his poems. On his tomb is this verse, written by himself:

"In lovely Mantua was my child-hood's home,
'Till my ambition lured me forth to Rome;
Flocks, fields and heroes have inspired my breast,
And now on Naple's sunny slopes I rest."

Here Brutus stabbed to death the mighty Caesar, lord of the whole world. Across the bay yonder at Capri-Tiberius, Emperor of Rome, came when broken with age and disease, brought on by sin and shame, to spend his closing years burying his soul still deeper in debauchery and vileness than he had done in his youth. Here he fortified himself against all his enemies, human and superhuman, believing he was powerful enough to fight them all. He built twelve villas and supplied them with all the luxury wealth could lavish and a sin-cursed soul could concieve. He spent a month in each villa, keeping his sinful soul intoxicated with sin and shame that he might feed his fiendish desires and keep away the call of conscience and the shadow of eternity that was fast coming across his bloody path.

On the high hill overlooking the rocks and the waters, they show you now a point called the "Leap of Tiberius." After putting his victims and prisoners and all whose conduct did not suit him through the most awful tortures his soul could conceive, and tiring of their agony and groans he had his soldiers plunge them from the cliff upon the rocks below, where more soldiers waited to continue their tortures if they were not dead before their mangled bodies went to the fish. Here, this sinful old Roman whose life for cruelty and debauchery almost equalled that of Nero was living his closing years when the Romans and Jews in Jerusalem crucified Jesus. When the news came to him from Rome that Jesus had suffered at their hands, doubtless, he gloried at the picture and wished he had been there to lend a helping hand.

The shame and sin of Roman life is unspeakable and cannot be told. Nowhere save in Rome was more of it seen than along the shores of Naples. It does seem strange that scenes so peaceful looking now and so richly blest with nature's hand should be so cursed with the sin of man! Yet it is ever so. Where is the sun-lit slope, breeze-swept hill, or wave-washed shore made beautiful by nature that has not been stained with blood and cursed by the sin of man? The flowers have been stained, the streams crimsoned, the quiet night made hideous with shrieks and curses; and the balmy days polluted with human crimes, and It is man who does it. His sinful feet have stopped no-where. His bloody hands have passed over no object. His fiendish appetite has preyed on everything. Rome, Athens, Jerusalem, the Temple, the Altar, Calvary, every thing and every place cries out to heaven how the sin-cursed soul of humanity's vile vandals have carried their slimy reeking stream of filthy sin over every thing and every body.

Not only has the sin of the race marred the fair picture of Sunny Italy but it seems that a super-human power has conspired to punish the race for so sinning on its fair shores by constantly tearing down its works and making the people live with the constant fear that at some sudden moment, volcanoes, earthquakes, pestilence, or plague, the lives and homes of the people may be ground into the dust. Time after time through the centuries, these fair hills have shaken in the throes of mighty earthquakes that left ruin and desolation in the wake of its trembling waves. Many times cities and country districts have been utterly destroyed. A few days after our departure, these hills shook until thousands were dead and still more were left homeless.

In 1883 a mighty earthquake shook the beauti-ful Island of Ischia, out in the Bay of Naples, as the people listened to the singing of the sirens. They were on the flood-tide of their social life, after supper, when without warning the island reeled like it had grown drunk on the wine they were drinking and when quiet from its spree, desolation and ruin came upon the stage instead of the gay festivities of the moment before. The organist was found dead at the instrument and the dancers in their last embrace upon the ball-room floor. As strange as it may seem the music they were making for the gay to dance by was "The Funeral March." How strange is the irony of fate that should thus turn the tables on those who, in burlesque, were dancing to "The Funeral March."! And yet fickle and sinful man has ever been so. He constantly passes from the stage of earth into the shodows of eternity, dancing to "The Funeral March."

When King Humbert, father of the present king of Italy, heard of the great disaster, he came in person to the scene to direct the work of relief and rescue as was his custom and as is the custom of many European sovereigns in times of public calamity. The present king came down to the ruined cities last summer to help the people with his deeds and words. When the old king reached the stricken island and looked upon the scene before him he cried, "My God, I never dreamed of such misery." The horrors of a buried city must be unspeakable.

The people live in constant dread of a return of such calamities and yet they rebuild again upon the ruins of the past and go on sinning and living

as the victims of the past had done. It was believed
by the ancients that these hills rested upon some
huge monster who grew tired of the burden he
carried and shaking himself to be rid of his load,
he caused the destructive earthquakes to come.

The Plague also has often preyed with mighty
havoc upon Southern Italy. In 1884 death and destruction followed in the wake of this dread disease and thousands were dead. King Humbert at
once made ready for the stricken country against
the wishes of his friends and physician. He can-
celled important engagements of state and bade his
friends good-bye, as it was not at all improbable
they would never see him again. He worked faith-
fully until the plague was over. The ancient poets
had a saying, "See Naples and die." They perhaps
meant that the beauties and attraction of the city
were so great that you need not hope on earth to
excell them, and when you had seen it you had no
more on earth to see, and yet there is irony in the
saying. When you think of the way Naples has
been preyed upon by earthquake, cholera and volcano, you can but feel that if you are not in a hurry
about seeing it you may die.

It is a strange kind of human nature that men
will build their homes and spend their lives on the
very edge of ruin. The green slopes of Vesuvius
were covered with homes and vineyards when the
first upheaval came and it was covered again as
soon as the wreck could be cleared away. People
live and walk today upon its edge, climbing over
the fields of lava it cast up. These hills that have
so often been shaken and devastated by pestilence

are soon refilled with folks, and yet why wonder
at the folly of silly men in so doing? Has not the
race always been so? Do we not do the same?
There is a feeling of security in the peaceful promise of Nature. We hide from a storm behind a hill,
when the storm can tear up the hill. We ride out
on the ocean when it has swallowed its thousands.
We trust Nature like a child trusts a mother. It
is hard to believe the scenes we love can treat us
ill. And if, per chance, Mother Nature does send
danger down upon her child, we believe it will not
come again, surely not this time and not on us. So
Italy's children build again tomorrow on hills that
shook with death on yesterday, and plant their
Vineyards and build their homes upon the side of
Vesuvius, that mountain of murmuring fire with
the confidence you have when you sleep above your
furnace that warms you in the winter time. And
then to be familiar with a thing means not to be
afraid of it. I once had a friend who was so scared
of a coffin that it gave him cold chills to see one;
later on he worked in a coffin factory, handling
them all day long. Soon he was eating on them at
noon and taking an after dinner nap upon them
every day. Italy has become so well acquainted with
her volcanic hills that she sees no danger in them.

And then, in the enchanted dream that leads men
on, they forget the rocks, listening to the song of
the sirens and think not of the fate that awaits
them in their effort to grasp the fruit before them.
So men camp on the brink of ruin and gamble even
with death, and pitch their tents where angels dare
not tread, in their efforts to taste the sweets of sin.

As Italians sleep above the roaring of Vesuvian flames, heedless of danger, our sons sleep on the flames of eternal ruin, thinking not of judgment. As long as men fight, cheat, sin and trifle away their years and sleep on the edge of eternity, unprepared to meet their God, there is nothing strange in Italy's children planting grapes near the crest of burning Vesuvius.

We visited all the points of interest in and about Naples; the museum, shops and public buildings. Volumes could be written on these but I must pass by these, stop briefly at Pompeii and hurry on to Rome. Pompeii stands out alone in the world with a history all its own. There is no city the earth has ever built with a story at all like it. Seventy-nine years after Jesus was born in Bethlehem, this city of thirty thousand souls, in the midst of its gay life, was buried without warning under a mass of ashes and red hot melted rock, hotter than any fire of earth could make them. This destruction came from a peaceful old mountain near by, up whose slopes they and their children had often gone to look upon the hills around, and far away stretches of the silvery sea beyond the Bay of Naples. Upon the mountain's very top, they had often walked and rested, seeing no sign of danger because then the mountains had no sign of internal disturbance. After the complete burial of the city with many thousands of its people, who, overtaken with the flood of fire and burning lava, and lost in the clouds of smoke and darkness, could not find their way to the sea, they remained in this tomb while eighteen hundred years rolled over them. Then science reached forth its hand and opened the tomb and let the world look upon, not a buried person but a buried city, dead and resurrected not to a better life but to a stately death.

Your feelings in Pompeii are unlike those you have anywhere else in the world's works or its ruins. In the tombs of Egypt or amid the dust and white stones of other ancient lands, your feeling is like that, that touches the wondrous life of a day long gone but not forgotten, but when you walk the streets of Pompeii, this buried and destroyed city recently lifted up to the light of the sun, you have a feeling of sympathy and human interest as though you were looking upon the deeds of yesterday. Here are the streets with grooves where the carriage wheels ran; the stepping-stones from one side-walk to another; the public bakery where half done bread was found; further on is the market-place and the Forum with its court of justice; then the temples to the Roman gods, nine of them; then two theatres with seats for five thousand each, and a great amphitheatre with seats for twenty thousand. Posted on the walls are signs advertising big features at the theatre and the ampitheatre for the night, and history tells us the gay people were there at their games when the cloud began to rain its fire. One of these games scheduled was a "Roman Hunt." The stage was changed into a forest where the people set at large three lions, one elephant, six tigers, a crocodile and a boa-constrictor. Gladiators were then put into the arena and given weapons with which to hunt down the furious beasts while the people in the crowded theatre looked on; the scene was doubtless bloody enough to suit their depraved tastes. The crushing of bones, tearing of flesh, flowing of blood, mingled with the groans of the dying men and furious screams and snarls of the hungry beasts who fought over the human flesh and tore it to pieces like dogs would a hare, must have furnished a comedy (?) of entertainment that caused the Pompeian ladies and gentlemen to linger over the tea cups of the morrow as with uplifted jeweled hands and smiling faces they talked of the things they had seen.

On this fateful night there was something in the air that made the animals strange and restless. Instead of showing their teeth and leaping on the hunters, they ran nervously up and down the side of the cage, lashing their flanks with their tails and sending forth anxious growls as they sought an exit that they might flee for safety to the hills, for instinct was telling them of a coming doom the stupid people could not see. To them the world was the same and life as sweet and sinful as ever. Presently, a distant rumble was heard. It increased with a roar of thunder that shook the hills and made the rocks tremble. The theatre shook, the walls fell and behind them the old mountain was burning. High into the air rolled a column of smoke and flame and then upon the world around, the clouds rained fire. Several feet of burning ashes followed by rivers of red hot melted rock ran down upon the city. Many escaped and many did not. The city was buried and preserved like we can fruit. Eighteen hundred years it was air tight. When excavations were undertaken many objects were found just as they were buried, others that had disapeared, leaving a perfect shape where the now hardened lava had formed about them as it turned them into dust, were saved by the excavators by opening a hole and pouring in plaster. When it was hardened it produced the exact form. The lava was then cleared away and the object saved.

Many wonderful objects are seen in the museum. They speak with pathos of a people destroyed in sinful pleasure. One is an old man decrepit and bent. About his body is a heavy loaded money-belt; perhaps he turned back to save his treasure and lost his life. A woman likewise was found trying to carry her jewels away with her. A dog was found in the street twisted in contortion, with his mouth open, where he perished by his master rather than leave him and flee for safety. A dove is seen upon her nest protecting even in the face of such a storm, the life beneath her breast. Tables set with food, families in the home circle, babies upon their mother's breasts add to the pathetic scenes. We went into the prison where three poor victims were found chained to the wall. The prison key was found near them on the floor where the keeper in his flight had left it. The key that unlocked the door that led them to safety was not quite in their reach. Tradition has it that these men were condemned to the arena later in the evening of the fatal day. Pompeii was indeed a wicked city and must have rivalled

Sodom for unspeakable evidence of its debauched life
and revolting sin is seen in a section of the museum.
You are almost forced to believe God destroyed this
city as he did the city of the Plains long ago.

Pompeii must have been one of the most beautiful cities of the world, for it has much evidence of
that after being in the grave eighteen centuries. In
the background was the mountain and at its front
door the wonderful bay with its shores dotted with
so many points of interest. The city was on an elevation that enabled the people to see all the land
around. Many of the homes speak of luxury and
grace. The streets are beautiful, the buildings great.
As it stood centuries ago adorned with all the glitter
of Roman grandeur it must have been indeed a
grand city.

One of the greatest novels ever written is "The
Last Days of Pompeii" by Bulwer Lytton. He spent
a long time in Pompeii studying the history, life and
setting of the place that he might give a full account of the city and its people in their latter days
and weave through it all his charming story. How
well he has done the work the world knows. His
descriptions of its life and especially the awful destruction, is the best to be found anywhere, and is
hardly excelled in the literature of the world. As
we walked through the streets of the city and were
shown the house of Glaucus, we could almost see the
living forms of Arbaces, the Egyptian; Glaucus, the
Greek, Ione the fair Neapolitan and Nydia the blind
girl who in the awful hour of death and darkness,
needing no light to guide her feet over the streets

she had learnd so well in her dark days, found her lover and guided him safely to the sea.

From Naples we took the train for Rome, one hundred and fifty miles back further in the hills. Every foot of this ride was over historic ground; the hills and fields seemed rich and full of life and everywhere, Italy seemed to be putting on her best clothes. The crops seemed to be good and the fields were dotted with white cattle with long horns, and the hills were covered with vineyards. As the sun was setting we came in sight of the Eternal City sitting on her seven hills, where for so long she ruled the world. The first view we had of Rome was of the ruins of the Claudian Aqueduct of other days. Then there burst upon us the vision of modern Rome nestling on the bank of the Tiber with the sinking sun falling in blazing splendor upon the dome of St. Peters.

In the short space before me it will be impossible to even touch upon the things of supreme interest in this city so full of charm for the human race. Volumes could be and have been written on the life and history of this old city. All these books of the masters would fill a library and they have not told it all. It seems folly for me who am no master to try. I shall pass by history, art, and Rome's great relics and mention only a few points of interest and the things of peculiar interest to me .

The first morning after our arrival in Rome we got in carriages and started sight-seeing. Our course soon brought us to the Tiber. We halted beside the yellow slow-moving stream and meditated. Great old river, for beyond the legend days of Romulus and Remus when there was no Rome you were going on your journey as you are to-day! Of all the rivers that have found their way through the hills to the sea, none can tell the tales you can! What secrets you have buried in your bosom! What treasures you could bring to light if you would! your banks have lured the wooing lover, and your stream has run red with blood! No stream has ever known such horrors, heard such bitter cries or borne away so many victims. When the secrets of the earth must be given up what stories you will tell!

We crossed the Bridge of San Angelo at the end of which stands the massive circular tombs of Emperor Hadrian, one thousand feet in circumference. We rode over the seven hills of the city. The most noted of these seven hills upon which Rome stands are the Pincian, Palatine and Capitoline. The Pincian hill is now as in olden times the haunt of high society; it is a beautiful park, restful and peaceful, giving little indication of the bloody horrors that it, like the other hills of Rome knew in the olden days. It was on this hill, while the sister of Napoleon rode in her chariot, one of her rejected lovers stabbed himself so near her, the blood spurted on her chariot. Every inch of land here has known dark crimes and vileness. It is said Nero's ghost wanders here now because its history suits so well his taste. But the soul of that vile Roman finds no such a pleasant place to travel.

The Palatine Hill was the part of the city where the aristocrats and royal families lived. From the buried ruins here, recent excavations have brought great wonders to light and more are yet to follow. The Capitoline Hill was the portion of the city devoted to the capital. On it now stands the great museum. Among the great wonders of this building the thing that struck me most was a selection of marble busts made from life of the Rulers of Rome. It was a matter of much interest that thirty-one of these rulers were horribly murdered and two committed suicide. This is another commentary on the vile life of that day. One of the most striking faces in this lot, to me, was that of old Nero with his thick bull-like neck and face. Truly licentious and devilish, he haunted me for days. Of all the men who have made history, none was more depraved than he. He consireded himself divine when he was devilish. In the heighth of his power he used to drive out of Rome along the Apian way with one thousand wagons carrying his baggage while five hundred she asses followed, to supply milk in which Mrs. Nero bathed to preserve her youth and charm. No scene of blood and shame was bad enough to suit this old monster. In his restlessness for excitement he conceived the idea in his depraved and drunken brain to burn Rome and look upon the drama or comedy of a burning city. History tells us he fiddled and sang his silly songs as he watched the horrors of the burning city. He then blamed the Christians for the fire and started the bloodiest persecutions the world has ever known. But his day came, and to save himself from a worse fate at the hands of his enemies he fell upon his dagger. His soul to-day wanders in a place not so fair as the Pincian Hill.

Our path soon led us to the Protestant cemetery which is a point of peculiar interest to all Protestants. As its name would indicate it is the resting place of many—some of them heroic souls—who found their sleep by facing their foes. In this beautiful spot upon which nature has turned on the light if peace rests the dust of those two great poetic souls and bosom friends, Keats and Shelley. In other years their souls had struck mine through the songs they had sung and I lingered by these graves with reverent heart to read the words upon their tombs. I copied in my notebook the following from the head-stone on the grave of Keats: "This grave contains all that was mortal of a young English poet, who, on his death-bed, in the bitterness of his heart at the malicious power of his enemies, desired these words to be engraven on his tomb, 'Here lies one whose name was writ in water.' "

Below this his friend Shelly had written the following beautiful tribute:

"Keats if thy cherished name be writ in water,
   Each drop has fallen from some mourner's cheek
   A sacred tribute such as seek
Tho oft in vain for dazzling deeds do slaughter;
   Sleep on not honored less for epitaph so meek."

I was amazed at the scale upon which the ancient Romans built. Their works of art it seems would take all the genius of an age to create and it was said of the Rome of old that there were as many marble statues, in the city as there were inhabitants. These are masterpieces and their greatness and profusion is so far beyond me I shall not try to write of them. The public buildings, streets and roads were built as if they were to witness the end of the world. With all the faults of the old Romans they did not do things in a half-way slip-shod manner. History tells us of one architect who, so poorly built a theatre that it fell, killing several thousand people. All the future history of the builder is summed up in one short chapter, "He was banished." If we had such a custom, doubtless, we would build upon a more lasting foundation!

The water supply of Rome is wonderful. The city is full of fountains, public and private baths. Its great water system is supplied by streams brought down from the mountains. In ancient days the water was brought through massive over head aqueducts which ran into the city like great railway trunk lines. In the old days of Rome it is said the water system was greater than it is now. The per capita supply of water was 110 gallons, the greatest any city ever had. In this day of sanitation and cleanliness, London has only thirty gallons per person and Paris seventy. The old Romans were badly stained in their morals but they believed in keeping their bodies clean.

When my feet stood in the Forum in Rome my feelings were such that they could not be recorded. In all the earth there is no place like this. It was the seat of Rome's life and government. Here they made history while you wait. Here still stands the "Golden Mile Post," marking the centre of the world. From the farthest confines of the then known world, all roads ran to the "Golden Mile Post." To the forum and from it, all distances were measured. Here the world was ruled, kings were made and unmade, kingdoms set up and put down. Here the mighty brains of the Roman Empire in its great days, wrought their deeds and plans into a mighty structure, whose influence will never leave the earth. Here the flaming tongues of Rome's orators swayed the people. Here Cicero made the speech that cost him his life, his enemies cutting off his head and carrying it to the Rostrum where so often he had sent forth his mighty and lasting orations, which for ages to come were to be the models of eloquence and rhetoric for armies of students to study in their schools. Holding up the bloody head they spat in his face and pulling out his tongue, its eloquence now hushed forever, they cut it to pieces as though it had been leather.

Here they murdered Julius Caesar "The noblest Roman of them all," and brought his mangled, bleeding body to gloat over. I could almost see the blood stains still upon the Rostrum. Caesar didn't have our religion and civilization. He was harsh and bloody and yet he stands out as one of the greatest men of the world. He certainly had some great and noble traits. He was not a renegade like Tiberius, nor a sneaking traitor like Brutus. He was a world-builder and a world-ruler to the manner born. When the dire plot was mature to take his life, and in the Forum they bore down upon him like wolves in the night upon a helpless traveler, he fought them single handed with a greatness and a heroism true to him. Men who owed their lives and fortunes to him were slashing at his heart with their knives. The hand of Brutus who owed so much to Caesar reached forth to take his blood, and as it pierced his flesh the mighty Roman turned his eyes full on him and said "You too Brutus"? Whatever faults Caesar had, he would not have done to them what they did to him. It made the heart feel strange to stand where all these things were done.

Just below the Forum the street runs into a large circular building which would set your mind to wondering if you did not recognize it from the many pictures you have seen. It is the great Coliseum, where the streams of Roman life used to come to see the games.

The building is on such a tremendous scale it overwhelms you to look upon it. It is built of stone, several stories high with many entrances. A large part of it is in ruins because many people of modern times got the material from it to build their homes in Rome, but not until they had used powder to loosen them, for the old Romans built it as they did their other works. That portion of the building not preyed upon by the vandalism of man is standing in fine state of preservation. Passing in one of the entrances we looked upon what might truly be called one of the wonders of the world. Tier on tier rose seats where the life of Rome used to sit until there was room for nearly ninety thousand people seated in the great theatre, all facing the great arena in front, which was in plain view to all. Often, this place was full, and it must have been a sight beyond power to imagine, to see the tremendous crowds of Rome's gay life pouring from the seven hills of the Eternal City into the entrances of this great building which stands where several streets meet. The vision that meets the eye as you gaze upon that brilliant throng in its gayety and gorgeousness, and the great building finished with the art and wealth of Rome's fine hand, produced a scene that has never been equalled in the history of the human race.

Passing into the center we stood upon the arena, where the eyes of Rome used to look down on blood as it flowed in rivers, and in the calm gathering of twilight we prayed. What a difference in this place then and now? Now it is a place of desolation and stillness while peace casts her mantle down. But then what was it that met the gaze of heaven? Yonder is the place where Nero and his Royalty and Nobility sat along with the vestal virgins, who directed the games according to their fiendish whims. When a foe was cast to the ground, if they raised their thumbs he was spared, if they held them down he was thrust through with a sword. Here are the trap doors leading to the dens. These dens were kept filled with the fiercest wild beasts. Large numbers of men at great expense were kept busy hunting down these beasts in sufficient quanity to entertain the Emperor and his people. What a task it was to gather up these ferocious beasts and get them alive to their dens below the arena? Many gladiators fought to the death on this arena to entertain gay Rome.

Several thousand were kept in training all the time. They were glad to run the fearful risk of the awful fate that sooner or later was sure to be theirs in the hope of receiving from those galleries the applause of Rome. What will men not do for a little applause? Many criminals were condemned to the arena where they fought with the beasts as Rome looked on. But the reason this place is dear to every Christian heart and brings to you the feeling you have at Calvary, is not because deluded fools met to shed one another's blood in quest of the approving smile of Rome's fair ladies, or because criminals were limbed by lions, while the crowd cheered. The reason is that this is the place where more Christians met their death to vindicate their faith than any where else in the world. It seemed to me as I stood there after eighteen centuries the earth was so black and soaked in blood that you could almost take a handful of dirt and squeeze it out. The fights of gladiators and criminals became too tame for Rome's fair ladies and gallant gentlemen. Old Nero, having burnt a section of the city, felt an aroused public would hound him down on account of this and other deeds too vile to mention. He had poisoned his own mother and kicked his wife Poppea to death for another young face, upon which his crime-soaked soul had looked, and, desiring some new excitement and entertainment he had the Christians accused of the base deeds he himself had done. They were arrested by wholesale, cast into dungeons, where in starvation, filth and disease they awaited their turn at the arena. Day after day large numbers of them, men women and little children were cast in the arena for Rome's entertainment and subjected to shameful treatment too awful and revolting to tell. Disrobed, they were tied to the horns of wild bulls and the heels of horses, or soaked in oils and tied to stakes about the arena and set on fire, that their burning bodies might give light for the games. They were put in the arena and those awful trap doors raised so the half-starved lions, leopards and tigers could come out to feed upon them. Rome laughed and cheered at their dying groans and prayers, mingled with the snarls and roars of the devouring beasts and gazed enraptured as the beasts tore their flesh, crushed their bones, drank blood and satisfied, slept upon the sands. It is said it took a small army of men the rest of the time till the next entertainment to clear the arena of loads and loads of mangled forms and blood and put it in shape with clean sand and perfumery and incense, for sometimes the odors were almost too much for the depravity of Rome.

It seemed to me in the gathering night as we stood there, I could almost see a ladder let down from heaven to that blood-stained arena, while down it came an army of angels with Christ Himself the Leader. When the Master's holy feet, still showing the place where the nails were driven, rested on the ground, He raised his hand pierced and bleeding still. From the bloody dirt below, I saw an army of souls rise up in garments white and glistening. Their faces were filled with heavenly light and their foreheads crowned with beautiful crowns of everlasting life. They met their Savior singing "Hallalujah, hallelujah, redeemed by the blood of the Lamb." An angel took each one by the hand and Jesus leading the way, they started up the golden ladder, while from the top of the ladder of gold came a volumn of song that shook the stones of Rome, and the song they were singing was,

> "Up to the bountiful giver of life
> God's children are gathering Home."

And then I saw another vision: old Nero was making his last retreat, followed by those enraged souls who sought his blood. His throne was lost; his power gone. No one in all the world loved him, but all the men hated him. No heart had a tender feeling of respect for him but all loathed him. He was followed by his enemies and by red-eyed devils hot upon his trail to close out the mortage they held on his sin-soaked soul. The bloody ghosts of all his crimes that night bore down upon him in an army he could not drive back, while they reached out their bony hands clutching at his throat. And conscience, that great white spirit that cannot be driven off forever but after all crime and sin known to man has thrust him away, will come back to press with a hand of iron his eternal claims upon the soul, was there, white but strong. This dauntless spirit gripped the soul of the doomed victim until his breath was almost gone. In the darkness that gathered about him he drove his dagger into his bloated, polluted carcass once decked in royal robes. With an eternal darkness falling on his eyes and a multitude crowding down to grind his filthy flesh under their heels in the dust, a legion of devils gripped his soul and bore it beyond the confines of hope into outer darkness, shouting in triumph over the trophy that they bore.

It has been wondered how the human race can become so repraved. Without the saving and restraining power of the Gospel of Christ, with all the culture and greatness the world can give, it is a downward course and humanity has fallen to the bottom and it will do so again without this saving power.

On the other side of the Forum is a dungeon. We climbed down these narrow steps into the stifling air of this underground cell, whose only means of light was a little overhead window through which a feeble little stream of light made its way. This was where the Apostle Paul spent his last days in Rome. Here by this feeble light, chained to a soldier, his limbs shackled until they were chafed and raw, he wrote some of that wonderful portion of the Bible that has so richly blest the world. Here, it is supposed he wrote portions of Galatians, Ephesians, Phillipians, Colossians and the Epistles to Timothy. Here, he spent his last days isolated from friends and loved ones. After a life of wandering and hardship he was closing out his days,

deprived of the communion and sympathy of his
brethren. His only attendant was the Roman guard.
He knew full well what his end would be. Perhaps
his reason in appealing to Caesar was to claim his
right as a Roman citizen and get the privilege of
preaching the gospel in Rome. After preaching
with the power of the Spirit to the Eternal City he
waited in his imprisonment for his earthly end.
The last word he wrote was to his son in grace,
Timothy, and through him to the Church for all
time. He is speaking his last word; his nerve is
steady; his heart is strong; his head is clear. Casting a backward glance along the road he had already come, he writes, "I have fought a good fight";
(you can almost hear the clank of the chains as he
drags them along in writing). Of course he had
fought a good fight; few men under such tremendous odds had fought as hard or a better fight. "I
have finished my course." Glorious thing to say. He
had run his race and finished the work he had to do.
"I have kept the faith"; how well he had kept it!
All the power of earth and hell had never been able
to make him lose faith. Blessed is he who can
say these three things as he looks back. Then
quietly he looks at the present. The axe is in the
hand of the executioner and will soon add his blood
to the stream that flows in Rome: "I am now ready
to be offered up." To all the sacrifices the earth
had known, including Calvary, he was ready, glad
to offer his own life. "The time of my departure
is at hand." The wonderful vision of this man had
swept beyond the realm of death; to him there was

no such thing as dying; he was just waiting, tired and worn upon the shore, for the ship to come to take him to the blessed home that awaited him beyond the storms and troubles of earth. "My departure," what a wonderful conception of death! Then sweeping the clear and cloudless sky of the vast future, he added: "Henceforth there is laid up for me a crown of righteousness, which the Lord, the Righteous Judge shall give me at that day." Of course there was. No man who had the past and present experience that was his would fail to get the future reward. "And not to me only but to all them also that love His appearing." Wonderful assurance. Greater than all the greatness of Rome, the Eternal City, is the promise God gives His children in the Heavenly City.

I did not write the Pope I was coming to Rome, for I did not want him to go to any extra trouble for me. In fact I hardly expected I would go to see him for I did not take any low-neck clothes or pontifical pantaloons, and felt I did not have sufficient duds and dusters to be nosing in such quarters.

I ventured to visit the king of Italy in his gorgeous palace, and drop in to look at the dazzling house of the Kaiser and even peep through the premises of the Sultan of Turkey, with such clothes as I wore, but then the pope of Rome is different! He puts himself up above all kings of the earth and sits down on the throne of God to be ruler of heaven and earth. Besides my clothes, I didn't have credentials. It is true I had a passport as an American citizen, signed by William J. Bryan and other certificates to tell from whence I came and who I was, but what are such poor papers in the presence of the pope of Rome? I knew no priest or cardinal to sign my pass to St. Peter's throne, and while there was a strong blue stream of good old Irish blood coursing through the crimson tide of my life, it was that tide you do sometimes find in the Emerald Isle that bears on its flood no cargo of love or homage to him who sits on Peter's (?) throne and holds the keys in his hands. In case I should see him, I had the rheumatism of Protestant independence in my joints and could not bow to him, and I had a fever blister on my lips and could not kiss his toe, no matter how clean it was. Thus handicapped by circumstances and heredity, I did not write him I was coming, but thought if I did go to see him, I would take him by surprise. However, one of the most unexpected and highly enjoyed pleasures of my visit to Rome was seeing the pope. It did turn out to be a pleasure and this is how it came about and why it was a pleasure.

One Sunday afternoon, the great Italian Mureski was to sing at St. Peter's. During the week we had heard him sing in St. John's and so thrilled were we that we desired to hear him again. His voice is one of the most wonderful of the world's singers. It sounds like a big choir of female voices completely filling the building. When told he was to sing in St. Peter's on Sunday afternoon, we finished our dinner and Williams, Gibson and myself made our way toward St Peter's. Enormous crowds of people, on cars, carriages and afoot were moving that way, among them a large number of priests, more than I had ever before seen in my life. We thought they were going to the service in St. Peter's but when we saw the crowd going into the right wing of the Vatican instead of the Cathedral, we enquired the meaning of it and were told in Italian that the people were going to see the pope.

For a while we thought it was one of the fakes they serve you so often in these countries and we paid little attention to it until we were assured by several, who seemed to know, that it was true and the pope was giving a public audience in the court of the Vatican. We were still in doubt and felt that if he was to be seen, we must be counted out as we had no ticket and had no pull to get one, but with that curiosity that makes one follow a crowd we fell in, determined to go until we were halted. This was not long, for we ran into two Swiss guards, dressed up like dancing monkeys with drawn swords. They demanded us, in Italian, to halt. At least, that is what I suppose they said though they may have told us they were glad to see us. Anyhow, we halted. We finally understood we could not be admitted unless we had tickets, and not being able to get any intelligent information as to how and where the tickets were to be secured, we turned back toward St. Peter's.

Presently we met a stout Italian, who, in a whisper, asked us if we wanted to see the pope. We said we were trying to see all the ruins of Europe and would like to count him in if we could, but could not see him because we had no ticket, and didn't know whose coat to pull to get one. The rascal then informed us he had some tickets, and while it was against the law to do it he would sell us some for two lires, 40 cents each. This made us indignant and we turned away in disgust. But on second thought we decided it would be worth while for us as free-born American citizens to pay the forty cents and see one of the greatest shows of the earth—a deluded multitude bowing down to their man-god. And looking back upon it now, I consider it one of the best investments I ever made. We paid the fellow and took the ticket which I have saved as a souvenir, for I somehow got by the guards without giving up my ticket. Here is the ticket:

No. 4355.   Gratis.

Anticamera Pontifica

Permesso per assistere all 'Udienza di Suc Santita nel gromo di Domenicia 2 Agosto alle on 17,30 5½ P. M. Dal Vatican 31 Luglio 1914 L'engress e dal por— Vittorio Ameded Rannuzzee De Beanche tone di Brongo.   Arcevescove tit de Tiro.

Maestro De Camera De Sua Santita.

Notice it is gratis. Of course Rome could not afford to advertise such a show of the pope and charge for seeing him perform. So to save their faces they pretend it is a free religious service in which the pope partakes, and that it is against the law to sell tickets, and that the blame for the selling is on those who secure them illegally and sell them themselves. But how do the men who get them, get them in such large quantities?

My number was 4355, which means I was the four thousand, three hundred and fifty-fifth, and there were twice that many more almost that followed. And yet the pope is welcome to my forty cents and I will not even ask him how he spent it. I got the worth of my money, and learned more lessons for forty cents than I've learned in some schools. But, Rome, don't come to me advertising your monkey show as a gratis religious service, and then have the town full of ticket agents selling to everybody.

After we bought our tickets we fell in line with the crowd that grew larger every second and were borne on the tide through the door of the Vatican, out into the large and beautiful court. Everything was grand and imposing. Such an array of cardinals, priests, seers and bead counters could not be found anywhere else in the world. All about us Catholics were counting beads and clasping costly crucifixes in their hands. On one side of us was the company of Swiss guards with uniforms of gold and glory it would be hard to surpass, and heavily armed. On the other side was the Royal Italian guards with costumes and swords in keeping with the occasion. Officers and guards were lined up all about the enclosure. The crowd from behind pressed us until we were near the center of the great enclosure. Above us on the first balcony stood the red-hatted cardinals, prominent among them, Merry Del Val, who, on one occasion locked horns with Roosevelt and Fairbanks. And whatever faults you find with Mr. Roosevelt,—let us remember in passing, he gave the pope and cardinal a good stiff black eye when they served notice on him that he would have to refuse to speak in the Methodist Church or not come to the Vatican. We all know how he went to the Methodist Church and cut the Vatican. Some statesman would not have done it.

After a while the great court was full, containing perhaps ten thousand folks. Several bands began to play music that charged the air and thrilled the soul. There was a flutter in the balcony in front and a still greater flutter through the crowds, men bowed their heads and moved their lips, women closed their eyes, hugged their crucifixes tighter and counted their beads. Then a silver trumpet appeared from a window above as if an angel from heaven had come to blow it; for, looking into it, I saw no man. Then out upon the air, from the mouth of that silver trumpet came the sweetest strains of music it seemed to me I had ever listened to. All eyes were lifted to the door above, and the crowd was as still as death. Then into the doorway stepped the snowwhite figure of Pius X, pope of Rome. When the crowd saw him it almost took my breath away, for I had not expected what happened. I had supposed they would be still and reverent. I have never seen anything like it. I have seen the political conventions of the olden days. I have been in the crowd when Roosevelt came to town, and among a hundred thousand I have seen him show his teeth. I have seen Bryan send up his guns from the trenches in a multitude that shook the earth; but I have never seen anything like that Sunday in the Vatican. It seemed to me a dozen bands turned loose an explosion of accumulated music that jarred the Vatican, and the yells and screams that rose from the crowd seemed to make the Tiber tremble. Above the roar I heard many cry, "Papa, Papa," which in their language meant father or pope. After Pius had received their acclaim for a while he bowed his head and raised his hand, and as though a hand from heaven had paralyzed the crowd, their music ceased, their lips were still, and hugging to their hearts their images, they fell upon the ground. They threw kisses at him, since they were too far away to kiss his foot, and mumbled out their prayers to him as though they had suddenly met the Lord God Almighty face to face. While the preliminaries were going on we held a conference to know what to do. All were supposed to bow. Guards and soldiers, as well as priests and fanatics, were all about us. If we declined to do homage to their god we knew not what they might do to us. There came charging through the flood-tide of my blood the Protestant fires back along my ancestral lines from the days of Cromwell; there rose before me the silken colors of my country's flag, and above all there rose the Christ of God who died for me and alone deserved my worship. I am sure my brethren felt as I did. So when the crowd went down we rose straighter and stood higher, looking beyond the white form of the pope of Rome to the pure, free skies above his head, where God our Father receives from earth the worship of His children. We three were the only ones in that part of the great crowd we saw standing. There may have been others behind us, but none in front stood. Many Protestants stood for a few seconds, but could not endure the strain and went down. All the time I expected a blow on the head by an officer or worshipper because we did not worship with them, but it did not come. When he had whined out his droning Latin prayer the people arose; the pope, leaning on the arm of his body guard, passed back into the Vatican, and the crowd dispersed, scattering itself through the streets of Rome. We made our way back to the hotel happy. We had seen the pope of Rome, and our knees had not bowed to him.

CHAPTER XVI.

ON THE SHORES OF CANAAN.

The long looked-for moment in the journey had come. On the morning of July 6, 1914, our boat cast anchor off from Joppa, and our eyes rested on the hills of "The Promised Land." Before us lay that wonderful little strip of land that has wrought its name in the fabric of human history as no other land the sun ever shone on. Other lands have been great in the world's history because of the might of their brains and the skill of their hands. They have built lasting monuments and left their names written forever on the pages of history. But whatever other lands have done since the world swung out fresh from the hand of God, it remained for this little plot of earth along the Mediterranean Sea to earn in the record of history the title, "Holy Land." In the soil of these hills God selected the place to plant the Tree of Faith, whose shade was destined to shelter the world. Here is the only place of which history has any knowledge that the Lord God walked and talked in living form with men. Around these hills and historic mountains He tied the mighty chain of His never-failing love and moored the world to His eternal throne so it could never drift away. Here He built with man His nation and set up His kingdom, sitting in all the councils of His people, giving them their laws, and handing down from heaven the patterns by which they should build. Here was the cradle of

His church; here His own Son was sent to save the people, and they shed His blood upon the hills God loved so well.

Every hill, stream, stone and tree in this land has a history of joy and sorrow, light and shadow, life and death, that would fill a book. Upon these hills the Bible was made, and its mighty characters lived in flesh and blood and wrought and died. Is it strange that this land should be so near to the heart of the Christian? Is it not natural that to look upon it and set foot upon its shores should give feelings that cannot be recorded? We felt that morning, gazing on that shore, that we were coming now to the goal of all our travels, and it seemed we could almost see the living figures of the giants of this land standing on the shore to meet us.

The length of Palestine is one hundred and fifty miles, and its area, both east and west of the river Jordan. That this little country should have had a history above all lands is of course due to the fact that in gaining the title, "Holy Land," it records the history of man, God and the devil contending for the mastery.

Is it not strange that the beautiful and peaceful hills God selected to plant a lovely garden for His children and build their home, should have been the scene of the worst bloodshed and warfare the nations have known? This country was repeatedly been overrun by armies which have wrested it from one another. It has been invaded by the Scythians, the Persians, the Parthians, the Persians again, the Turks twice the Mongols three times, by Alexander the Great, by the Romans, by the Crusaders, and by the Turks again, who have held possession for nearly eight hundred years. The wonder is there is anything left after the invading hosts and heartless vandals have preyed upon it so long.

Perhaps this is a good place to remark what more and more seems to me to be a strange stroke of the hand of Providence. We have been taught from youth that "God moves in mysterious ways His wonders to perform." How He does take some of the works of the devil and make them work for His glory is a mighty evidence that His hand in on the pilot wheel. It seems to me the rankest fatalist could not have the heart to accuse God, our Maker and Father, of being the author of the sin, shame and misery of the earth. None would insult heaven and earth by claiming God was in league with the low and vile government of Turkey, and yet how God has put His hand into the affairs of the Turks and other evil people and worked out things for His glory is a study great and true. If Palestine had not fallen into the hands of the Turks, who believed in no advancement, and refused to let its sacred shrines and objects be explored by modern mer-chants; even preserving almost entirely the very life and customs of the olden times, because they believed in nothing new, we might have lost forever from the earth the Bible land as it was. For the greatest value of Palestine to Bible students is that it is not modern, but is almost as it was before the days of Jesus. Modern changes have only recently begun to take hold, but soon will sweep the country as the Turks pass forever from the stage of history and modern nations occupy the sacred hills. What they will do with it remains to be seen.

We were now ready to land and begin our long trip through the holy hills. Long had my heart throbbed in anticipation of the days now before me. The dream over which I had planned and prayed so long was ready to come true. This was really the Promised Land, and now my feet would walk upon it. I wondered if it would be disappointing? I almost dreaded it. Would closer view and real touch take away any of the sacredness of that history? Would what I should see of sin and common clay lower my idea of the Bible and weaken my faith in God and Jesus Christ my Savior? I had heard of those upon whom this result had come. I heard some of my friends say they did not want to go for fear it would thus affect them. If the journey would bring this result to me I wanted then to turn my face the other way and go home. Behind those hills my faith was anchored to the truth they knew. On the mighty rocks out there my soul was moored to the faith that arose one day. The breeze of this land had swept my soul, and its songs sounded in my heart. If aught of charm should pass away; if one whit less the chain of faith should hold me to the truth; if a single cloud should pass across the sun of hope that shone from over these hills upon my soul because of this journey now before us, I wanted to say "good-bye" to my friends and let them go on without me, leaving me to return deprived of the journey, but possessing still the cherished charm of the things of God.

I am glad to say, now that the journey is over and I am back again pursuing my humble course over the hills herding my Master's sheep, that no such result came to my soul. Whatever the result may be to those who make that journey, it has done more for me than my fondest dream had pictured. My faith has been reinforced with the iron bands of living reality; the truth has come for my eyes to see and my hands to touch; my soul has been lightened with a radiance I could find no where else on earth; the Bible and all its history is covered with a charm it never had before. These are some of the results that came to me as I traveled through the Holy Land, my Bible in hand, reading the history, life and gospel it had made in those places, with a prayer upon my lips that God would make it real.

One essential thing to a pleasant and profitable trip through Palestine is to have the right kind of a dragoman and guides, for much depends upon them. Our dragoman was Philip Jallouk, and his assistants were his brothers, George, Charlie and Abashia. I don't think it is putting it too strong to say nobody in Palestine or elsewhere ever had a better set of men to guide them. This is proven by the fact that they had charge of Miss Helen Gould and her party a few years ago when she made a tour of the Holy Land, and they received

from her the highest commendation. They are
Syrians, and descendants of the best families of
the days of the Crusaders. Perhaps their race even
goes back and takes up the blood of Abraham.
They are intelligent, cultured, educated Christian
gentlemen, being faithful members of the Episcopal
Church in Jerusalem. They were kind and friendly,
doing everything possible for our welfare and comfort. They spoke English with as much ease as
they did their own tongue. In fact, they were at
home in any tongue they found in that land. Philip,
especially, was one of the most attractive person-
alities I have met. There was a charm about his
manner, his mellow voice, and the warmth of his
soul that drew us all to him. He was thoroughly ver-
sed in the Bible as well as all the life and custom
of Palestine, and his reverence and devotion to his
Lord and His land was beautiful. We cannot feel
too highly our debt to Philip in making our journey a pleasant and profitable one. Philip was the
general director and lecturer, while George looked
after the business side of the trip, and Charlie and
Abashia attended to the personal needs of the party.

Much has been said about the rough landing at
Joppa, and perhaps it all is deserved. There is no
harbor here, and the water is nearly always rough,
since there is nothing to break the waves. The
boats anchored out some distance from the shore and
little boats came gliding like ducks through the
rough and jagged rocks to take us ashore. About
two hundred of them ran alongside our ships and
their owners came onto the decks like rats in a bin,

climbing over one another and up the sides of the boat like squirrels. They beseiged us and seized us, clattering and clamoring in their jabbering, until we almost had to fight to keep them from taking us bodily away.

After awhile we found our guides, were assigned to our boats, and started for land. The boats lay along side the ship rising and falling with the waves. It seemed to me they rose as high as a house. We were started down the ladder like cattle, and as the little boats rose on the crest of the waves we were shoved into them before the waves receded and they went down. Sometimes people would hesitate, and they were picked up and pitched over like sacks of corn. When our boats were full we made our way through the jagged rocks, guided by the skill of our oarsmen, who saw to it no evil befell us. Yet, in spite of their skill, many accidents occur in these rough and dangerous waters.

Joppa is noted in Bible history for several things. It was in these waters here that Jonah went down in a submarine. He was swallowed because he got on the wrong track, and many men to-day get swallowed because they get on the wrong ship. I recently met an educated (?) youth who wanted to question the orthodoxy of this Bible story. He said a whale could not swallow a man for his throat was only six inches wide. I told him that was easy. If he was to meet a whale in the road it would scare him so he would shrink up until he could go through an inch auger hole, and I guess Jonah did the same thing. I then called his attention to the fact that the Bible did not say it was a whale, but "the Lord prepared a fish" for the occasion. If God could make some things He has made, does it not seem that he could fix up a fish to swallow a sinner? But Jonah didn't stay down. You can't keep a good man down, and I reckon some sinners would taste so bad a fish could not keep them down. My same young friend, who was tainted with higher or lower criticism, I don't know which, was also puzzled over Baalam's experience. He said it was unreasonable to think of an ass talking, and asked me if I had ever heard one talk. I replied that I had a great many times. I was listening to one then.

Joppa is also noted because it is the chief seaport to Jerusalem. From the interior commerce comes to Joppa to be exported, and into Joppa comes a large amount of the imports for Palestine. Here Solomon landed the timbers for the temple in Jerusalem. They were brought by ships down from the Lebanon Mountains. Here also was landed the gold and silver from Tyre. In those days of limited machinery it must have been a task to get these timbers out of the mountains, down to the boats, and then get them from Joppa fifty miles over rough hills to Jerusalem.

We landed in the midst of confusion. Traders, beggars, donkeys, camels, and other things bade us welcome. The poor beasts were groaning under heavy burdens. It is a land heavy laden and full of burdens.

Through dirty streets we made our way, passing camels and donkeys who poked their noses into us uninvited and almost ran over us. We stopped to get a picture of the street cleaning department of the city, which consisted of an Arab boy loading garbage in a basket on a donkey's back. Some buildings we passed we were told were soap factories. If so, the people there must be like our doctors, who will not take the medicine they prescribe for other folks.

We came presently to the house of Simon the tanner, who lived by the seaside; and climbed to the top of the house where Peter saw the vision of the sheet descending from heaven and was taught the great lesson that God is no respector of persons. God brought Cornelius to him there to be converted. (Acts 10). This may not be the exact site, but it is surely near it. It was here also, that Peter raised Dorcas from the dead, as her friends gathered about her, showing the garments which she had made for them. We visited her beautiful tomb erected by the Greek Church, which has honored this faithful woman. A greater honor to her memory would be to organize Dorcas Societies here, as has been done elsewhere in the world, and try to lift the people up. But they think the building of great tombs is the greatest way they can honor the memory of people.

Joppa is one of the oldest cities of the world. It was given to the tribe of Dan in the distribution of Palestine, and has been in existence most of the time ever since, though sacked, pillaged and destroyed many times. Napoleon seized the city, and the mighty Saladin captured it in the days of the

Crusaders. Not far from here, while Saladin's army was camping, Richard led 2,700 prisoners on a hill where they could be seen and cut them to pieces in his sight, the soldiers trying to recover jewels they believed them to have swallowed. Their galls were cut out and saved for medicine. This gives an idea of what has occurred on the holy hills in the name of religion.

Joppa is a busy, active city, and while it is full of filth and poverty, as all these cities are, it has much magnificence. There are two Turkish churches and a Greek church that are imposing. In and around the town are some of the finest orange orchards of the world, as well as other orchards. The crops are raised by irrigation. It is crude, but it answers, and it shows what all Palestine could do if the custom was followed.

We boarded the train at the little station in the edge of the city in the early afternoon, and turned our faces across the Plain of Sharon. Wonderful plain this is. It seems that it could feed the entire country. As far as eye could see was wheat in the harvest fields and flocks of goats and sheep. These Syrian sheep differ from ours chiefly on account of the big tails, on which the fat accumulates until often it weighs several pounds. Their tails often hang almost to the ground. The fat is hung up to dry and used for cooking purposes, as it is needed. From the moment of our arrival until our departure from Palestine we were hardly out of sight of sheep and goats, and many times our minds turned to the many beautiful and important truths the

Master taught from these domestic animals. David's herds fed upon this plain. (1st Chron. 27:29). Beautiful beyond description is the plain when in springtime it is carpeted with a mass of many flowers glistening with dew in the sunbeams. Chief among these flowers is the Anemones or Rose of Sharon, which tuned the songs of Israel's poets more than once. In Song 2:1, the Bride speaks of herself, "I am the Rose of Sharon, a lily of the valleys." In Isa. 35:2, the prophet speaking of the future of Zion, says, "The glory of Lebanon shall be given unto it, the excellency of Carmel and Sharon." In other prophecies the Book deals with Sharon. "Sharon shall be a fold for flocks." How true that is.

On this plain we first saw the natives threshing their wheat—for it was harvest time—in the same way they did before the days of Christ. They pile their wheat upon the threshing ground and drive cattle over it until the wheat is separated, then they throw it into the air and the breeze blows the chaff away. As we saw this scene there came to our minds the solemn figure of the Lord's description of the Judgment, when the righteous should be separated from the lost.

After a journey of fifteen miles we left the Plain of Sharon and passed into the hills. About us the olive trees were white and green in the sun. Figs, apricots and sycamore fruit were in evidence. At one of the stations I bought a little tin pan full of this fruit for a penny or two. I gave the boy his money, but he began to cry as the train made ready to go, thinking I intended going off with his pan.

There is a great deal of this fruit in Palestine and in the days of the country's glory there was still more. It is eaten especially by the poorer classes and is similar to figs. The taste is not very pleasant. These trees are small and bushy and it was easy for Zachaeus to climb one when Jesus passed by. When the Prophet Amos was called to his work he was a dresser of these trees. Amos 7:14. We also saw for the first time the Carob tree or Prodigal son tree. It grows a bean that is used for food by the poorer classes and for feeding purposes, and it was to these husks that the Prodigal turned for food as he fed the hogs.

Our route brought us through the scene of the most of Samson's career and with my Bible I read of his rough and shadowed life as we came to the places linked with his name. There was Zorah, where he was born, and his mother dedicated him to God with high hopes for his future. On the mountain side, to the left, we saw the cave pointed out as the place where he met the Philistines as they crowded him and hurled thousands of them down and slew them with a jaw bone. Here was the place he tied the tails of the foxes together and set fire brands on them and burned the Philistine corn. It perhaps would have cleared up the matter to those who have wondered how Samson caught three hundred foxes, to have heard Philip say jackalls have always been called foxes and that they go in large numbers and can be easily caught. Not far from where we passed, this giant met his doom. Like the pure and singing brooks of his native hills, he went a downward course until he sought the low lands, where, though strong and mighty, yet polluted, he entered eternity's boundless sea. There has not been a more pathetic figure in the path of history than Samson facing the Philistines the last time, shaking himself with his old-time confidence as he raised his mighty arm to strike them down, only to find that arm had lost its strength while he slept in the lap of sin.

Our little train also took us by Bethshemesh, where God slew fifty thousand Philistines because they tried to capture the Ark of Israel. 1 Sam. 6; also the supposed home of Joseph of Aramathea a faithful friend of Jesus in whose tomb Jesus was buried. Joseph and Nicodemus were the only two friends Jesus found in the Jewish Sandhedrin's seventy Elders of Israel.

The course of the train as it made its way slowly through the mountains of Israel crossed the Valley of Ajalon, noted because it was here Joshua ordered the sun to stand still that he might finish destroying the Gibeonites before the night came. These mountains were barren yet, in many places covered with olive trees and showing the ruins of terisses, where in olden times the trees grew in such abundance as to cover the mountains.

Our train made a halt at a little station near Philip's fountain, where the Apostle Philip baptized the Eunuch. Here we had the laugh on our good Baptist friends. Our guide Philip, was describing the event to us while we listened. All around it was desolate and barren. One of our Baptist brethren asked, "Where is the fountain"? Philip replied there was no fountain here and never had been. Then he added "They didn't baptize by immersion in those days, everybody was baptized by sprinkling."

On we went by the spot pointed out as the home of the old Saint Simeon, who blest the infant Jesus in the Temple at Jerusalem and with wonderful prophetic insight called Him "A light to lighten the Gentiles, and the Glory of Thy people Israel." Luke 2:32. Philip pointed out to us the hill upon which David was when God gave him the signal to attack the Philistines, which was the moving among the mulberry trees. 2 Sam. 5:24.

We had climbed to the top of the mountain plateau and were nearing the Holy City. Our path had brought us through the territory of Dan and the section occupied by the mighty Philistines who were the strongest enemies Israel feared and whom they never completely conquered. Palestine received its name from this tribe and was known as the land of Philistia later Philistin land, and then Palestine. What strange feelings came to us this day as we passed over the scenes of this Bible history. But what greater experiences were yet before us? We were nearing Jerusalem! I stood on the platform of the little train and looked out to get the first view of the Holy City! Who could describe the feelings at the first vision of Jerusalem! Around a hill the city came suddenly before my eyes as if it had been let down from heaven. There was the Mount of Olives with its churches and olive trees, the Kedron valley and Gethsemane, between it and the city walls; the city on a hill with the mountains all around; the dome of the Mosque of Omar, the cite of Solomon's Temple. There came to my mind the words of the sweet singer of Israel "As the mountains are round about Jerusalem so the Lord is round about his people from this time forth and forever more." Ps. 125:2.

The train moved slowly into the station and half dazed we got off. A crowd was here to meet the crowd that the train had brought. Many pilgrims of Jews and Mohammedans as well as American and English tourists crowded this little train into Jerusalem. In the crowd that surged about the little station I saw a very touching scene.

A bright-faced, happy looking Jewish girl was coming home after two years absence in a Christian school and her mother was there to meet her. Oh how she did break down and weep with unspeakable joy! Words came not to her lips. Her old mother's face was full of love and down the wrinkles of her cheeks the tears ran in little rivers. These scenes made me think of another day and another city—the heavenly Jerusalem instead of the earthly one. The old ship of Zion after perilous journeys over many seas and through many storms is nearing the Haven of Rest on the Shores of the River of Life. The host of heaven from the City not made with hands come down to meet the ship that is coming in and welcome those on board to the heavenly home! Those who land are searching the heavenly throng for the faces of their loved ones and those who have watched the ship come in are looking for the faces of those they love. The mother sees her child and they fly into each others arms. Mothers clasp again to their hearts the little ones they have "long since lost but not forgot." Sisters and brothers, husbands and wives and friends are meeting and greeting one another in that happy land. No tears are in any eyes, no trouble on any face. Above them stands the blessed Savior with the light of eternal love upon his beautiful face and the words of welcome on his lips while the blood-washed throng of a hundred and forty and four thousand burst forth in singing

> Up to the bountiful mansions—
> Gathering Home! Gathering Home!
> Safe in the arms of His infinite love
> God's children are gathering home.

CHAPTER XIX.

RELIGIOUS AND SOCIAL CONDITIONS IN PALESTINE.

Published in Methodist Quarterly Review January 1922.

The world has never been more interested in Palestine than now. This little piece of land between the river Jordan and the Mediterranean, about the size of South Carolina, has given to the world three of its greatest religions and all things worth while that go to hold earth's constitutions and civilization together. It seems strange that a land that won the title of "The Holy Land" because it was the birthplace of the world's religion and the world's Redeemer should have been for ages a seat of war and bloodshed. The land has been overrun by conquering armies fifty times, and there is hardly a square inch of dirt or a stone that has not been wet with human blood.

Palestine has gained a new and important place in the geography and history of the world because of its part in the great World War. Few students of world issues with causes and effects of the late war have realized the importance of Palestine in the great stuggle. This is one of the most interesting and fruitful fields of modern thought, but can now only be alluded to in its bearing on the question before us. The thunders of the guns in Flanders and France so filled our ears that we did not think much of the entrance of the gallant Allenby and his brave army through the breach in the walls of the Holy City made twenty years before for William Hohenzollern to enter in royal pomp. This was the rebirth of Palestine and a new era for the people who live there. We are looking now toward Jerusalem and giving ourselves with new zeal to the study of the country, its people and its history. Among other questions, we are asking, "What are the social and religious conditions of Palestine?"

It was my privilege to travel through Palestine in 1914 and also in 1921. In the interim, I eagerly devoured everything that came to me. Having just returned from Palestine and having been asked by the editor to contribute an article on this subject, I am happy to call one of my choice hobbies from the stable and ride him some. The message will be plain and simple, and many things will have to be left out as we glean in such a wide field for so short a time; but if the interest of any person in Bible Lands and their people will be quickened, the effort will be worth while.

In studying the present conditions in Palestine, it must be remembered that the Turks dominated the land for nearly a thousand years. Behind the Turks was the siege of the crusaders and behind them the dark ages of Israel's lapse from the religion of Jehovah into heathenism. It is not necessary to undertake any tirade against the Turk or any description of his morals and his manners. It is a marvel that Palestine has survived so well under his heathen rule. John R. Mott says: "If the Turk cannot find a desert to live in, he will make a desert out of something else and live in it." He also says that Mohammedanism is the most formidable foe Christianity has met since Jesus was born. Mohammedans are known the world over for their low ideas, their debauchery of life, their degradation of womanhood, and their guilt of all the blackest and lowest crimes known to man. A thousand years of such rule must produce a deplorable state in religious and social life.

It must also be remembered that the Christain Church put forth but a feeble effort to counteract this Moslem curse and make the Holy Land a Christian Land. We have been greatly interested in taking the gospel to China, Japan, Africa, and the islands of the sea, but it seems that we have thought little or cared little about seeing it triumph among the hills where it was born and where our great Redeemer first spoke its golden words of life and light to the listening ears of man. This neglect of the very home land of our Lord and our religion has been a strange, sad blunder on the part of the Church of Christ.

Missionary efforts have not been entirely lacking, but they have been far below what they should have been. The American University in Beirut has been a strong factor in influencing the life of Palestine and Syria. Missions under the English and the Presbyterian Boards have operated with small stations in Bethlehem, Nazareth, Tiberius, and Safed, but they have been weak and lacking in support. The Christian Alliance has long had a very active work in Jerusalem. All of these have done great good in keeping the light from going out in the homes and among the women, where their main efforts were, but they have been hampered by their weakness.

The Roman and Greek Catholic Churches have been strong, but have been so honeycombed with superstitution and formality that they have not been a great force for morality and godliness. They have, like the Moslems, spent much money gathered from tax on their subjects to build gorgeous churches. There is great need of large sums from the Protestant Churches to build imposing and attractive churches and schools in commanding places and equip them with a strong force of prepared and consecrated workers. We could then compete with the Catholic and Mohammedan Churches in our appeal for attention and following. These people are very susceptible to such impressions; and as great fools as we take the Catholics and Moslems to be, they have built churches that are appealing to the Oriental mind and put them at the shrines and commanding places rather than having a poor shack on a side street like we have in some cases. If we were wise here as we are in other places, we could soon make Palestine a really Christian country, for there is no mission field with doors wider open and a stronger Macedonian call.

The people of Palestine are naturally and constitutionally a religious people, having descended from a long religious line that traces its path back to the olden days of Israel's altars. The native mind of this Oriental world is inclined to believe far too much. The supernatural appeals to them more than

the natural, furnishing fertile soil for the fake
priests, who have ever plied their trade in superstitious trickery. The crop has been a wonderful
collection of miraculous performances and legends.
You are shown the rod Aaron used and are told that
it still has magic power. Stories of the divine fires
that fall at intervals, the print on the rock Omar
where the Prophet bumped his head (he must have
had a hard one), the suspended rock that tried to
follow him to heaven, sacred bones, blood spots, and
pieces of garments with wonder-working power are
a few of the multitude of supernatural stories they
believe as they believe that the sun shines. But,
strong as the impression this superstitious religion
has made, it has had in it little that gives moral tone
to human life. A religious mind like this, however,
furnishes good soil for the real things of the gospel.

The most deplorable thing about Mohammedanism
is its blight on womanhood and home life. Women
were chattels without soul, little less than slaves,
confined most of the time at home; and when they
left the confines of their prison homes, they went
with heathen veils over their faces. It was considered a curse for a girl baby to be borne in a home:
the mother was scorned and the father snubbed. The
Koran allowed four wives to each husband, and added
the liberal provision, "If he wanted more, let him
have them, for Allah was merciful and kind." Girls
were married when mere children. There were few
schools open to boys, and still fewer open to girls.
A few years ago it was estimated that nearly nine-
tenths of the natives were illiterate. The women

then seldom went to religious services and had practically no social life.

Other awful fruits of Turkish sowing were the fearful health and sanitary conditions. There is now one reputable physican for every twenty-five thousand of the population in Palestine and Syria. Before the war, it would have been nearer the truth to place it at one for every one hundred thousand. Flies and filth caused the spread of malaria, typhus fever, consumption, leprosy, and that widespread malady that hangs like a pall over the land—blindness. I visited the new hospital in Shechem and was told by the superintendent that a majority of their patients were suffering from disease of the eyes and that nearly all of it was caused from flies and filth. The poor babies had no one to keep the filthy flies out of their eyes when they were helpless and were given all the germs that could be gathered by these scavengers.

There is one thing that must be said to the credit of the women of Palestine and Syria: with all they have had against them, they have a better moral standard than the women of other near-by-lands. Not once did I hear any member of our party say that they came in contact with any woman who bore marks of the underworld. This cannot be said of any other part of our pilgrimage.

But great changes are being wrought in Palestine. A mighty war like the last will shake the foundations of all peoples; and as great as the effect may be on other lands, it is still greater in Palestine. It took an awful toll of human life. One-third of the entire population of Syria died of disease and starvation. The population of Jerusalem was cut in half, being reduced from one hundred and twenty thousand to sixty thousand. Many of these were killed, many starved, and many drifted out, none but God knows where. As awful as this was, it had some good effects, because the country had always been overrun with beggars and mendicants, who were a menace to the nation. These disappeared first, leaving a better chance for those left behind. The general thought is that the land has more beggars than ever, whereas the truth is they are few compared with 1914.

On Christmas day, 1918, God's Christmas gift to Jerusalem was the coming of the British army and the going out of the Turk. And nothing is truer than that the retreat of the terrible Turk is forever and the British have come to stay. It is hard to refrain from remarking on the crime against civilization that the nations calling themselves Christian allowed the Turk to overrun Palestine and Armenia so long.

Our British cousins are master colonizers, and with their coming they bring better things. They make mistakes, but they build up. On the crest of the Mount of Olives overlooking Jerusalem is a beautiful palace erected by the erstwhile bragging bully of Berlin for one of his sons to occupy when the House of Hohenzollern ruled the world. Over that mansion now flies the Union Jack, for this is the home of Sir Samuel, British High Commissioner of Palestine.

Beside the Joppa gate is a breach in the wall, made there for ex-Kaiser to enter the city in royal splendor when in 1898 he rode into the Holy City in a chariot drawn by snowwhite horses. He was there on an official visit felicitating with his friend, Adbul Hamid, and he was dreaming of another day. Twenty years later the gentle and gallant Allenby led the conquering British army through the same breach on foot. He is reported to have declined to ride, saying that the Kaiser entered riding in a royal chariot, Jesus of Nazareth entered riding a donkey, but he felt unworthy to do aught but walk.

The modern tide is now sweeping over the Holy Hills and flowing through the Holy City. Traffic police stand guard in Jerusalem to prevent speeders from running over Arabs and tourists. Jerusalem has a telephone exchange, a splendid new water system, a weekly paper published in English, Hebrew, and Arabic, electric lights shine over the city, and in other ways the people are catching the spirit of Western life.

Great work has been done by the Near East Organization and the Red Cross. The war gave them great opportunities of service in the lives of the people. Closed doors were opened and walls of prejudice broken. The people were won to the influence of the newcomers. The British have established government schools open to all, and the churches now have about one hundred and fifty schools in the land. These are all full and more knocking for admission. This awakening has been one of the most noted changes.

But the most notable change to me was the blow that has struck Mohammedanism. A strange change has passed over the children of the Prophet. In 1914 the weird call of the muezzin from the minaret was ever in your ears, and when he called the faithful everywhere could be seen leaving off whatever they were doing, if they chanced to be doing anything, and turn toward Mecca for prayer. In 1921 I kept eye and ear open, but seldom heard the muezzin call, and during the whole summer I did not see a dozen folk at prayer. The mosques also were almost empty save for lazy loafers taking naps. It seemed that with the breaking of Turkish power in Palestine there has also been a breaking of Mohammedan influence. If this is true, it greatly strengthens the plea for the Church of Christ to hasten.

Along with this is noted the wonderful changes that are taking place among the women. They are fast throwing off their heathen veils and are turning their faces to the sun. They are donning skirts almost as short as those worn by their Western sisters. They are also going about in high-heel shoes. Redemption has come to the Palestine women after centuries of weary waiting.

Palestine is governed by a mandate from the League of Nations that gives Britain the power of government there. It is one of the wisest and most statesmanlike papers of modern times. In keeping with the first order issued by General Allenby, it establishes religious freedom, protects all sacred places, permits each sect that controls a shrine to continue to do so. Ecclesiastic courts and bodies

The Author and Members of the Party in the Street of Samaria.

Troupe of the Saffourys. Mother and father in top row. Moneera (who recovered the author's Bible), to reader's left; Ameer, the brother, in center; Kareemy, eldest sister, at right.

are recognized; but there is a wise provision to the effect that where any dispute arises Great Britain reserves the full right of settlement.

Palestine is to be known as the "Jewish National Home" and Jews were permitted to return along with all others who come, but the rights of all must be maintained. Last year, which was the first year of the real working of the mandate, ten thousand Jews entered Palestine seeking an asylum and home. It is interesting to note that three hundred of these came from North America, while the most of the others came from the stricken sections of Europe. In voicing a strong and united protest to this invasion of their land, the natives claim that they have lived there, it is their home, and it is manifestly unfair to allow such strangers to overrun them. They claim also that the most of these newcomers were dependents, bringing nothing to help the country, but coming after what they could get. Palestine was weakened and drained so that it could not support its own people, not to mention these thousands. It was pointed out also that many of them were of such low type, possessed with Bolshevistic natures, that they would prove a serious menace to the country. Few of them were people of Christian ideals. If they had come into a country with established business and economic conditions strong enough to absorb them and give them a place to live and earn, where society could control them, it would have been different; but Palestine was too weak to do this for them and would soon fall a victim to their preying. This feeling and resentment became so strong, and the Christians, Mohammedans, and natives protested so much, that riots broke out in the spring. In Joppa nearly a hundred were killed. England at once saw that this was a question of such gravity that she put a stop to all immigration until a satisfactory agreement could be reached.

While this action, which the natives looked upon as a serious blinder, lost friends for England, the people of this land still believe in English and American civilization and believe that these two countries are the only two countries that are able and willing to render them an unselfish service. There was a strong demand for America to take the mandate over Syria, and the people voted three to one preferring our nation over any other. They threw the doors wide open and called loud and long, but our seats of the mighty were at that time filled with political checker players, and not missionary statesmen, who were so absorbed in their petty selfish games that they heard no Macedonian call.

But still the doors of service are wide open and the call continues loud and long. These people want the blessings we have. Sitting in the shade from the heat of the Syrian sun I talked with my friend Joe Jabes, an Arab from the far-away Hills of Hauran. As the soft light of his deep brown eyes fell on me, he spoke the call of the heart of Palestine and Syria: "We no want our Religion man; we want America Religion man. Our Religion man tell us to hate one another: America Religion man tell us God is our Father and we are brothers and must love one another. America help weak and suffering. We want America."

If the Church of Christ in America hears this call and answers it, we can lift up this stricken land from which came all our hope, and bring those people into the heritage that is ours. Then the Master, who spoke all our words of life in that land, will say what once he said over there, "Inasmuch as ye have done it unto one of the least of these my brethren, ye have done it unto me." Failing in this, what will He say?

CHAPTER XX.

MOTORING OVER HOLY HILLS.

(1921)

We were happy to sight land and to know the end of our journey was near. For three weeks the ship had been our home and we were land hungry. We sailed along the course Columbus sailed over the trackless, uncharted seas, looking for land. Some man spoke up and called him the greatest far-seeing prophet of the century but as I thought over it all, he seemed to be the greatest Nut to try a trick like that.

The Syrian hills gave us a welcome as they stood there in the twilight glow as our ship dropt anchor and we faced the rabble and the scramble that comes when you disembark in an Eastern port. There is nothing like it in the world. You hear the shouting and see the commotion long months after it is over.

I found George Jallouk our trusted dragoman of the past and we were soon in his boat pushing for the shore. The war told on George and he bore the marks of hardship. True gentleman, good friend, the best guide, is George Jallouk. He took us to the hotel, which we found to be a delight sitting in its Oriental charm, hard by the tide washed shore, in sight of the lofty Lebanons. Beyrout has a charm that was wonderful. It is the seat of the American University, one of the greatest institutions in foreign lands. Here also is the place where St. George slew the dragon.

Bro. Welch was wild when he hit the ground. He kicked up his heels, gave a snort and started. In a minute, he was drinking some sort of home brew peddled out by a street vender, who sold it out of something that looked like a skin of a yellow dog. But when a hill billy has been jailed on a boat for three weeks, he will do most anything.

After a delightful night, supper in the court—rest on good beds, with Oriental music and sounds about us, we started toward the Lebanons in autos. What an experience! Motoring over the Holy Hills! We climbed the mountains amid scenes wonderful and fascinating to Baalbek where we spent the night. We found no place more charming. The finest fruits and the grand old ruins, and a homelike hotel with rooms opening into the Court where we ate. We had a table to ourselves, thanked God for our food, as we always did, and had a good time.

I was retiring when there came a knock at my door. The proprietor was there saying a Mohammedan woman wanted to see me. I found in the Court a spooky figure, heavily draped in dirty black. I could see neither nose, finger, ear or toe. I supposed it was a woman. I asked the proprietor to ask what she wanted. She said a member of our party came to her home in the afternoon entered the yard where she was baking bread and ate some with her. When he departed he invited her to the hotel to see us that night and she was here. I asked her to describe him and she indicated he was a long tall gentleman for she stretched her hands up and down as far apart as she could. I knew at once

Welch was the culprit and called him forth to face the music and receive his Mohammedan lady caller.

The preacher was informed he had committed a grave offense in entering the private quarters of a Mohammedan woman and in the eyes of her tribesmen, it might be considered cause for mobbing us. Such things had led to war and massacre. We were pictured held as prisoners by superstitious moslems until our country could discuss our case in Congress and come to our relief if we were not killed before help could reach us. And to eat bread with a person forever binds you to them by the law of friendship in the East. Whatever they demanded after that, must be done.

The preacher was pale and looked like he was listening to the bishop read his appointment. At last I suggested to him a good gift of back-shish might mend matters and he gladly emptied his surplus change in the hand of the black-robed blackmailer, who went away satisfied. Welch drew a sigh of relief when we got out of that town without any aftermath.

We left Baalbek for Damascus early in the morning and rode swiftly down the rich and historic Baca Valley. We expected to reach this oldest city of the world ere noon rolled in. But alas the plans of mice and men got oft awry when you figure on cats and cars. I have never been in love with gasoline. I detest the way it smells and the way it sells. Motoring over the ancient caravan paths of the East upsetting the equilibrium of stately camels, kingly billy-goats and demure asses is out of place. It seems sacriligious to see Fords hooting and tooting along the roads where Rebecca leaped from her camel to meet the timid Isaac. I have never known why Isaac wept. Perhaps because he was afraid she would break her neck in her haste to meet him or maybe because he knew he was caught at last. But I have missed the path in the Ford.

We started buoyant and full of life with spirits keen and faces clean. We didn't get there that way. All went well until it didn't. There was an explosion of air—and Arabic. The car stopped and the Arabs got out. One fellow with a fez and big pants raised the flap and looked in Mr. Ford's right lung, while another took the blood pressure. A number of loafers nearby came up, looked on and said things. One said "mofish benzine", which meant, "are you out of gasoline." We were!

I have never seen anything more impressive than these Arabs, driving Fords over these Syrian hills, snorting, staving thru caravans of loaded camels, droves of plodding donkeys and hundreds of sheep and goats. I have never seen anything more thrilling and exciting. They did not slacken speed or give quarter. With a hoot and a toot, they went straight on into the solid mass of animals, men and cargo, leaving them to get out of the way or take the result. I shut my eyes and stopped my ears to keep out the tragedy. Such excitement among goats, camels, sheep and shepherds, I have never seen. Billy-goats and slow donkeys climbed up banks; loaded camels leaped from the road falling down and bellowing, while the men said things. I expected to be shot and mobbed but they seemed to think we had right of way.

We made the trip without accident save several times turning animals around and starting them back the other way and bringing with us hair and wool on our fenders for souvenirs. My, I wish I could have been in the first auto that went thru that country!

The camel and ass resent the coming of the auto. It upsets their oriental poise. The billy-goat also shows his contempt. They protest at being upset and driven from the caravan paths their sires have gone with stately tread for centuries. But the auto seems there to stay. Where ancient priests burnt incense in the Ark of the Covenant, they now burn gasoline in Fords. The Shah of Persia is dickering for a Ford and will rig it up with Oriental splendor. King Fiesal already has his. Sheiks and shepherds are after them as the East and the West are meeting together.

Who would ever tire of Damascus? Not if you are interested in folks with eternal variety and surpassing mixture. We had two extra days and we spent them in Damascus. I am sure no one was sorry. Our Hotel, the Damascus Palace, was in the heart of things. A Mohammedan Mosque was on each side of the hotel. One minaret rose hardby the window where Rev. A. L. Stanford slept. Five times a day the Muezzin climbed up there and gave forth his weird call to prayer. Stanford gets his best sleep at the very time the Mohammedan sends forth their first morning call, as it penetrates and shivers over the world. This Presiding Elder had a voice like a Bishop and he stood in ten feet of Stanford's bed. Now Stanford is a fine fellow and splendid preacher but he does not like some things. What he thinks of Muezzins who bawl at 4:30 A. M. and of Samaritans in Shechen is not at all in keeping with the General Rules. There was nothing on the whole tour richer than the way these two divines Rt. Rev. Muezzin and Rev. A. L. Stanford exchanged glances and compliments at the time of morning and evening prayers. Stanford did not appreciate the rare privilege of having a minaret at your window and a private priest to tell you when to get up and say your prayers.

All about us were the bazaars. They are the joy of a woman's heart and the sorrow of a man's pocket book. The merchants sit on the floor on their feet in Eastern style with a great display of goods about them. It seems impossible to pack so much stuff in such a compass. A store the size of a stateroom will be a regular department store. There seems to be no end to the articles both in quality and quantity. One man usually sells one thing but you never know what the man next door will have. The finest silks will be hardby a store full of stinking cheese that must have been old when Nero fiddled over Rome. Saddles and brass, macaroni and wine, rugs and rags and everything in endless array and display are before you. No man could describe it. To trade with these fellows is rare past time and if you know how to do it, you can carry good bargains home.

One of the most interesting experiences in this city was buying some Persian rugs from a rug dealer. Four of us desired to take such rare trophies home to our wives and we set out to buy them. We found a boy, who was a good interpreter and located the rugs we wanted. It takes much dickering to drive a bargain. The rugs we selected were gems and rare and costly at home. He wanted $80.00, each of them. We offered him $25.00. He became incensed, put them up, spat, stamped and laughed. For a part of the two days, the trade was in soak. He came down to $40.00, and we stuck to our first offer. It seemed our bargain was doomed, but I felt in the last test he would fall. We got what he claimed by his Holy Shrines was his last and lowest price, and we departed to another rug man nearby. We selected some from his lot and started a deal when the first man came to us and whispered, he would take our price.

We left Damascus early in the morning. Our host was at the station, telling us goodbye. The train went out on the rich fields and plains, passing thousands of camels, donkeys, sheep and goats. I never saw so many in one day. They were grazing on the plains after the crops were harvested. The owners are not too friendly and great care must be used in dealing with them. When an animal got on the track, the engineer stopped with all haste, almost throwing us on our heads, but this was better than hurting a billy-goat. The car of the Governor was fired on some days before and the bridge over the Yarmouth near Galilee had been burned down. This was the nearest to a danger zone we had come but we went thru to Lake Galilee without trouble.

We visited Jericho, the Dead Sea and the Jordan in autos this time in order to hurry out of the heated zone back to the good air of Jerusalem. Of course, we took a bath in the Dead Sea. Everything was progressing well, when we heard a pitiable wail and a loud call for help. Bro. Welch had drifted far from the shore and said he was caught in a current that was swiftly bearing him to the Moab shore. I pictured the sad sight of the poor fellow, being beaten and held a prisoner in his present plight until we could form a rescue party and go after him, takin sufficient dry goods and notions to induct him again into civilization.

Frank McKenny went swimming to his rescue, but made the sad mistake of approaching footwards rather than headwards. His long feet were churning the water like the old-mill wheels and he was kicking like the mule Maud. He beat Frank under the water and pounded him without mercy, and to have your head put under the Dead Sea water is not as pleasant as eating Charlotte Russe But Frank flanked him and hove him in. He went swimming with his burden up in front of an Arab hut when all the inmates came forth in loud and explosive protest. They didn't propose to be disgraced by having any such derelict wreck drift up at their front door.

This second visit to the Holy Hills was greater to me than the first. It was a great privilege to stand on these Holy places where the Bible stories

and truths were born and read the record from the
book. Every morning when the day was dawning,
I stole forth with my Bible. One morning, I sat on
a rock half way between Jerusalem and Bethlehem,
and as I read, I tried to picture the scenes. I saw
the Wise Men following the Star to the manger in
Bethlehem. I saw Solomon ride his royal chariots,
and David lead his army down that road. There
Rachel, whom Jacob loved, drifted out into the
other world as little Benjamin came into this one.
I heard the angel choirs sing on the plains while a
lost earth listened to the first Christmas Carol. I
looked back at the Holy City, sitting on the hill in
the glow of the rising sun and as I read of her past
glories, I could see the pictures before me.

Then I looked behind me far over into the desolate solitudes of the Judean Wilderness while I read
of David fleeing from Saul. Here he was hunted,
hiding alone away from home and friends, but he
was not alone nor discouraged. God was with him
and while in the lonely wilderness, he gave us some
of our sweetest music. It was down here one night
all alone, he looked into the shining stars of that
Syrian sky and tuned his sharp to sing, "The Heavens declare the Glory of God and the firmament
showeth His handiwork. Day unto day uttered
speech and night unto night showeth knowledge.
There is no speech where their voice is not heard."
And down here all alone, and hunted by his enemies,
he burst forth into glorious song, and striking the
chords of his harp, he gave the world its greatest
gem of literature—the Twenty-Third Psalm. To

sit here and read these two Psalms is worth the trip over the ocean.

The next morning by sunrise, I stood at the foot of Calvary, reading the account of the crucifixion as I looked upon that skull shaped hill outside of the city wall. Then I followed the venturesome Dr. Squires in an adventure few people have ever accomplished. We climbed the steep slopes of Calvary and stood with bared heads and solemn hearts on the spot where the cross was raised when the Lord was crucified to save the world. Here was the very spot where his blood ran out on the ground. It was easy to picture the scene of the disciples and the multitudes on the surrounding slopes, watching the greatest sacrifice ever made in the history of the world. I have never experienced anything like that visit to Calvary and I came down almost overcome, humming,

"There is a Fountain filled with blood,
Drawn from Immanuel's veins,
And sinners plunged beneath that flood,
Lose all their guilty stain."

On top of Mt. Calvary we saw a strange and gruesome relic of a brutal battle lost. It was an old rusty German cannon made in the Krupp factory in Germany. The Turks have always had a superstitious reverance for Calvary and would not let others tread on its ground. But when their German comrades came to the defence of the Holy City, they who had no respect for sacred treaties

and life and virtue of course had no reverance for
Calvary. So they fortified Mount Calvary with their
guns. The Turks were driven out and the Huns
fell but in the retreat this relic was left, where it
stands and rusts, a strange reminder of the brutality
and barbarism of Prusianism defeated and corod-
ing away on the very spot where the blood of Jesus
ran out to save a lost world. The Prince of Peace
has triumphed over Prusianism.

CHAPTER XXI.

STORY OF THE LOST BIBLE.

On July 16, 1914, I visited Cana in Galilee. About the village fountain the natives were gathered watching us. Leaving our carriage we visited the spot pointed out as the place where the Saviour performed His first miracle, when at the wedding "the water saw its Lord and blushed."

When we returned to the carriages my Bible, which I had left on the seat, was gone. My heart was sad, for I loved this Book of mine. With it in my hand I had walked the Holy Hills, reading from the Divine record what transpired upon the very place before my eyes. It was one of the greatest blessings of my life. I had made valuable notes in the margin which I felt would be of untold value when I got home. Then the Bible was a much prized gift from dear friends, and through many months had been my constant companion of comfort and cheer.

Of course I felt some little Turk had stolen it and I would never hear of it again. With a sad heart I proceeded over the hills the Master traveled, on by the Horns of Hattin down to the blue waters of Galilee.

On March 1st, 1920, when the mail-man handed in my mail my eye fell on a strange foreign looking envelope. I saw it was a Turkish stamp and was posted in Nazareth, Palestine. I eagerly opened it and read:

"Kerf-Cana, Galilee, Palestine, January 8, 1920.
To the Pastor of Thomas Chapel,
        Cartersville, Va.
Dear sir:—

On September 26, 1914, I bought from a Turk who happened to pass, an English Bible, in which is the following inscription, "Presented to Jos. M. Rowland of the Virginia Conference by the Sunday School of Thomas' Chapel, Cartersville, Va., Christmas, 1906."

Owing to the world's war I was unable to write and if the above mentioned Mr. Rowland is still living and desires his Bible I will be glad to return it to him, if you will kindly get in touch with him, if he has changed his address.

Awaiting his instructions and reply, I am
                Yours truly,
                MISS MONEERA F. SAFFROURY."

My heart was thrilled with this message from far off Galilee. Who was this person who had bought my Bible and kept it as a sacred trust to return to me, while for nearly six years war and famine swept about her and her people? I was strongly impressed with the feeling that God was bringing in this peculiar way our two lives together. Far off yonder in that little village where Jesus attended the wedding with his mother, lived a woman or girl who held my Bible for over five years waiting to send it to me. I wondered who she was living there in the land I loved. Was she a girl or an old woman? Was she a Jew, Catholic or Mohammedan? Perhaps she was a mission teacher there.

I wrote her at once, enclosing a check for $10.00 as a gift in appreciation of her fidelity. I requested her to write me about herself, her people and her land, giving any information she liked about conditions there and how they fared during the war and since. I told her we were greatly interested in the land and people there. I asked if she was a Christian and connected with the mission in Nazareth. I gave opportunity for her to trust me as a friend and confide in me as such.

On May 25th, 1920, I received an answer posted in Jerusalem and dated April 4th. It reads as follows:

"Dear Sir:—

Ever so many thanks for your kind gift enclosed with your most interesting letter received yesterday. I am a young girl of 17, born and brought up in the village of Cana. My parents sent me to school in a town called Safel, beyond Tiberias. There I stayed three years where I learned English. When the war broke out the school had to be closed as it was English and I had to go back to Cana. You cannot imagine how sad I was to leave. I had to go back to Cana and stay all during the war.

It was a very miserable life we had to go through. I have one sister, two years older and a brother four years younger. My sister was also in school with me, and both of us had to stay together at my parents. Our little family is the only Protestant one in Cana connected with the C. M. S. at Nazareth (a mission of the Episcopal church of Enland.)

There is a very kind Syrian minister at Nazareth who used to come to Cana for a service and give us communion during the war. He had to come walking every time as no cars or horses could be found, as the Government took them all. Sister and I were not confirmed and did not take the communion. As soon as the war was over the Bishop of Jerusalem came to Nazareth and confirmed a number of boys and girls with whom we were also confirmed.

You wish me to relate about the war, through which we had to go. It was a very miserable time under the Turkish tyranny that I don't like to remember it again. My father who was about fifty years old, was obliged to serve as a Turkish soldier. The first and second year they accepted fifty pounds (equal to about $200) for any who wished to pay instead of a year's service. So my father paid one hundred pounds for the two years. The third year they would not accept any money and forced every man to join the army. My father had to go then.

Every thing was dear and scarcely found. We spent all our money during that dreadful war. I do thank God it is over now and hope we will have a better time now under the British rule, though things are still dear as before. I cannot tell you how great was our joy to see the British army. It was on October 20th when they came to Cana. You would have heard about all that in the newspapers.

The first Enlish Military Governor of Nazareth was a very kind one. He gave my sister work as a teacher at Cana for 5 pounds a month (equal to about $20). Of course the fee was very bad but it was the only work she could get. The English mistress of our school at Safel came to Jerusalem to teach in the British High School. She wrote and asked if I would go there to finish my schooling, as it is the highest school in all Palestine. Sorry to say I couldn't as the fees were too much and we had no money. My sister saved money until she got enough for half a year fees for the school and sent me. I have been here two months. Examinations were held March 14th. I was so pleased, I passed it all.

After that we had Easter Holiday for a fortnight. The first week we spent very nice with walks and so on. The first day all the girls went out for a long walk to the Tombs of the Judges, which no doubt you would have visited when you came to Jerusalem. On March 31st in the evening the Lord's Supper was served as usual at the Arabic Church and all the big girls which were confirmed went with the school mistress to take it. I was, of course, one of them.

After it was over we went on a long walk in the beautiful moonlight to Gethsemane. A lovely sermon was preached there that made all the people drop tears. We sang several hymns also of which "Jesus Lover," was one. I can't tell you what strong feelings I had to think I was in the same place where my Lord spent that terrible eve of agony for my sake.

Yes, I count myself lucky to be in the land where Christ lived. I sincerely hope you will come next year and I will be most delighted to see and meet such a gentle and nice friend as you are.

Well, to finish about the news of Jerusalem. The next week of our holiday we spent very bad as a great trouble arose between Moslems and Jews, and even a fight. Lots of them were killed on both sides. Thank God it did not last long for many soldiers were brought and scattered here and there and airplanes stayed two days hovering down the town to see that was right.

Now I have written a too long letter and told you all about myself and people. Sorry I haven't any of my photos here but will promise that as soon as I get one from home will post it to you. I will soon be going back to Cana for the long holidays so you better answer me if you like at my address there as you did the first time.

I wonder if I will be able to come back here next year to finish my schooling to learn typing, shorthand and French. I do not know if I can get money enough. Of course I will keep the money you sent me and see if I can get any more—enuogh for it. I do thank you heartily for it. I trust God will manage as He did this year. I wish I could find somebody who would pay for me and as soon as I finish my education and get work will pay him back. I wish you could help me, Sir.

I am enclosing you here a frame of my needle-work lace which I trust would be interesting to keep as souvenir of Palestine. I will write and tell my sister to post you your Bible as I left it at home at Cana. I will come to the end of my long story, wishing you all the joy of this world and the best of luck.

Thanking you again for your kind gift, I remain,
Yours Sincerely,
MONEERA F. SAFFOURY."

and then, true woman that she is she adds a

P. S. I bought your Bible from a Mohammedan, as you will see written on it when you get it.

CHAPTER XXII.

DINING IN GALILEE.

In my second visit to Palestine in 1921, I looked forward with keen anticipation to a visit to the home of some friends in little Cana of Gallee.

It was the home of Moneera Saffoury, the little girl who recovered my stolen Bible in 1914. She bought the book from a Turk, who stole it from the carriage. She kept it until the war was over and she could send it to me. This started a correspondence that led me with the assistance of friends to undertake the education of Moneera, who has a passion and a call for mission work in this land from which our Gospel comes. She believes the beautiful story I have already published about it is the working of our Father's hand bringing friends to her in answer to her many prayers, and she believes it no more than the one who writes the story.

When I found I was coming again to Palestine I wrote Moneera I would certainly visit her home as I passed through Cana. She answered at once, extending a warm invitation with all the warm Oriental hospitality, seconded by all the members of the family. I must come and bring all members of the party and we must not spend a few minutes but stay at least a day and a night. This stirred my heart, for I longed for such a visit as this, and having never dined in an Eastern private home, I longed for the time to come. The providential manner of our acquaintance and the interest I had in

the future of this girl added to the interest of this
looked-for visit.

It was in the early morning light of July 28
when our carriage climbed the hills from the hotel
on the shore of Lake Galilee. How powerless is
the hand of man to write of the glories of these
hills as the light of a new day shone on them. We
looked down on the historic waters and the shores
on which moved so much of the gospel life, and
tried to see the pictures as they were in the days
of Jesus. We paused at the Horns of Hattin long
enough to read the sermon on the Mount, where it
was preached. Then over a good road being built
by the Jewish immigrants, we jogged at a good
rate in sight of Mount Tabor around to the edge
of little Cana.

The folks had been looking for us for two days.
I had to change our plans in Damascus, and could
not advise them we would be two days late. All
their hearts were beating with the highest anxiety
as they put the big pot in the little one, dressed a
kid and watched down the road toward the lake
for a cloud of dust that would herald our coming.
Of course, it is not good to keep ladies waiting a
meal two minutes, not to say for two days. As
anxious as they were, they could not have been
ahead of me very much, for in all my life they have
not had to do much waiting when they wanted
eating done. I am there waiting. But to keep
these folks waiting and wondering for two days
must have been hard on them.

At last our carriage swung around a hill into a

grove of figs and olives, and we were in the gates of
Cana. Here a great surprise awaited me, for the
girls had published to the inhabitants that distinguished visitors were coming, and a large number
of folks turned out to greet us. As I alighted from
my carriage, trying to catch the manner of Oriental
salutation and tell the folks how glad I was to come
to town, I felt the governor, when he came, had
nothing on me.

After bowing and scraping and going through
other bodily forms of greetings, I located Moneera
(from her photo) as she stood almost breathless
with excitement and timidity among the folks. I
took her hand and bringing her forth presented her
to the members of our party. She led the way down
the little street to their home. We saw the church
on the supposed site of the Master's first miracle
and I was thinking as we walked that somewhere
nearby Nathaniel sat under the fig tree when Jesus
called him out into the light and called him the guile-
less one.

The Saffoury home from without looked like the
typical Oriental home. It was built of dingy limestone, with flat roof, and walled about. But when
we crossed the threshold, looked on the interior and
saw what marvels the tender touch of woman's
hands can do for the inside of things, our hearts
were warmed. For a month we had not seen inside
of a home, and we felt a thrill at seeing this one.
We felt like giving three sheers for woman and
joining in the toast of old, "Woman, God bless her,
we can't get along without her, and we can't get

along with her." But we do not want to be where her refining soul and tender touch comes not.

It was a cozy, cheerful home, with nice handiwork, carpets and pictures. Mother Saffoury and Father Saffoury, with other kindred, including an old grandfather, who wore the prophetic looks of Abraham, all bowed low, speaking softly in the Syrian tongue, their age-long welcome and sending forth to God prayers for their guests. As I acknowledged these, I said, "Peace be unto this home," and I remembered I was in the only Protestant Christian home in the whole village. How would you like to be in the only Christian home in a village, with few of the others friendly and sympathetic?

We spread our lunch we brought from the hotel and it was supplemented by other things our good friends brought. They had at my suggestion brought laces and things for us to buy, and as we lingered here, the time passed far too swiftly. When time came to go, I was told I could not go. Moneera and Kareemy, the sister, and Mother Saffoury said I must remain for the night. It has always been hard to disobey the word of women and I didn't know what to do. We were to spend the night at Nazareth, seven miles away, and I must be there at 5:30 in the morning to see that the folks were up, get breakfast at 6:00 and start on the days journey at 6:30. When they were told this, they did what woman always does—they found a way out. I was told I must remain here the rest of the afternoon, eat dinner with them and they would see I reached Nazareth by bedtime, and as I always do, obeyed.

We saw the folks in the carriages at the village well where the girls were filling their water jars and bearing them homewerd on their heads, and as the horses trotted up the road I turned back with the two girls. We passed the village threshing floor where they were threshing wheat as they have done for centuries, by driving cattle over it, and the folks made remarks about us. Being kin to women, and somewhat like them, I wanted to know what they were saying about me and asked the girls. One said, "Look at that American with the teacher. Isn't he handsome." This remark brought great comfort to my heart, and as night wore on helped very much toward crowning the ending of a perfect day.

I sat under a fig tree with Moneera and Kareeny and they asked me of America, and spoke with shining eyes of their ambition to live lives of service for God and His children. Their tender gratitude for what my friends had done for them was one of the most touching things I ever saw.

When we reached the home, I found a nice clean bed all ready for me to take my afternoon nap or siesta as they call it. A canopy was drawn over it to keep out the mosquitoes. When the lady, with all the gracious manner of the East, pointed out the bed, I thanked her, but told her I would be ashamed to sleep these precious hours away. I was here to talk, not sleep. I could sleep any time.

The old grandfather could not talk English, but the girls acted as interpreters. He was a pious seer and gave me more light on some points of the Bible

land than all the commentators. He told me of the
persecution of his people by the Turks, because they
were Christians. His grandfather fled from a massacre—the only one who escaped and settled in Cana.
I felt like I was sitting at the feet of God's prophet
of old. When I left him with tears running down
his white beard, he leaned on his staff and prayed
the blessing of God to ever rest on me and mine, because of what I had been for them.

When supper was announced, I could not prevail
on the others to eat with me. They seated me at the
table and five women served me. The King at Buck-
ingham Palace, when Princess Mary had her wedding supper, didn't beat me much. We had seven
courses, and no better meal ever faced me. Soup,
chicken and cream potatoes, mutton and rice, pudding, goat clabber, fresh milk, cheese, coffee, figs,
grapes and nuts, came and went before me as I sat
there like a presiding elder down in Southampton at
the third quarterly conference, with all-day meeting
and dinner on the ground. What could make the
soul of a Methodist preacher glow like a meal like
this, with five women waiting on him? In the house,
at the door and windows, crowds of Mohammendans
had come to watch the circus with open eyes and
mouths. It was the first time they ever saw a
Methodist preacher eat and they seemed to find no
fault with the way he did it.

Before our party left the home I read the second
chapter of John about the first miracle of the Master performed nearby and we prayed together. Then
the girls recited and sang for us. They sang "Galilee"

and it seemed to me I never heard it sung with such
heavenly sweetness. Then an impulse seized me and
I asked Moneera if she would not say a few words
to us before we went. I wanted her to tell us about
finding my Bible and some of the troubles through
which they passed during the war. She began in a
timid, hesitating way, but her heart caught fire, and
her words seemed to come from God. In a simple
way she made one of the most powerful speeches I
ever heard. She told us of the clouds of war. Tourists ceased to come. Things were scarce and high.
One day a Turkish officer came and took their money.
The father gave all he had to keep out of the war.
Then they came and took him off. There he sat, old
and broken from the trials of Turkish trenches and
he did not love the Turks any more than we do. Then
an officer came and took everything else they had
and ordered them not to speak English, write letters
or receive any. She had my Bible and through those
awful days they read it while they watched for the
officers. Then one day the horrible threat every
woman dreaded worse than death happened. A
Turkish officer told them tomorrow they would line
up these Christian women and start them off on the
long march of deportation to Constantinople, about
1,000 miles away. Christian women knew the horrible death and things far worse that lay on this road
over burning sands, through torture, starvation and
abuse. Four million Armenians were driven out on
this trail of hades and their bones are bleaching in
the sands. Many of their women now are prisoners
in Turkish harmens, with the name of their owners
burned in their cheeks with branding irons.

With tears running down her cheks she pointed out a little room where she and her mother and sister lay on the floor all night praying to the God of all to send some power to stop this horrible calamity. They could not read my Bible, but held it in their hands and wet it with their tears. The night wore on and the day dawned as it always does, no matter how dark the hours and heavy the burdens. But the sunrise brought no hope. The hours wore on until at last they heard a shout and commotion in the streets of Cana. Thinking the officers had come earlier than expected, they looked from the window and flying in the air was the British flag. General Allenby's army, working up from Egypt, piping water as they went, had reached their home and deliverance had come, just a few hours before the cursed Turks were to start them on the road to their awful doom. God had answered their prayers and deliverance had come to Palestine. Not far from there the British overtook the Turks and captured 100,000. When she finished her story, tears were in all eyes and those of us who were there will never get away from the influence of that hour.

That night I parted with my friends, and mounting a pony with Father Saffoury and a neighbor as comrades, rode out by the spring up the hill in the glorious starlight of the East on the road to Nazareth. Prophets of old and the Savior walked this road. The stars nowhere seem so bright as here. I could not talk to my comrades. We did not know the same lip language, but our hearts understood what the other thought. I was sorry when the gleaming lights of Nazareth shone before me and that wonderful ride was ended. I told my friends good-bye at the hotel door and joined the party at the end of a perfect day.

One word more to any friend who reads this story. Moneera is in school in Jerusalem. She has made a fine record there. She finishes the work next year at this British college. I will bring her to this country to finish her preparation for mission work in her home country. The brother is also in school there. I am standing by them. With what I can contribute and receive from friends, I have faith in God to believe I can see them through. If any one who reads this feels moved to have a part in this fine deed, I will be glad to receive the contribution.

CHAPTER XXIII.

IN JERUSALEM.

"Last night I lay a sleeping there came a dream so
  fair,
I stood in Old Jerusalem beside the temple there;
I heard the children singing and ever as they sang
Me thought the voice of angels from heaven in an-
  swer rang.

> Jerusalem! Jerusalem!
>   Lift up your gates and sing
> Hozanna in the highest,
>   Hozanna to your king.
> Jerusalem! Jerusalem
>   Sing for the night is o'er,
> Hozanna in the highest
>   Hozanna forever more."

This great strain of music, one of the grandest
ever tuned to song ran through my soul with thrilling force as we made our way to the Fast Hotel
near the Joppa Gate, where our home would be
while in the Holy City. We found the hotel clean
and comfortable and the fare good. Brother Williams and myself were conducted to our rooms,
where as we always did at such times we sought
our mail. What matters dusty clothes, dirty faces
and uncombed hair when far away from home with
no word for many days, your mail is placed in your
hands! Even the charms of Jerusalem were put

aside. How good it was again to get messages from loved ones and friends and know their prayers were following us! How pleasant was the sight of a Virginia newspaper even though its date line was nearly a month behind the date!

We took a short walk out into the streets after supper but soon returned to get off some mail, and spend the hours till bed time meditating and reading from our Bibles, the portion relating to Jerusalem. What a privilege to sit here in Jerusalem and read these things from the Bible on the ground where they happened? We knelt by our beds and thanked God for blessing us with this cherished privilege, and then we tried to sleep. But who could sleep on their first night in Jerusalem? How pictures arose before our minds! How the mellow voice of Israel's singing Shepherd rang in our souls! How strange things climbed the steps of memeory and knocked at the door of our hearts and pulled the latch strings with all their might! Why, right on this spot the Wise Men came enquiring of the Holy Child; here David and Solomon ruled; here Jesus walked and talked and died. Who could sleep when such history of many centuries clamored for attention? We went to our window and looked out on the city with its flat top houses, and down on the white road that wound like a ribbon from over the hills of Dan into the Joppa Gate. Caravans of stately camels with measured tread and unlifted solemn heads were coming into the city with the products of the land, just as they had been doing since the world was young. All night long we heard the jin-

Climbing the Great Pyramid in Egypt.

The Jews' Wailing Place.

the body of Christ in the greatest sacrifice history ever knew. Thus the world was forever linked to the throne of God with a golden chain of Eternal Love sealed with the Blood of Christ.

The history of Jerusalem runs far back in the beginnings and loses its trail in the shadows far away. The name is a combination of Jebus and Salem. It is supposed to have been founded by Jebus, the son of Canaan, who was Noah's grandson and for a long time bore his name. Then it took the name of Salem and that mysterious character, Melchizedek, was its king. Its first name signfied "trodden down" and Salem meant "City of Peace." Well do these names blend in Jerusalem, for while it stands for peace it has been trodden down as no city on earth. It has been beseiged twenty-seven times and in and about its walls rivers of blood have flown. No city ever founded has experienced so many unspeakable horrors as the passion of the nations inflamed with the fires of hate have charged about its walls.

Our hotel was just outside the Joppa Gate so naturally our first steps would be through this historic gate into the city proper. In the big gate we saw the little one called "the needle's eye" which was open for footmen when the big gate was closed to traffic. Some have thought this is what Jesus meant when he said it was easier for a camel to go through the eye of a needle than for a rich man to enter the kingdom of heaven. A camel could squeeze through this little gate if he removed all his baggage and got down on his knees. So if the rich man does that he can

gle of their bells and the call of their
our window.

We were up early the following mor
mind and heart to see Jerusalem, and
breakfast of cold bread, butter and coffe
out to see the Holy City. Is there in all t.
any city like it? In classifying the cities n
not put it in a list all alone? Other cities be
empires and kingdoms, Jerusalem belongs
world. Other cities belong to certain races, Je
lem belongs to the human race. Other cities
shrines for certain faiths, Jerusalem is the H
City for all. The Jew loves it, sings his home-s
songs about it in exile far and wide; speaks it wi
accents of devotion and when he comes to it weep
over it like the Savior did whom his people rejected as their Lord. The Mohammedan often
spends all his means and strength and gives his
life in his effort to make long pilgrimages to behold
its sacred scenes and worship at its shrines. The
Armenian, Abasynians and Copts count it the
greatest joy in their lives to pass beyond its walls.
The Catholics, both Greek and Roman, have so
adored it that they bow down in worship to its emblems and objects. Far and wide the hearts of
Protestant Christians have brought them here to sit
upon the ashes of its former glory and call up before
them visions of things dear to their souls. It is even
used as a type of heaven. Jerualem gains this distinct place in history because it was the city where
heaven and earth touched, and the spot where the
life of God and the blood of man met together in

enter the gate of the Kingdom. Traders and beggars in abundance were at the gate waiting for us. We halted only a moment as we were out for other things and would go shopping later. We did return to look over the goods and make purchases.

We visited Mt. Zion, the portion of the city occupied by David as his headquarters. Zion means "sunny" and this point being the highest ground in the city, was full of light and sunshine, thus well-suited for the fortified home of King David. Near here stands the Tower of David. It is an old castle whose history is in doubt and it is now used for barracks for soldiers. The walls of the city at this point show clearly three eras of building, Hebrew, Roman and Modern. We then passed down David Street and Christian Street, two prominent streets of the city. They are like all streets, very narrow and crowded with venders, beggars, tourists, camels and donkeys.

Our next visit was to the Church of the Holy Sepulchre, one of the far-famed shrines of the world. It is not my purpose to say much about this church. It may seem gross sacrilege to those who count it the most sacred spot of all earth and would die to stand on its holy ground, but I must say I took little interest in it. I came to Palestine determined not to deal in question marks of faith-destroying criticism. My eyes and ears were not to give their precious time to those places and things that mar and spoil and stain the real life and meaning of the Holy Land and its glorious history. I would look beyond the spoils and desecrators of the Temple and the Tabernacle. I would throw the ashes aside to find the buried gold. I would look beyond the clouds to the sun that shone in light and life, and above the growl and grumble of fanatics and dirty beggars' empty hands. I would hear the voice of God speaking and see the bleeding hands of Christ. So the shams and lies bothered me not. The fact that they grouped in this church all the world's history was no concern of mine. I saw Adam's grave and his skull, the real cross on which Jesus died, the rock on which his body rested, his tomb and all his history. Here in a dark church are many candles in golden candle sticks burned, casting solemn rays on gold and silver crosses and altars whose glitter and profusion might bemuddle a cardinal; but beyond all this prison, I looked to the hills where Jesus lived the outdoor life and died the outdoor death. There never was any convent dust or monastery mildew on the garments of Jesus Christ. There was the smell of the fields on his garments, the dust of the road on his cheeks. The Master was no monk, he was a man; a manlier man than any of the masters have painted Him or Theologians have pictured Him. His life was in the market place, fields, lake side, high ways and not in dungeons and cloisters, and yet the Catholics have taken every thing sacred they could find, built over it a gloomy, dark old church, sprinkled about it their incense and lighted their pitiful little candles, instead of turning on the sunlight and incense of Nature's sweet atmosphere. I must be excused if I took little interest in these prison churches but looked beyond their gloomy walls to the great Outside.

There is one thing, however, that did impress me about the Church of the Holy Sepulchre. It is the joint property of the Greek-Catholics, the Roman-Catholics, the Armenians and Copts. These religious bodies have fought many a bloody battle here on its shrines in jealous rage to control its altars. The dome was dirty and needed cleaning but they were unable to decide who could be trusted with the work. Every Easter people are killed in their fiendish contention about its shrines. The Turks hold the keys and only by their consent can these worshippers get access to their own altars. These Turkish soldiers are ever on guard to see that the devout worshippers do not kill one another!

We then went through the city to St. Stephen's gate, out of which the enraged crowd thrust the young saint and stoned him to death because he preached the Holy Ghost. Here was the very place where he knelt down under the shower of crushing stones that mangled his body, praying for those who did the deed, committed his spirit into the hands of God, while Jesus stood at the throne of God (at other times He is represented as sitting) to welcome the martyr home. For a long time the gate that was baptized with his blood has borne his name.

We visited the scene of Pilate's Judgment Hall, where Jesus was tried and condemned to death. A Catholic monastery and orphanage is now on this site. The sisters in charge were very courteous to us, received us kindly and put before us many little things made by the children. Many of them showed skill and were very attractive. Our party gathered in the chapel that is said to be on the spot where Jesus was condemned and scourged, and had a little prayer service. It may seem odd for us to have service in a Catholic church, but we did. We had brass enough to do it without asking permission.

Our next move was to leave the city for a visit to the Mount of Olives. Wonderful, beautiful hill is this Mount of Olives! The finest vision of Jerusalem is seen from this hilltop. When Jerusalem was in her glory, sitting as a queen upon her hill there, with the rising sun shining upon the sides of Solomon's Temple and all her greatness, it must have been like the city John saw let down from God out of heaven. You can always get better visions from a mountain or elevated place. You feel more in a spirit for seeing and things are more prepared to be seen. What visions do rise up to the soul standing on Olivet! How Jesus loved this hill and how oft He found comfort and communion in the shades of her green olive trees! There are a great many of these beautiful trees on Olivet now, and in the days of Jesus, when the country was more flourishing than it is now, Olivet must have been covered with olive trees until it presented one of the most charming pictures to be seen anywhere. These trees were His friends.

"And still they stand above the Holy City
A rugged road of hoary-headed trees
Among whose boughs the wind with heedless ditty
Bloweth from out the far off skies.
All thought is here of Him, and fancy sees
The love-lit face the nights beneath the trees

In prayer for us; we hide rebellious tears
And pray that his sweet spirit
May guide our faltering years."

What he thought and the feelings that went through His soul in the days and nights of His retirement here, is well worth our pondering. This was the Master's rest room, His study, His retiring place. He went over into the city to do His work and face His battles, but down the slope across Kedron and up Olivet He came to the quiet of the olive trees where His soul could find peace and where His Father could speak to Him while the leaves of the trees made soft music to His listening soul. It was from this place, somewhere, when His soul was full to overflowing and His heart full to bursting with Jerusalem's hard-heartedness, he criel out, "O Jerusalem! Jerusalem! How oft would I have gathered thee together as a hen doth gather her chickens under her wings but ye would not."

Standing on the Mount of Olives, I read this passage from my Bible, and coming down the sides of Olivet we saw a hen spreading her wings about her little brood.

It was on Olivet or somewhere near the crest where we stood that His holy feet left the earth and He ascended into heaven. Luke says, Luke 24:50,-51—"And He led them out as far as Bethany and lifted up His hands and blessed them, and it came to pass while He blessed them He was parted from them and carried up into heaven." It would seem from this He ascended from Bethany as many suppose, and yet Olivet being so very close to Bethany,

He could have parted with them at Bethany and coming up Olivet to reach the highest point where the Holy City could be so plainly in view, He mounted on the chariot of God's love up to the gates of heaven. And yet, what doth it matter which theory of the doctors is right? We looked upon the spot where His feet last rested on earth, for it was somewhere near here. It is a wise provision perhaps that the exact spot is not known. The Catholics would cover it with a dark church and sprinkle incense over the shadows they cast. Let the spot be unknown. What might crazed fanatics do if they really knew?

Looking west from Olivet we saw almost at its base, Bethany, the home of Martha, Mary and Lazarus, the faithful friends of Jesus, who ever gave him a place in their home for rest and comfort. Near Bethany we could see Bethphage, where the disciples got the ass upon which Jesus rode into Jerusalem. His course was one of the three roads, either over Olivet, around the Southern slope near the foot, or the road still further west. What an assembly that was! The Savior of the world was in the dress of a Galilean traveler, riding upon an ass at the head of that great company, while palm branches were spread in his way and the men, women and the little children shouted (of course the children did) "Hozanna to the son of David! Blessed is he that cometh in the name of the Lord, Hozanna in the highest!" Matt. 21:9. Perhaps yonder through the Golden Gate, just near the temple, the procession entered the city. The Turks closed up that gate hundreds of years ago because of a report among them that a conqueror would come from the East, over Olivet, some day and enter Jerusalem through this gate and take possession of the city. What a sermon that closed gate preached to us that day! Of course a conqueror is coming from the East to rule not only over Jerusalem but over the world, and how his conquering coming will differ from His humble entrance to the city before! Do the silly Turks think they can wall up a gate and keep Him out? Cannot He who entered through the locked door to the prayer meeting of his Apostles pass beyond all the walls man may build?

On beyond Bethany, down beyond the foothills ran the blue stream of the River Jordan winding its crooked course to the Dead Sea. It seemed as it burst upon my vision it could not be over four or five miles away, but again I was fooled by the clear air of this land, for I knew Jordan was over twenty miles away.

We visited the two Catholic churches on Olivet and attended the services in one of them. The most striking thing about these churches was the windows. The words of the Lord's prayer were arranged in striking design on thirty-seven windows in thirty-seven different languages.

Passing from the Mount of Olives we visited the tomb of Herod the Great, also the Tomb of the Kings which is one of the most noted burial places about Jerusalem. These large tombs and chambers are hewn out of solid rock. There are two stories and many rooms in these tombs. Their history is uncertain. Perhaps they were for the Roman kings, or maybe the Jewish kings. I could but wonder as I beheld all these ancient burial places, what distinguished forms were put to rest within their walls. It would be interesting if the mind could call up the picture of all these burials.

We drove along the road over the slope of Olivet around to the Damascus Gate, passing two caravans of camels and a flock of sheep. They followed the shepherd and obeyed all his calls. A little lamb was tired and unable to finish the journey, so the shepherd took him in his arms and carried him on. Many times the Master saw scenes like this and from them He drew the finest lessons of the Father's love and care for His little ones.

From the carriages as they went along that afternoon, our eyes rested on a knoll outside the city wall northward of the city. It took no word from the guide to tell us this was Mount Calvary, where Jesus died upon the cross. Who could, with word or pen, describe his feelings as he looks upon that skull-shaped hill where our Savior hung upon the cross and died for our sins? Doubtless all of us were thinking of the day in the years gone by, far away from there, when groping through the shadows of sin, our souls sought the cross of Jesus. All broken, tired and sick with sin we came to let the blood that was shed on Calvary cleanse us of our sin. The children of God in the church of our childhood seemed to be singing again:

> "Just as I am without one plea
> But that Thy blood was shed for me
> And that Thou bidst me come to Thee,
> O Lamb of God, I come, I come."

We felt ourselves coming again to the altar of
the old church six thousand miles away, with broken
heart and tear-filled eyes, and kneeling at the altar
of our fathers, that had known so many tears of
sorrow and joy, the soul, hungry and sick, sought
the dying Savior in penitent prayer, while the
verse came sweet and low—

> "Just as I am Thou wilt receive;
> Will welcome, pardon, cleanse, relieve,
> Because Thy promise I believe:
> O Lamb of God, I come, I come."

And when the seeking sinner and the seeking Savior met, and the Savior had spoken "Peace"—
the sweet peace of forgiveness to the seeking soul
the people sang:

> "Just as I am Thy love unknown
> Hath broken every barrier down;
> Now to be Thine, yea, Thine alone;
> O Lamb of God, I come, I come."

In our hearts we had been to Calvary before, but
now we were standing by the real spot where the
Lord was crucified. I tried to picture the scene but
it was a poor effort, for my soul was too overcome
to picture or describe anything. The three crosses
were there on the crest of the hill and the soldiers
on guard near by. The surroundings would afford
a splendid theatre where the great crowd that had
come into the city to the Passover could see the acts
on the stage in the center. The mass of people
crowded around to see the performance—the public
crucifixion of three criminals who had proven them-

selves unworthy of living among them. Yonder, near the cross, was a little company more touched than the others, a poor, bent and crushed woman wept but she had not left her Son.

> "Near the cross was Mary weeping;
> There her mournful station keeping;
> Gazing on her dying Son;
> There in speechless anguish groaning,
> Yearning, trembling, sighing, moaning;
> Through her soul the sword had gone."

Then comes one of the most tender touches of all the history of men. The dying eyes of Jesus were turned toward that bent and troubled figure. In the midst of the most intense agony the body and the soul have ever known, He did not forget His mother. He was all she had, and she was all He had. He had no home or earthly store to will those He left behind. He need not even think about who would take his garments, the only earthly possession He had, for the soldiers who killed Him would take His clothes for the trouble. Yet He made a will, an additional will to the one He made in John 14. when as a last will and testament He left His friends a legacy of Peace and Titles to Mansions in the skies. This is a very peculiar will. There is no case like it. When the eyes of the Savior saw Mary His white lips moved "John, behold thy mother, Mother, behold thy son." He had willed his mother to His best friend and willed His best friend to His mother. Mary, leaning on the arm of her new son John. went down from Calvary. What tender pictures we would see if we could follow them through the rest of their earthly life and see how each one tried to carry out the Savior's dying request.

I think the greatest description of the crucifixion I have ever seen is that of General Wallace in Ben Hur. Over and over in my mind ran the words He uses and rose the pictures He draws as we stood about Calvary. It is not strange that the lips of those in our carriage ceased speaking and tears ran unhindered from the eyes that watched the scene that day.

Calvary is occupied by a Mohammedan cemetery and no alien foot is allowed upon its top. People have been killed for trying to reach it. While the Christian heart revolts at the thought of Turks owning Calvary, it seemed to me that it was better so than for the Catholics to own it and cover it with a gloomy church and let priests sling incense where Jesus died. Now it is bare and the sun shines on it while all who come can see it. Surely, no building ought ever be put on Mt. Calvery.

From Calvary we went to the Garden in which is located the tomb where Christ was buried. Of course, great controversies have waged over the location of these places. The Catholics have maintained all of them were to be located in the Church of The Holy Sepulchre within the city walls, while the great weight of Protestant scholarship has placed the crucifixion and the tomb outside the city walls. It is not the purpose of this writing to trace the arguments for this position. After much study of these authorities and looking upon the scenes with my Bible in my hand to see what it says, there is not a shadow of doubt to me that "Gordon's Calvary" and "Gordon's Tomb" to the north of the city wall are genuine. They fill all conditions and no other place could. These spots have General Gordon's name associated with them because by his labor and money the weight of evidence was secured that located them as the real places where Jesus died and was buried.

The garden in which the tomb is located is a beautiful one and is owned by some very devout Episcopalians from England. The old gentleman, who was the garden keeper was indeed an attractive Christian gentleman of culture and spiritual force. He seems to live in the atmosphere of the garden where Jesus was buried, providing an opportunity for followers of Jesus to visit these sacred spots and devoutly meditate, rather than using the garden for commercial purposes. How different was the atmosphere of this garden to other sacred places occupied by lazy Turks and Catholics who drone out their Latin and scatter incense! It was refreshing to find the tomb where Jesus was buried, occupied by devout Episcopalians.

We greatly enjoyed our visit to this garden and the lecture by the keeper. We entered this tomb that had the name "Joseph" carved on it and read there the gospel account of Christ's burial. What feelings came to our hearts, as standing with bowed heads in the empty tomb of Jesus, we reflected on the scene so dear to Christian hearts! We could almost see the weeping women coming in the gray dawn of the first Easter morning, their hands full of sweet spices, their hearts full of a sweeter love, and their eyes overflowing with tears. All others had left Him. Fearing naught that might be in their path, they sought His tomb with a question on their lips as to how their weak feminine hands could roll the stone away, but with a faith in their hearts that somehow God would attend to that. Then they went back with the first message of a Risen Saviour for a waiting, hungry world upon their lips. Peter and John were so stirred that they braved the dangers and ran with questions on their lips to see for themselves. "So they ran, both of them together, and the other disciple did outrun Peter and came first to the sepulchre, and he, stooping down and looking in saw the linen clothes lying, yet he went not in. Then came Simon Peter following him and went into the sepulchre." Jno. 20:4-6. John outran Peter I suppose because poor Peter was so weakened by his suffering since his awful sin of denial, and his eyes were so blinded with tears he made a poor runner. When they reached the tomb John halted for fear, but Peter overtook him, passed him and went into the tomb where his Lord had been. What must have been the feelings of their hearts as they came to the grave of the best friend they had ever had and found it empty, knowing that no power could open it and get the body away but the power that went in with His body when it was buried?

Of course the authorities tried by bribery and lies to prove his disciples stole His body away while the soldiers slept. But who would believe it? The disciples could not open the tomb, and they were too frightened and timid to try. The soldiers would not sleep, for it was a death penalty to sleep on duty. And the whole company would not sleep while such a robbery went on under their noses. Besides this, if there ever was a time and place when people were not inclined to sleep it was here and now. This was a weak and foolish theory, and the people did not believe it. They knew it was the hand of God and not human hands that opened the tomb.

What strange feelings came to our own hearts as we stood beside this tomb! Many times I had tried to preach to poor souls as they stood beside the graves of their buried treasures. I had assured mothers across the seas that their little ones were not dead but sleeping, and soon the Lord who rose from the dead Himself would raise them up and place them in their mother's arms. I had assured children they would see their parents again. I had said it was all wrong to say they were dead. They were only sleeping. I had comforted myself thus beside the graves of my own loved ones many leagues from here. What a privilege to have our faith thus strengthened by a visit to the empty tomb and looking in on the place where he arose and sing

> "In rising God forsakes the tomb;
> In vain the tomb forbids His rise
> Cherubic legions guard Him home
> And shout Him welcome to the skies.

Our approach to Jerusalem this time was from over the hills of Galilee into the Damascus Gate. Charles Jallouk met us at Shechem in a car and took me ahead of the folks to make arrangements for them, and have rooms assigned for our folks.

No event of the tour was more enjoyed than our evening at Tea in the Jallouk home. These folks are born noblemen. The Jallouk Brothers are the best guides in Palestine, and their wives and children are a credit to them. During the war news came to me that Philip, the Prince of them all, had died with Typhus fever in Moab. I waved Philip and George goodbye at the Beyrout dock in 1914. I looked down on George sad and alone at the same place six years later. He was broken and at times sad, but he was still the same true unselfish gentleman, ready to wear himself out for us.

It was several days until I had a good opportunity to hear George tell the details of his brother's death and recount some of the sorrows and horrors of the war. I sometimes wish I could reproduce the pictures he drew, and give the soft light in his eyes, with the shadows on his face and the quiver on his lips. It is best I cannot do it. My blunt interpretation is not equal to it.

When the war came, the tourists ceased to come. The Turks confiscated money and property and forced men in the army. Christians, who did not flee, were deported. Many starved, beggars died faster than they could be counted and a stream went along the roads all the time. None could help them. The Jallouks lost everything and fled to escape the Turks. They were taken in by Christians in Moab. Philip and his wife were sick of fever. He died while she was unconscious. When she came from delirium she asked where Philip was. They told her he had gone to Jerusalem. That Prince of God's Israel had entered the pearly gates of the new Jerusalem.

We entered the Jallouk home through the gate in the wall and sat under the vine and fig tree. The true real hospitality of the East met us. Mother Jallouk—a kindly sweet old lady—in whose heart sorrow had done its work—was in front of the receiving line. Philip's widow, her fine children, Mrs. George and the younger brother's wife, helped receive and serve. Culture and manners were in evidence. We feasted on tea, Turkish coffee, Oriental cakes (delicious) fruits and other dainties.

I talked to the old mother thru an interpreter. She held a locket in her hand which she wears near her heart and said, "Philip." The tears were in her eyes. I told her now many Americans, who knew Philip, loved him and grieved at his death. I told her what a great treasure it was, to have such a son and how happy she would be when she met him in Heaven. We will never forget that visit.

We had a busy Sunday in Jerusalem, going to church. We went to Mass in the Catholic church, the Greek church and the Armenian church. At eleven we worshipped in Christ Episcopal Church. Here we found a houseful of worshippers and the service made us feel at home. All the British soldiers were there. It was a good service and a fine sermon. In the afternoon, we attended services at the American Colony, and at night, we worshipped at St. George's Episcopal Church, the church of the Jallouks.

That day of church going in the Holy City was delightful and made up somewhat for times when we could not attend public worship.

CHAPTER XXIV.

ABOUT THE WALLS OF ZION.

We spent several days in the Holy City and were busy all the time to make every precious moment count. Of course I am not trying to give anything like a full account of all we saw. It would be impossible for me to attempt such a thing; I am merely giving some impressions of some things.

One morning, just after breakfast, we all assembled in front of the hotel for a donkey ride around the wall of the city. There were fifty-two of us and when we all got together it seemed to me I have never seen such an array of donkeys. We discussed the matter of how many donkeys were along, but were never able to determine.

Palestine and Egypt cannot be disassociated from the donkey. He is its national flower. He is everywhere. If you go out into the fields, he is there browsing and happy. If you go in the alleys, he is there asleep or in deep study over some solemn subject. If you go into the houses, he is there. If you walk the streets, he is stepping on your toes, rooting his nose in your neck, rubbing his back on you and switching his tail in your face when he has energy enough to do so. You can't get away from him. There are ten thousand in Cairo alone. You can hire him for a day's ride for a song or if you want to buy him you can do so for something like five dollars. He is usually mouse-colored but sometimes black or white. He is so small that your feet

will almost drag the ground when you mount him.
But notwithstanding his insignificant looks he can
and does carry immense burdens; for one of the
most pathetic sights of the country is the way they
burden their beasts. And when you get on his back
you will get one of the most pleasant and comfortable rides you ever had.

The world has never given the donkey his dues.
It has honored the horse in literature and even
mounted its heroes upon him on their monuments.
It has immortalized the dog in eloquent words and
touching stories that have touched the heart and
dimmed the eyes. It has honored the bird and
praised the cow, but what has it ever done for the
donkey? He has carried man's burdens and never
uttered a word of complaint save when Baalam tried
to drive him where he knew he ought not to go.
Sure-footed, careful and strong he has carried man
where other animals could not take him. He has
carried his owners' children, cared for them and
hurt them not. For all this service he has been
beaten, half starved, and his name used to curse with
for when we desire to put a person down as low
in the scale of brain and character as possible we
call him an ass. But the donkey does not deserve
such treatment, he has traits that are not commendable, the main two being laziness and hard-
headedness, but in the East he is the poor man's
friend and in our land he ought to be.

We all selected our donkeys and mounted them
in great confusion. The confusion, however, was
among us, and not them, for a donkey never gets

confused. He is at home anywhere and under all circumstances, he is nature's most cool-headed animal. He didn't even get excited in the Ark. I selected mine, mounted him. His name was Mohammed, and I think that was his faith, for he had some traits very much like that prophet. He did not believe in progressive doctrine but was a standpatter. He also, like the prophet believed in predestination, holding that whatever was going to be would take place whether he was there to see it or not, so he need not hurry. But he also believed in the perseverance of the saints, beliving that when he did start he would keep on until he got there even if the program was over.

The vision of that donkey party made impressions on the slate of my memory that will never wear off. The solemn little mouse-colored donkeys with fringes of many colors on their saddles, long-legged men with feet nearly dragging the ground, dignified D. Ds., professors and bankers, laughing lassies and solemn school marms, stout ladies and thin ladies with the bare-foot, baggy-panted donkey-boys, produced a picture I have hung high on the walls of my soul.

After all necessary preliminaries, we started around to the south of the Joppa Gate and down the Valley of Gihon, that moves on the south side of the city until it becomes the Valley of Hinnom and runs into the Valley of Jehosaphet, which is formed by the brook Kedron, which runs between Olivet and the city walls on the east side. Thus the city is almost entirely surrounded by these valleys which vary in depth from almost a level where they begin to over six hundred and seventy feet at the juncture of Hinnom and Jehosaphat. A ride along these valleys, around the city walls, over ground historic as no other ground can be with landmarks that stir your soul, is a privilege never to be forgotten.

I got along very well with my donkey, Mohammed. I hope I will not be considered sacreligious or disrespectful to the prophet when I shorten his name to "Ham" for all of it too much to say when hurried. He was very hard to get started, for he seemed to have a great deal of pious meditating to do before he began his journey. After you had exhausted about all your energy to get him under way you had equally as much trouble halting him when and where you chose. He was like one of the old-time freight trains before the days of air brakes. You had to begin to put on brakes as soon as you saw the station and then you were sure to go by it and have to back back to it. To pull on the reins was like pulling on the guy-wire of a telegraph pole. It seemed to make no impression on him. To speak to him was worse, for he did not seem to understand English, or if he did he paid no attention to it. I did not try Turkey talk to him, for I never did like to use that language. I did devise a method of management before the day was done. I had wondered what his long and ponderous ears were for and I thought I would experiment some, so when I wanted him to stop at the Hill of Evil Council and he seemed bent on a through trip to Jehosaphat with no stop-overs allowed, I caught a big ear in each hand and swung back on my stirrups with all my might   Ham stopped with grace and dispatch. After that I dispensed with the bridle and when I wanted him to "haw" I pulled his left ear and when I wanted him to "gee" I pulled his right one and when I wanted him to "whoa" I pulled both, and I had no more trouble save in getting him started. I didn't learn how to do that. One of the donkey-boys ran up while I was swinging on to Ham's ears to keep him from going into a cavern and protested. I think he was trying to tell me in Arabic that this was not the proper way to manage a donkey. I argued to him in English that it answered the purpose and I proposed to continue it.

Our dignified divinty, Williams protested because of my treatment of my donkey and said I ought to talk to him in his native tongue. So he called a boy and asked him what to say to the donkey to get him to stop. The boy said it and the doctor repeated it all day. At the end of the journey the guide smiled and asked if he knew what he had been saying to the donkey, he replied he had been telling him to stop, like the boy told him. Imagine his feelings when the guide told him he had been telling the donkey to "go to the devil" all day. I told him I'd rather pull his ears than to cuss like that.

Doctor Gibson had turned out his whiskers for reasons best known to himself. Perhaps he had associated with goats until he wanted to look like one. When his donkey got to the highest place in the Valley of Hinnom (from which we get our word

"hell") he started down the precipice. I told the
doctor I had seen a good many things but never saw
a Baptist preacher on his way to hell on a donkey
before. It was suggested that the donkey looked
back and saw the whiskers and thought his passenger had some interests in that place, and he wanted
to take him home.

One reason we had trouble guiding our steeds was
we did not have enough donkeyboys. Each donkey
is accustomed to having a boy following behind him,
beating him with a stick to make him go and using
his tail as a rudder to guide him in the true course.

We paused to view the hill of Evil Council, where
Judas met the Chief Priests and the Scribes and in
secret planned the destruction of Jesus. What a
sad sidelight on human nature? The leaders of
Church and State, in secret plot to kill the Son of
God when they should have been helping Him do
His Father's work! And saddest of all, Judas, one
of the Apostles whom He had trusted, loved and
befriended, sneaking through the city in the night
to join the company to sell his Lord for a little silver! What sadder verse has the Scripture recorded
than that that says of Judas "He went out and it
was night." Yes it was night, a dark and awful
night to his soul and to the world. Their deeds
could only be done in the night. The devils creep
forth at nightfull to ply their trade, for as Jesus
said of them, "They love darkness rather than light
because their deeds are evil."

Not far from the Hill of Evil Council, further
down the valley is Alkedema, or the Field of Blood.

What a history, has this barren, rocky field? Bought with the money for which Judas sold his Lord, it furnished the grave that was to hold the body of the Traitor himself! Many men buy their own graves with the money they have loved more than they love their Lord or their souls! What thoughts came into our minds as we beheld this awful place! Judas Iscariot! What a history he has? How strange such a black chapter should come into the history of the beautiful life of Jesus? What is the meaning of it all? Strange, sad mysteries! It is strange there will grow in the same soil, fed by the same rain and sunshine a food that gives life and the poison that destroys it! It is stranger still there will grow up in the same home, reared by the same parents a child that will honor his parents and one who brings their gray heads down in sorrow to the grave! But stranger than all is the fact that in the family circle of Jesus Christ there should be a Judas and a John!

The great lesson that comes to us is—If from the side of Jesus the devil could drag one of his apostles down to ruin and hell, there is no place on earth where his fiendish feet may not go, and there is no mortal who may not fall a victim to his assaults. Judas did not go the depths at one leap, but sure and swift were the steps he took down the stairway of his doom—covetousness, jealousy, listening to the jingle of the money more than to the words of his Lord; resenting his Lord's correction, keeping company with his Lord's enemies; putting a price on holy things and he had reached the bottom. But the money burned him. He had gained his paltry purse, but on the other side of the balance were the things he lost, his peace, his reputation, his place in the church, his soul.

Poor Judas, thy accused dust will be here in barren Alkedema until God calls time on the world! No vandal's hand will bother thee. All who go this way will pause with a feeling of revulsion and disgust; Friendless, lost, abandoned, thou hast gone down the valley of darkness. While the judge crowns Peter for his martyrdom and John for his life long love he will reward thee for thy treachery and suicide. What a scene that judging time will be! The men thou didst help will have no sympathy for thee and in hell the devils and the damned will sneer at thee while across the great gulf in the city of God angels will welcome thy comrades to everlasting peace.

Another thought came to me in this dark place. It somewhat crowded out my condemnation of Judas. If he fell from the place he held I may fall from mine. Who is exempt from hell's assaults or proof against its alluring lead? May God help us to be true, and if we can never do great deeds for Christ help us not to sell our rock-ribbed loyalty for any glittering bribe. Some men say they hold aloft from Christ and the church because of the hypocrites that are among his people, but somehow more than ever that day as I reviewed the career of Judas on the ground where it was enacted there came a stronger band about my soul that bound me to my Lord because of his failure. If your mother had two sons and your brother brought the family in disgrace and sorrow to her grave after a life of vileness and shame, would you leave the bent form of your weeping and broken-hearted mother at the grave and go off to disown her because of the sin that was in your family? Wouldn't you rather put your arm about her broken-hearted form, kiss her weeping face and say, "Mother, your other son has disgraced you and broken your heart, but I will stick to you closer and love you better because of it." I felt like saying something like that to my Saviour as I stood by the Field of Blood.

Just below the Field of Blood is the valley of Hinnom from which comes the words Gehenna and hell. Jerusalem represented heaven and the valley of Hinnom represented hell. Into this valley the garbage and filth of Jerusalem was dumped, and set on fire. Here, also, the offal from the slaughter pens nearby was thrown. The fires never went out here. The worms died not but ever preyed upon the putrifying mass. The wild dogs and jackalls came up in the night with their hungry howls and gleaming eyes seeking prey. This was in outer darkness for the valley is deep and no light shone save the fires that smouldered and sent up the awful odors toward the skies. In this valley was inaugurated the worship of Moloch. In the arms of a great iron god made hollow so internal fires could heat it as a stove the people placed their little children.

These things account for the references Jesus made to the home of lost souls. Hell was to be the dumping place of all the filth and vileness of the Universe. Everything that was not fit for heaven would be cast into it, and set on fire. If Russel or anybody else can get any consolation from the contemplation of such an eternal abode they surely have accomodating minds. I could but notice how fitting it was that the Hill of Evil Council and the Field of Blood should be so close to Gehenna.

Our journey around the city walls carried us by the village of Siloam and the pool of that name where Jesus made the blind man go and wash that he might receive his sight. Also we made stops at the Virgin's fountain, the tomb of Zecheriah and St. James, reputed to be the burial places of these distinguished characters. Not far from these we came to the pillar of Absalom, a rather imposing, yet gloomy looking, monument. This is supposed to be the grave where Absalom was buried and when the natives pass by they usually spit at it and throw stones at it to show their contempt for a son who treated his father so. Now and then the piles of stones cast about the tomb become so great they have to be cleared away. Near this tomb is the tomb of Jehosaphat where the good king is supposed to be buried. From this fact comes the name of the valley.

We left our donkeys outside and made a visit to Solomon's quarries. The entrance is not large and one would never think of the marvelous scheme of this underground work. There seems to be no end to the caverns and tunnels which the workmen of the great King Solomon dug under the city. Some of them open into large rooms which are very high. It is said the full extent of these underground passages has been explored by very few, if anybody, and much of their regions, is unknown. Here is where the stones were secured for the building of the Temple, and all the stones were quarried so that in putting them together there was heard no sound of instruments. The stone is light gray granite, almost white and everywhere is seen the signs of the workmen's hands, where the stones were hewn out and in many places half finished stones are found.

The whole earth under Jerusalem seems to be filled with this stone.

When the force of Solomon's workmen was at work getting out these stones, bringing them up the incline to the entrance and conveying them to the temple grounds it must have been a wonderful sight. We visited a Masonic lodge in one of these caverns.

A visit to the Jews' Wailing Place brought strange feelings and made lasting impressions on all of us. There is not a more touching place in or about Jerusalem than this place where the Jews come to shed their tears, sing their songs of lamentations and pray to the God of their fathers. There are those who see in this nothing but an exhibition of ceremonial ritualism, but it did not seem so to me as I looked upon it. There may have been a few in the crowd that day who were there just from custom or because of other reasons than sincere devotions, but the large majority of them seemed to me to be pouring out of hungry and sick hearts sincere lamentations and prayers. It was a sad sight. An hour in which there was no note of rejoicing, naught of peace in any heart, and no smile on any face, and is it not a sad hour for any people when their worship comes to that?

The wailing place is just inside the city beside an old wall of the ancient city which is said to be a part of the original wall of Solomon's temple. It is the beginning of the Temple Area, now held by the Turks who will not let a Jew pass over the ground. Their fathers used to worship there. Their incense went up on the air to their God. Their songs went wide and sweet upon the winds. Their prayers in streams flowed heavenward in the good days of Israel's glory and now the heathen Turks will not let them enter the grounds. So they come here every day, but in large numbers on Friday and mourn and pray, kissing the stones and placing their foreheads against them. When we were there they were chanting like a solemn dirge the words of Isaiah 64:9-11, "Be not wroth very sore O Lord, neither remember iniquity forever; behold we beseech thee we are all thy people. Thy holy cities are a wilderness, Zion is a wilderness, Jerusalem is a desolation. Our holy and beautiful house where our fathers praised thee is burned up with fire and all our pleasant things are laid waste."

They repeat other such expressions equally as sad and mournful from the major and minor prophets. Psalms and lamentations are poured forth from their lips with tones, manner and looks of the most intense interest. Some of them seem to be going through severe internal sufferings.

How history and prophecy rolled down upon us at this sad place that evening. For everywhere you go in Palestine you are impressed with the literal fulfillment of the prophecies. The glory of Israel had departed, and her beautiful land laid waste. These Jews were coming back to Jerusalem, the city of their fathers, and praying for restoration of their greatness and were trying to reoccupy Palestine. What a great thing it would be for them to accept the Lord they rejected and then claim the Promises of God!

The day was drawing to a close and we made our way back to our hotel feeling that it had been a day of peculiar interest and pleasure. It being sometime till supper, Williams and myself walked out about the Joppa Gate to study the life we saw there. The usual amount of begging and trading was going on. Almost every stand was supplied with stale bread and watermelon seed which were bought by the poor people for some miserable-looking pennies. Upon these they made their meal. Four Bedowen had partaken of this poor meal and were sitting down upon the ground talking. They were children of the hills, shepherds of a few sheep, roamers far and wide. They had come into the city on some mission, and like we were doing had come to the gate with the crowd to take a little interest in life. They were rough-looking men and they were unkempt and dirty, yet their faces were friendly and their eyes were kind. Three seemed to be happy and one sad. It was easier to guess reasons for the sadness of the one than it was for the happi-

Rock Moriah in Mosque of Omar. See chapter on "The Temple."

Garden of Gethsemene.

The Walls of Jerusalem.

ness of the three. The three were busy trying to cheer up the sad one. They laughed at him, slapped him on the back, called his attention to everything of interest in sight. They told him stories and laughed at them themselves, but the sad man did not laugh, nor did he smile. He did not even look up or take any interest in what was going on. I was thinking their mission to the city was in some way in behalf of their troubled friend. We could not, of course, understand anything they said, but we could read the meaning of what was going on.

We had watched them with much interest because there was much of human life in the picture. I was standing near them with some smoked glasses in my hand. The sun was sinking over the Holy Hills and throwing the beams of its good-night upon the city. The light was soft, the glare was gone, and I had removed the glasses which all travelers must wear to keep the glare of the sun from burning out their eyes. One of the men saw the glasses in my hand and called the attention of the troubled one to it. They all then began to talk to him about me and they became so interested they stood up and came nearer. One of them reached forth his hand for the glasses. I gave them to him and he put them on the eyes of his troubled friend, and as he did, I saw the cause of the man's sadness. His eyes were red and water was running from them. One of the great curses of the land, blindness was pressing down upon him. From constant contact with the burning sun and glare of rock and sand as he looked after his sheep, with no protection for his eyes he was going blind.

When he put the glasses on he looked over the hills of his fathers toward the sunset. His friends were speaking to him. From his troubled face the shadows were passing and in his red, sad eyes a new light was shining. One of the men reached forth his hand and took mine, giving it a vigorous shake. He then took the hand of his afflicted friend and put it in mine, the while making signs and speaking in his native tongue. I understood it all. He wanted the glasses for his afflicted friend thinking this invention of Western civilization would have magic power to save the poor man's eyes. Perhaps his friends had come with him to Jerusalem to seek some aid for their friend in his affliction. I shook the man's hand and also the hand of his friend, which according to the custom of the country was sealing the bargain in the presence of a witness that I had given him the glasses. He went his way rejoicing in his gift and hoping it would save his eyes. I went my way feeling happy that I had had the privilege of taking part in such a little act of kindness at the historic Joppa gate. But my mind turned back to the one who used to pass in the gates of the city and when he saw such poor afflicted eyes he touched them with his fingers and spoke a word to them, bringing to them the blessing of sight. Oh that he were here to-day to bring the same help to the many eyes this glare was burning out. And then there came the thought that our poor, blind souls coming to Him receive sight and see the blessings of forgiveness, peace

and everlating life.   So we went to our supper
from the Joppa gate singing:

> Amazing grace, how sweet the sound
>   That saved a wretch like me;
> I once was lost, but now I'm found,
>   Was blind but now I see.

CHAPTER XXIII.

ON THE SITE OF THE TEMPLE.

Our hotel life in Jerusalem was the most home-like of any we found. By this time in our journeys we had begun to feel like a big family, and somehow the other tourists at the hotel were of the same mind. So our fellowship was very pleasant. Our dragoman, Philip, and his faithful brothers left undone nothing that would add to our comfort and the hotel authorities were as thoughtful, kind and attentive as they could be. The waiters were unusually attentive to us, so much so that one day at our table we raised a tip for our boy. He was a pathetic looking Armenian who seemed to feel that his standing on earth and Heaven would be determined by his attention to his table. When the boy received the tip he went to the chief waiter with that matter. The chief waiter came to us at once and informed us the boy would have to return the money or be dismissed from the hotel, for the rule of the management was that no tips were to be accepted by any employee. This was a new thing under the sun to be found in hotels, and we felt like taking off our hats to the Hotel Fast, and yet we were sorry for the poor boy who wanted the money, and no doubt needed it.

The water we drank was very good but hard to get. They seemed to be stingy with it, as they are everywhere, and well they might. Still when we demanded it we got it in such quanities as we wanted. It is hard for the people to understand the thirst Americans have for water. They drink very little, perhaps the main reason is that it is so scarce and hard to get. It is much easier to get wine than water. One day I asked the hotel man where his supply of water came from. He told me to come down to the entrance the next morning at six if I was up, and he would show me. That morning a company of Arab girls came up the Bethlehem Road by the Joppa gate with large stone water pitchers on their heads. These pitchers seem to hold four or five gallons, and they keep the water cool and fresh for a long time. The girls filed into the hotel and putting down their burdens received their pay of a few pennies, and went on their homeward way. The hotel man informed us this water came from a cool, pure spring near Bethlehem. Think of girls carrying water on their heads in huge pitchers for six miles! When I learned that I was ashamed that I had been such a pig as to demand so much of it to drink.

All over Palestine we saw the women and the girls on those long journeys with their water jars, carrying water home. We also saw hundreds of men carrying water, but they were carrying it in goat skins. It is considered a gross breech of conduct for a man to carry a pitcher. Thus when Jesus sent the disciples to find the ass upon which he would ride into Jerusalem he told them to follow a man whom they would see carrying a pitcher. Had he said "bottle" they would have been confused, as they would doubtless see a large number carrying these skin bottles, but when he said pitcher it was clear, for it would be so unusual to see a man carrying a pitcher that it would attract much attention, since it was likely the only such case they would see.

It was a mystery to me how they got the skin off the goats without so far as you could see any rent in the hide. The head and the feet were cut off and thongs of hide tied to them, and these thrown over the shoulders. The neck or a leg was used as a mouth to let the water out. I thought they scared the goat so he jumped out. The most of these carriers of skins of water seemed not to be carrying it for family use, but for sale to public places or on the street by the glass. We saw a great many of these goatskins and once we saw a man selling water on the street in a dogskin. No, I didn't drink from this bottle ("not as I knows of," as a colored witness said to the court), and don't know how it was, but those who knew said it was fine. There seemed to be a great demand for it.

We spent part of the hours in the evening and during the mid-day hours when it was too hot for much travel about the city in writing postcards and mailing them to our friends. I sent about five hundred, mailing one into every home in my church and to my relatives and friends. These cards, beautiful souvenirs of Palestine, cost us seventy cents a hundred, and the postage when less than five words were used was a cent and a quarter (one matelick), which made the card delivered to friends at home cost a fraction less than two cents.

The visit to the temple area is always of peculiar interest to every Christian traveler. The section occupied by Solomon's Temple, courts and chambers connected therewith occupied a plot of thirty-seven acres in the most commanding section of the city. The temple stood in the center of this section and faced Olivet and the sun rise. To picture the glories and splendor of this temple and its surroundings in the time of Solomon is beyond the power of man to grasp. We visited the temple area early in the morning and took our time going over the sacred ground and thinking of the history that was made here in gold and glory and blood and fire. What spot on earth has witnessed over and over such a train of mighty events? Its first history comes to us from that pathetic chapter in the life of Abraham when God ordered him to take his son Isaac (Gen. 22) and take him to Mt. Moriah and offer him as a sacrifice. The home of Abraham was then several miles to the south. He came to Moriah which the main authorities of Bible History now agree was here in Jerusalem and was the crest of the hill upon which the temple of Israel was destined to stand. God had a plan and purpose in these strange events which are well worth our careful thought and meditation.

Isaac was the only son of Abraham. In a peculiar sense Abraham, the father, stood for God our Father, and Isaac, the son, represented Christ the Son. Abraham took his only son to Mt. Moriah and was in the act of sacrificing him to his God when he was ordered to stay his hand. This was on

the very spot where for centuries the sacrifices of
Israel would be offered. All these things pointed to
the time when Christ would die on the hill of Calvary a few leagues away. God would allow His son
Jesus to be offered up as the fulfillment of all prophecies and accomplish the salvation of all who
henceforth had faith in His blood.

The next mention we find of the temple site is
in 2 Sam. 24. It is now called "The threshing floor
of Araunah the Jebusite." God tells David to go to
Araunah and buy this spot for an altar. David did
so and built there an altar unto the Lord and offered burnt offerings and peace offerings and called
upon the name of the Lord and he answered him
by fire. 1 Chr. 21:26. Then David said, "This is
the house of the Lord God and this is the altar of
burnt offering for Israel." 1 Chr. 22:1. This settles
beyond question the fact that King David, who instructed Solomon as to the building of the temple,
also selected the place and he did it not of his
own fancy, but by the order of God. This threshing floor is declared to be the site where Isaac was
to have been offered.

The first temple that ever stood here was Solomon's Temple, the first permanent dwelling place of
God among the people after the Tabernacle passed
away. The active work of building was eight years.
The principle material was rock from the quarries
under the city, cedars from Lebanon and gold, silver, brass and cypress from Tyre. Large numbers
of the most skilled workmen to be secured in the
world were busy bringing to completion this the

most wonderful building of the world. The height of the temple was two hundred feet. Its body was of white granite. The floor and the roof were of gold. Its pillars were of brass (hollow), two of them were twenty-seven feet and their circumference sixteen feet. The altar was of brass. For the temple service there were twenty thousand silver cups and forty thousand of gold, and ten thousand golden candlesticks. There were also eighty thousand vessels for water for purifying; one hundred thousand golden vials and twice as many of silver; also eighty thousand golden dishes for kneading flour and twice as many made of silver. Of large basins for mixing unleavened bread there were sixty thousand of gold and twice as many of silver. The golden censors for carrying incense to the altars were twenty thousand and those for carrying fire from the altar were fifty thousand. The garments of the priests were of white and covered with a thousand precious stones. There were ten thousand pretty garments of fine linen, two hundred thousand trumpets and as many white robes for the choir of singers. What was it to hear the music of such a choir? This gives but a faint glimpse of a part of the glories of Solomon's temple. Critics have said there was a far too free use of gold and silver, but we must remember in those days it was not money but "goods" and the supply was great and it was all in the hands of a very few who alone could use it.

What a picture this temple must have presented to the view of all the surrounding hills as the morning sun rose over Olivet and shot its shining rays upon its walls of white and domes of gold! Or sinking behind the hills of Judea it threw upon all that marshalled glory the soft light of a dying day! Travelers coming from afar could behold the vision. On the banks of the River Jordan and the shores of the Dead Sea over twenty miles away people could see the white temple and crown of gold shining in the sun. From far and wide pilgrims and caravans as well as shepherds who watched their flocks would rest on a hill and shade their eyes with their hands as they gazed on the glories of Israel there upon the hill and in their hearts longed to realize their highest hopes and stand within its courts.

The dedication of Solomon's temple was an event of such magnificence and display that it has never been equalled in the annals of the nations. People came in multitudes from all parts of Israel's domains and there was hardly room to pitch another tent on any hill around. The Bible tells us Solomon used as sacrifices one hundred and twenty thousand sheep and twenty-two thousand oxen. The blood from such a multitude of slaughtered victims must have run like a river down the Kedron Valley. That much meat on the markets to-day would sell for about twelve million dollars. There are those who think these numbers too high and yet in the days of Israel's highest wealth and prosperity it is not at all unreasonable to suppose the people could have secured from their pastures as many sheep and oxen, and that so many priests in several days could sacrifice them. It must have made a wonderful impression on the people of Israel to see all these slaughtered victims and the blood that was flowing and feel that it in some strange way represented a sacrifice God would make to save their souls.

The prayer of dedication delivered by Solomon ranks as the longest and one of the most eloquent and touching prayers in all literature. The Lord was surely near the king when with uplifted hands he prayed. Standing near the spot where he must have been with the Bible in my hand the last sentence of that prayer came so clear to my soul that I could almost hear the voice of the king ringing over the hills. "If they sin against thee (and there is no man that sinneth not) and thou be angry with them and deliver them in the hand of the enemy, far off or near; yet if they shall bethink themselves in the land whither they are carried captive, and turn again and make supplication unto thee in the land of them that carried them captive, saying, 'We have sinned and have done perversely, we have dealt wickedly;' if they turn unto thee with all their heart and with all their soul in the land of their enemies, who carried them captive, and pray unto thee toward their land, which thou gavest unto their fathers, the city which thou hast chosen and the house which I have built for thy name, then hear thou their prayer, and their supplication in heaven thy dwelling place and maintain their cause; and forgive thy people who have sinned against thee and all their transgressions wherein they have transgressed against thee; and give them compassion before those who carried them captive that they may have compassion on them (for they are thy people and thine inheritance which thou broughtest forth out of Egypt from the midst of the furnace of iron); that thine eyes may be open unto the supplication of thy servant and unto the supplication of thy people Israel to hearken unto them whensoever they cry unto thee; for thou didst separate them from among all the people of the earth, to be thine inheritance, as thou spakest to Moses thy servant when thou broughtest our fathers out of Egypt, O Lord God." 1 Kings 8:46-53.

It would be hard to find a more touching and thrilling prayer anywhere. It must have greatly effected the great concourse of people. Does it not seem from the tone of the great king's prayer his soul had in a sweep of prophecy seen a vision of the time when his people would forsake their God and be scattered over the world while the glory he now beheld would be blown away on the winds?

I could but feel deep in my soul the contrast between those days of Solomon and now. There came a time when Israel's glory was departed and not a vestige of her greatness left behind. Her proud priests and prophets were led away in chains; her fair daughters sold in the market as slaves; her children dashed to pieces on the rocks; her temple prostrated in the dust; her sacred vessels bartered for merchandise. Unhallowed feet of an alien race walked in her Holy of Holies where once the High Priest of God went to pray for the sins of the people. Heathen curses rose on the air where once the sweet insense from Israel's altars rose on the winds

to God. In the courts of the temple where the
Jewish maidens once sang the song of Miriam arose
the heartrending cry of the souls as they were
borne from the hills they loved so well to return
again no more. Over to Babylon they went footsore,
tired and weak until after a long journey they sat
down by the river of Babylon and with their faces
buried in their hands and their heads between their
knees they wept when they remembered Zion,
"Upon the willows in the midst thereof we hanged
up our harps. For there they that led us captive
required of us songs, and they that wasted us required of us mirth, saying, 'Sing us one of the
songs of Zion.' How shall we sing the Lord's song
in a strange land? If I forget thee, O Jerusalem, let
my right hand forget her cunning. Let my tongue
cleave to the roof of my mouth." Ps. 137.

No they couldn't sing the Lord's song in a strange
land. The day of their singing was over and their
harps were hung up forever. Strange people,
lonely, homeless in the earth, driven from among
men, persecuted, oppressed and ridiculed, they have
been unwelcome anywhere but have gone everywhere. They have ceased to herd sheep, but have
hoarded the world's gold. Sneered at in every mart
of trade, they have had a mighty hand in the commerce of the earth. They are a byword among nations and outlawed from social circles and yet their
fathers were priests and prophets in the service of
Jehovah when our ancestors were naked savages in
a wilderness that knew no law. All of this was
caused by sin, that fatal scourge that has wrought

its havoc and desolation in the earth since the time it broke down Eden's garden gate. Everywhere you turn in Palestine you see the literal fulfillment of the prophecy which foretold Israel's doom, because of their sin.

These were our meditations as we walked about the Mosque of Omar, the Turkish temple, that now stands on the site of the wonderful Temple of Solomon. It gives one a strange feeling to see these dirty heathen where Israel's glory reigned. They met us at the door and put dirty, germ-laden slippers on our feet to keep us from defiling the holy place. This mosque is one of the most noted buildings of the world, not only on account of its location and history, but also on account of its construction. No attempt at description will be undertaken. It is gorgeous and gaudy and imposing. The windows were designed by the finest expert to be found and tradition goes that so well pleased were the Turks with his work and so fearful were they that he would duplicate it somewhere else in the world that they had him killed.

The most interesting thing in and about the place is the Rock Moriah. It is something like sixty feet long, fifty feet wide and ten or twelve feet high at the highest point. This is the very rock on the crest of Mt. Moriah where the uplifted hand of Abraham was ready to sacrifice his son. On this rock was Israel's altar and here the blood of the sacrifices ran through an opening in the rock out to the Kedron Valley. On this rock the blood of Saracen and Christian has flown in streams as they slaughtered one another in multitudes and piled about the sacred place their mangled bodies. What a rock! What a history! How it represents that Rock, Christ Jesus! All through history God speaks of a Rock, solid, great and mighty upon which the truth, hope and life of the world must rest and on which men and nations must build. This rock has been wet with the blood of sacrifice. Nearby that Great Rock was placed on Calvary with the promise that the gates of hell should not prevail against it. What a glorious promise this is. Enemies have prevailed against Israel's rock of law and sacrifice. Solomon's Temple was swept from it. Zerubbabel, after years of toiling, built another which was borne off in a storm. Herod then built one which also fell a prey to enemies. Now for many centuries the Turks have had their temple here. But the promise comes to us that no enemy can sweep the Structure of Truth from the Solid Rock. As long as our faith rests on Him we are safe.

The Lord's our Rock, in Him we hide,
A shelter in the time of storm;
Secure whatever ill betide,
A shelter in the time of storm.
O, Jesus is a Rock in a weary land,
A shelter in the time of storm;
Be thou our helper ever near,
A shelter in the time of storm;
O, Jesus is a Rock in a weary land,
A shelter in the time of storm.

CHAPTER XXIV.

IN THE GARDEN OF GETHSEMANE.

"Choose thee out a cell
In Kedron's storied dell,
Beside the streams of love that never die;
Among the olives kneel
The chill night's blast to feel,
And watch the moon that saw thy Master's agony."

We visited the Garden of Gethsemane more than once during our stay of several days in Jerusalem, but in many respects the most impressive visit to me was that made by a few of us at night. The moon was full and the city was still. It seemed to me I had never seen such light from the moon. It was bright and soft as it shone through the clear Syrian atmosphere upon the white limestone rocks and the many historic spots we passed. The night was enchanted and a voice seemed to call from the long gone ages the mighty souls who had lived upon these hills and was marshalling them and their wondrous history before us. We met them in the road and brushed their white garments on the way that night as we made our way to the garden gate.

Almost overcome with feelings I sat upon a rock. Perhaps there upon one of those rocks my Savior fell prostrate as with breaking heart and white upturned face he prayed to Heaven, and met single handed all the evil spirits of earth and hell and here upon the world's great decisive battlefield fought to set our souls free from the bondage of sin. The troubles of all the souls of earth were pulling his tender heartstrings. The weight of all the hearts of earth were resting on his tender soul. To add to his cup already full there was no sympathetic voice to whisper comfort, and no friend's hand to hold His as he went through the flood alone. He trod the wine press alone, and what that awful word means we will never fully know until we see Him face to face. The disciples were sleeping and his mother was gone. His was a bitter loneliness. There is a loneliness that is sweet and soothing and there is a loneliness that breaks the heart and crushes the soul. Oh, to be lonely when the heart is bleeding and the soul is being crucified upon a bitter cross! Then the cold, trembling hand reaches out in the dark for the warm clasp of the hand of a friend; and then it is the eyes look through the shadows, for the light of a sympathetic face. If only in the darkest hours of trouble we could have the companionship of a sympathetic friend! But so often the hardest battles must be fought in a lonely place where no one can come to help.

In the awful hours there was a foot fall in the Garden, and a man came stealing cautiously through the shadows of the olive trees. It was one of his disciples. Ah, blessed be the sight of a friend at a time like that! How much lighter it makes the burden. He comes to the prostrate form of the suffering Galilean and speaks to Him, "Hail Master." The white face looks up at the man. In those eyes shine a light the world had never seen before. It was the light of a Savior's dying love. For a moment the man hesitated, and then he stooped and kissed that white face! Ah! beautiful sight of tenderness and love! How sweet is the kiss of a friend in the Garden of Trouble! How comforting to know a friend will seek you out in the shadows of suffering and place a kiss of love and trust upon your face!

Beautiful act did I say? That kiss was the darkest act of treacherous infamy ever born in hell. If in all the annals of crimes the devil has found one thing to be ashamed of it is this! It was the traitor's kiss instead of the kiss of a friend! It came from one who had been befriended and helped by the Savior. Dark is the night when the hand of a friend becomes the hand of an enemy and thrusts a dagger into the trusting heart of Love! Awful hour when a kiss, that seal of purity and trusting affection has behind it a plot of shame and ruin! And yet how many faces in other places than Gethsemane have received the kiss they thought was love's sweet seal only to learn it was the sign of their sale by the traitor they trusted?

How that kiss burned the face of Christ with a fire like that of hell itself! Of all the pains and insults heaped upon Him this was the worst of all, but the Savior bore it without a word, nor did he rub off that burning kiss. Then the soldiers came to take Him. Cowards of perdition! They could not, they dared not do it in the day, but chose the night when he was alone and the city was asleep. A whole company of armed soldiers coming to take a lone meek and unarmed Galilean! Wonderful bravery! In keeping with the reputation of Roman heroism. When they saw his upturned face they fell back in confusion, and well they might! He could have raised His eyes to heaven for help and every stone in Kedron's Valley would have been turned to a soldier to defend Him. That upturned face would have made the Roman Empire tremble and no wonder it startled them. There was a light in that face they had never seen before. There was no resistance there but tenderness and love. And oh, what marks of suffering! Upon the white features tricked drops of blood instead of sweat! The agony of the soul had broken his heart and His blood was running out through the pores of His skin. The sight of that face was enough to startle anyone. Then the unexpected happened. Peter who with James and John had been asleep instead of keeping friendly watch as He had expected of them, roused by the noise of their intrusion in their sacred haunt, leaped to his feet with his sword and single handed leaped into the conflict to fight all the cohorts of Rome and defend his Lord. Whatever blame you heap on Peter for sleeping, and later denying his Lord and being unstable and impetous you must give him credit for a bravery that few men have. It may be poor judgment to leap single-handed at the throat of Rome for unkindness to a friend, but surely it is the act you do not look for in a coward. But the Lord ordered the sword put up and even stopped to heal the wound that was made, and ever since then the swords that have been drawn have been drawn against His will. Then they took Him in the night and led him away from the garden he loved, to come back to it no more.

Great old olive trees are growing in the garden and they are very old. If they are not the trees that witnessed the Savior's agony surely they have grown up from the roots of the ones that did. It was a great event on a night like that—a night like the one when He was here—to see the moonlight shining through the olives. At other visits we read the account of the Lord's agony in the Gospels; tonight we meditated and prayed while running through our mind were the words:

> "Into the woods my Master went
> Clean forspent, forspent,
> Into the woods my Master came
> Forspent with love and shame.
> But the olive trees were not blind to Him;
> The little gray leaves were kind to Him;
> The thorn tree had a mind to Him
> When into the woods He came."

Who could describe the feelings on a visit like that to Gethsemane? Not even Calvary touched my soul more than this. Sweeter, clearer, stronger came the Master's love to me that night. And the peace that was in my heart as I climbed the hill to Hotel Fast was softer and brighter than the light of the moon that flooded the city that night. There is no money could buy the great privilege of that visit. May its influence ever abide in my soul, and may I have the power to impart some of it to others.

As we turned from the garden to my room, my soul was singing with the angels:

> "Paschall lamb by God appointed
> All our sins on thee were laid
> By Almighty Love anointed
> Thou hast full atonement made.
> All thy people are forgiven
> Through the virtue of thy blood
> Opened is the gate of heaven;
> Peace is made 'twixt me and God."

CHAPTER XXVII.

BETHLEHEM AND HEBRON.

"O little town of Bethlehem,
How still we see thee lie;
Above thy deep and dreamless sleep
The silent stars go by.
Yet in thy dark streets shineth
The everlasting light,
The hopes and fears of all the years
Are met in the night!"

We took one full day for our drive to Hebron. After an early breakfast, we started for the twenty-mile drive through this historic Southern border of Palestine.

Our horses turned their faces across the valley of Gihon up that highway toward Bethlehem. Oh, if these stones and hills along this historic road could speak! Who could they tell us they had seen pass along the way our horses went? Abraham, Isaac, Jacob, David, Solomon and armies too many to count. Here is the valley of Rephiam where David fought the Phillestines.

Yonder is the hill where old Goliath marched up and down letting off steam and defying Israel. David, a shepherd lad, came down to bring his brothers food and taking some stones from the brook yonder he dove one into the head of the bragging giant and brought his proud form to the dust. God uses little people and weak instruments to lay the giants low every day. Better throw a small stone, guided by the hand of God, than be a giant with a staff like a weaver's beam and blow off gas for the devil. God will guide our feeble efforts and make them bring down the giants of sin.

Not far from Jerusalem we passed the Leper Hospital and colony where the poor victims of that awful disease are kept until they die. If the earth can produce a more horrible sight than a group of lepers I know not where it would be found. The sight will haunt you for a long time. What a powerful truth the Bible teaches when it compares sin to leprosy? It is contagious; so is sin. It is loathsome; so is sin. It starts from a little spot and spreads through the system until it destroys the entire being; so does sin. It separates the victim from the congregation, friends and home; so does sin. It is a scourge that could be prevented; so is sin. There is no cure outside of the direct hand of God; so it is with sin.

They came to us begging for backsheesh, holding up stumps for hands, and crying from lips and throats half destroyed by the ravages of the disease. Their fingers, hands, ears, noses, eyes, palates and other portions of their bodies were eaten away. All stages of the disease were in evidence. Some were almost to the point where death would bring a merciful deliverance, others had yet a long seige of suffering, until their bodies were sufficiently rotted away for the disease to reach the vitals and end their misery. Long will we remember the weird, pathetic cries from half-destroyed vocal organs and the diseased hands held up for help. There was a time when Jesus walked these hills and with a look, a word, a touch cured these suffering souls. Thank God for the thought that the disease of sin that wrecks bodies and damns souls can now be cured by Him.

Joseph pointed out to us a well called the "well of the Maji," where the star reappeared to the wise men, and also a monestary built where Elijah slept when fleeing from Jezebel. At least these are spots which tradition ever hungry for spots and places have fixed upon. While of course these places along with many others pointed out are perhaps not exact, yet they do help the mind and heart to call up the great events that did occur very near by. The well of the Maji is surely near the spot where these strange men from the East as they pursued their journey searching for the newborn Savior saw their guiding star returning and welcomed it again.

And if this monastery is not on the exact spot it is somewhere near here that Elijah overcome with exhaustion, overwork and nervous strain fighting the devil single-handed in the form of Jezebel, Ahab and Baal, came overwhelmed with despondency and blues and God sent an angel to find Him and put him to sleep like a loving mother would a worn out child. When the old prophet awoke refreshed, God first taught him that in our zeal we often get faster and more violent in advancing His kingdom than is best. Thunder, lightning, earthquake and fire have their uses in the kingdom of God, but His best work is done by the still small voice of the Spirit. When God gave him this lesson he sent him off on a vacation and then sent him to work to help other folks. What a wonderful treatment for disordered souls! Communion with God, sleep, food, vacation and work.

In a few minutes we came to the town where Jesus was born. To the left of us lay the fields of Boaz now, as in days of Ruth's beautiful story, full of harvest. Here the Moabitess Ruth came from miles away clinging to her mother-in-law with those immortal words upon her lips, "Entreat me not to leave thee and return from following after thee; for whither thou goest, I will go; and where thou lodgest I will lodge; thy people shall be my people and thy God my God; where thou diest will I die, and there will I be buried. The Lord do so to me and more also if aught but death part thee and me." Ruth 1:16-18. Thus leaving her own land she joined the people of God and was rewarded by becoming an ancestor of Jesus Christ. It was here on these plains,

"While shepherds watched their flocks by night
   All seated on the ground,
The angel of the Lord came down
   And glory shone around."

Little Bethlehem is alive with history of the years. To the right of Bethlehem in sight was the home of Saul. Around here David wrought mightily and drove back the Philistines who beseiged the city. Here still stands the well called "David's well," because he liked the water so, and in the thick of a battle nearby one day being thirsty, cried for water, "Oh that one would give me water to drink of the well of Bethlehem that is by the gate." 1 Chr. 11:17. Three of his mighty men forced the Philistines who then occupied the city and brought the water for their king. But he was so touched he refused to drink it, and poured it out on the ground as an offering to God. On these hills here one day rose a pathetic heart-rending wail from the troubled mothers because old Herod sent soldiers to kill all their babies so that Christ whom he dreaded might be included in the number. "A voice was heard in Ramah weeping and great mourning, Rachel weeping for her children, and would not be comforted because they were not." Matt. 2:18. Rachel herself is represented rising from her tomb and weeping over the slaughter of her little ones.

But all other history of Bethlehem fades away in the light of the one event that will make the little town live forever. It is the birthplace of Jesus. Here heaven and earth came together in the strange blending of God and man in the life of the child Jesus. One day a tired and travel-worn Galilean came over the hills to Bethlehem walking beside his donkey upon which rode his young wife. That journey must have been a hardship to Mary. It took us two hard days driving over good roads from Jerusalem to Nazareth, and Bethlehem is six miles still further. In those days when there were no roads over the rough hills it was a long hard journey for the Virgin. They reached Bethlehem, their native city, and sought shelter, but the hotels were closed to people of such humble station, and the city being crowded on account of all the natives coming back to their tribe center to be taxed they sought the quarters where the cattle lived, a thing the humble classes do even now, many of them living in the tents and caves with the animals. "There was no room for Him in the inn" (Luke 2:7). And there has not been much room since for when the world, the flesh and the devil have been accommodated at the hotels there is not much room left for Jesus Christ.

That night to the tired woman away from her home in these humble surroundings came that heaven-sent Visitation that left in her arms her first-born child. Like babyhood has always done, the child's little blue eyes looked into the face of His mother. And like motherhood has always done, Mary looked into the face of her little one, and as she looked the eternal fires of motherlove were burning in the heart and the light that first burned in Heaven was shining in her eyes. As she looked upon her baby's face as mothers have always done, she took those little hands in hers and wondered what in the providence of God those hands would do out in the world some day. And as she felt the beat of the baby's heart, as mothers have always done, she wondered what that heart would bear and do in the battle of the world. Strange things had been said of her child and motherlike "she kept all those things and pondered them in her heart."

Nobody can ever tell the possibilities that lie hidden in a baby's little hand and brain and heart, for all the mighty men of the race were once helpless little bundles of infancy with no power to lift their heads and hands and with no language but a cry. But who dared to dream that night what lay before Mary's child? Those little lips would speak the Sermon on the Mount, that would live when Roman Royalty had gone to dust. Down by blue Galilee they would speak parables of light and life to thrill souls for all time. They would rebuke disease, sin and even death and at their rebuke these monsters that had cursed the world so long would sneak away. They would cause words of comfort and peace for troubled hearts in all lands and for all time. That little throbbing heart that made his mother's heart so glad when she saw it was living, would bear the weight of all the world's sin and shame in Gethsemane and break and bleed in sacrificial love to bring a lost world back to God. Those little hands and feet would be nailed to the cross, but those same nails would forever fasten a lost world to the loving heart of God so strong that no storms could tear it away. It is best mothers never know what is before the helpless little ones as they go down into the valley of death to bring them up the hills of life.

Strange visitors were there to welcome Him to the new world into which He had come, but none there understood that those little hands resting in His mother's helped God make the world, hang up the stars and strike the spark of life. Mary looking on was Love. The cattle standing by was Nature.

Then the wise men from afar came to look on His face, lay down their gifts and go back over the hills rejoicing. This was Wisdom. Then the shepherds came to behold Him who was to be the shepherd of us all. This was Labor. Then the angels hovered over as they do at every cradle, and that was Heaven. But there was another visitor. Out in the shadows sneaked the Devil, for he never sees mother-love looking in the face of a new-born child that he does not march about that scene with the tramp and tread of hell and set the blackest spirits he can find to the task of blighting that picture if he can. Especially was his eyes on this baby, and back to hell he went to perfect a plot as black as the walls of perdition, to destroy the life of the baby in Mary's arms. Those were the representatives about the manger watching the sleeping child, Love, Nature, Wisdom, Heaven, Labor, Satan.

These were the thoughts that came to me as I stood in the Church of the Nativity, and these thoughts outshone the light of the Roman, Greek, Armenian and Catholic altars with their burning candles and sullen priests here in the place said to mark the birthspot of my Savior. So much absorbed was I in these thoughts and the pictures that arose before me that I scarcely noticed the room in which Jerome spent his years translating the Scriptures, nor did I listen long to the story of Joseph that the Turkish soldiers we saw were there to keep the priests from killing one another. Religious hatred here where the Christ of Peace was born, is so strong that not long ago they fought to a bloody

finish and left nine dead bodies near the place where
the manger was. These things, along with all the
tinsel glitter, musty air and incense of the superstitious creeds that built their gloomy church over
the spot mattered little to me. This was where
Jesus, my Savior, was born, the first Christmas gift
to the world. My heart went back to that day when
the gift of His Peace and Love came into the world.

We visited other spots in Bethlehem and found
the people more kindly disposed toward us, and
with all better looking and brighter than we had
seen. Mission work has told on the people here.
After finishing our visit we turned our faces southward toward Hebron. On this journey we had a
fine opportunity to see the life of Palestine as it is
to-day. Sheep and goats by the thousand were grazing on the hills; large black lizards, over a foot long,
were sleeping in the sun; caravans of loaded camels
were coming and going along the road and paths;
fierce looking Bedowin wanderers were passing and
repassing us; women with big rings in their ears
and noses and water jars and other burdens on
their heads were journeying to and fro. Here and
there the threshers were treading out the grain. Far
and wide the gray and green of the olive trees glis-
tened in the blazing sun that poured from a cloudless sky. We passed two or three wells where women
were washing their clothes. They drew up some
water in a goat skin and poured enough on the garments to wet them. Then putting them on one
stone they beat them with another. Then they
poured on a little more water, wrung out the gar-

ments and spread them on the grass to dry. We tried to take a picture of one of these laundries, but only succeeded in bringing down upon us a rain of condemnation from the women who assaulted us with unknown tongues and threatened to cast stones at us. It is bad enough to have a woman quarrel at you when you understand what she is saying, but it is beyond all endurance when she expresses her opinion of you with fire in her eye and you don't know a word she says. But I didn't blame the women for not wanting their pictures taken in their present poses. It showed they had womanhood in them to resent it. What woman would want to have her picture taken without a chance to comb her hair and peep in a mirror?

About nine miles from Jerusalem we came to the Pools of Solomon, which that great king built nearly three thousand years ago for the purpose of supplying Jerusalem with water. This provided a water system which would be considered first-class today, and in those days must have been a wonder of the world. There are three of the pools or reservoirs, each one being below the level of the other. There were strong springs or fountains in the hills which ran into the first until it was full, then it over ran into the second until it was full and the second overflowed into the third. From the third pool the water was conducted to Jerusalem through a covered flume built of stone, like a mill race around the hills. These pools are well built on a massive scale, and are in a good state of preservation. The lowest is the largest, being six hundred feet long and two hundred feet broad. The second pool is four hundred feet long and two hundred feet broad. The upper one is five hundred feet long and two hundred feet broad. The capacity of these three pools was about ninety million gallons.

From the pools we continued our journey southward to the valley supposed to be Eschol, the place visited by the spies who came to bring the waiting Israel a report of the land. From this valley they carried back wonderful samples of the land's fruitfulness, among them a great cluster of grapes two bore on a staff between them. The valley was full of vineyards and heavy laden with grapes as we went through it.

The end of our southern journey was Hebron, one of the most noted places in all the land of Israel. This is a sacred city to Mohammedan, Jew and Christian. Here Abraham lived and reared his family, and here the Father of the Faithful and his family are buried. Here David was anointed king and at first had his capital during the seven years he was king over Judah, moving to Jerusalem when he became king over all the tribes. Hebron comes down to us through an unbroken history since the settlement by Abraham. It was occupied by Abraham's descendants without a break until twelve hundred years ago, when it was occupied by the Turks, who have held it ever since. The meaning of the name is something like "confederation" or "society," and it took the name because it was the home of Abraham, who received the greatest honorary degree ever given to man, "The Friend of

God." With Abraham and God living on terms of united friendship, how fitting to name the old patriarch's home Hebron or "Society," and what a society it was! How far it outshone all the society the mighty of the earth have ever invented!

We ate our lunch in the shade of the oak of Mamre, where Abraham entertained the angels. We turned to the eighteenth chapter of Genesis and read: "And the Lord appeared unto him by the oaks of Mamre (Mamre means vision, and what a vision Abraham must have received here!), as he sat in the tent door in the heat of the day." It was the heat of the day—oppressive heat—when we were here and sat in the shade of the oaks. The tent was a tent of goats skins, and we imagined it was just there before us. "And he lifted up his eyes and looked, and lo, three men stood over against him; and when he saw them he ran to meet them from the tent door and bowed himself to the earth and said, My lord, if now I have found favor in thy sight pass not away I pray thee from thy servant; let now a little water be fetched and wash your feet and rest yourselves under the tree, and I will fetch a morsel of bread, and strengthen ye your hearts."

The old tree, worn and shaken by the storms, there before us, is said by wise men to be the tree. Others claim it would be an impossibility for a tree to stand so long if the hand of man would let it alone. It is a very old tree—one of the oldest to be seen anywhere. Its main trunk has died away from age, and on one side of it another tree is growing. If this is not the real tree that has died away more than once that a new branch might grow on from its dead body, it is surely near the place before us where the Patriarch did entertain the three angels who had come as messengers from heaven to tell him his wife should bear a son. The angels also brought with the joyous message, one of sadness, as God's messengers often do. Sodom, the wicked city where Lot had gone, would soon be destroyed from the earth.

It was at this point the Prophet of God rose to the highest point his character had reached, and only once did it go beyond that, and the time was when, on the road to Moriah, he went to lay on the altar of Jehovah his only son. Out there somewhere before us, near that old oak, the old man fell in the dust, and turning his anxious face up to God, threw his soul out to God in such a challenge of intercessory prayer as the world has seldom witnessed. It is no sign of greatness for a man to pray for himself in the face of danger. The smallest and the meanest do that. But it is a sign of greatness for a man to throw himself between another sinner who has wronged him and divine judgment, and with a mighty faith and pleading prayer stay the hand of Judgment!

One day out there the young man and the old man stood gazing over the hills. The forks of the road had come, as it always does, to the old and young. Henceforth their ways must go apart, as ways so often must. The old man told the young man to take his choice. One road led through the hills, rough, rugged and sometimes bare; the other led over the hills to the plains so black and rich. The fields were heavy with harvest and the people gay with life. As the young man gazed first along the hillside road and then the river road, a woman came—as women often do—to help him make his choice. Her hand was trembling as she caught his arm, and her breath went hot upon his face as she whispered in his ear for him to take the river road. Its luxury called her; its society lured her more than the society of the old man and his angels. No man ever rose to heights of success or fell to depths of ruin that there was not somewhere in the shadows nearby a woman whose hand did its helping.

The young man took the River Road as young men often do and turned his back on the old man as young men often do. Youth gets tired of being bothered and bored with old age, but sad is the day for youth when it turns away from age and thinks it needs it no more. The young man pitched his tent toward Sodom. No he had no notion of going there, but the river road was a downward road as it always is and on a downward road we never know just where we can stop. He lived near the city and with his flocks and herds went into the dairy and meat business with the city people. His family got a taste of city society and grew tired of the suburban life. So one day Mrs. Lot and the girls decided on a fine home on Society Boulevard and they moved in. The girls became society favorites and daughters-in-law of Sodom. Mr. Lot was elected to the town council, and often in their home on the avenue and going to and from society functions, they smiled in joy and blessed the day they left the country to come to the city and wondered how the old man fared, whose old-time notions kept him in the hills. What greater society advantages had they in the city of Sodom, over the old man alone in his tent in the hills with his immaginary (?) angels! Yet the old man's home was Hebron, which meant society—yes, Society Hill—and what a society it was! In his tent he dined with angels. But people have different tastes. Some prefer Sodomites to angels!

Back in the hills the old man met God with promises in his hand. And in the light of those promises the old man lived and died. But the old man never forgot the young man; he missed him and he prayed for him. Any young man is to be pitied who goes to the city and has no old man in the hills who closes his eyes and turns his face heavenward in prayer for him. When the storm came, it was the old man back in the hills who saved the young man down in the city as he came, white-faced and weak from his agonizing prayer. Even his prayers did not save the young man's wife and the characters of his daughters.

These thoughts ran through our minds as we lunched that day under the shade of the oaks of Mamre, and when we finished our lunch we went to the grove where Abraham, Sarah, Isaac, Rebecca and Jacob are buried. There is no doubt about the locality. The Turks for over a thousand years have guarded it and if a foreigner's foot crosses the line, the price they pay is death. It gives one strange feelings to stand at the grave of these great saints. And yet I thought that their souls were not here. Abraham had been seen in heavenly company. He who had angels for his company in life, surely now is with them in the Better Land!

In front of Abraham's tomb is a Mohammedan cemetary, the dreariest place on earth; no flowers or plants; no inscriptions; just bleak, barren mud-covered graves, with mud-made head stones as gloomy as the Turks can make them. Nowhere is the superstition, degradation and filth of the Turk more in evidence than here about the tomb of Abraham. Strange Abraham, The Friend of God, should rest in the midst of all this shame, while the heathenish Turks control his tomb.

In 1921 we secured photos of the interior of Abraham's tomb, the first ever taken. After the fall of the Turks in 1918 the Mohammedans became more lenient and now with proper pull and backshish you may enter this sacred tomb.

On this trip we met Rev. Mr. Forder, a Wesleyan Methodist missionary in Jerusalem. He gave twenty-five years of heroic service to the Mohammedans in the Land of Moab, working under awful persecutions, but delivered by God in ways truly miraculous. The way the country was finally opened to him and he won the hearts of the people was touching in the extreme. His baby fell sick and died. They buried the little one in that far away strange land, the father the undertaker, the mother the chief mourner. The people gathered in great numbers to see them give their child Christian burial, so different from that they gave their children. The people seemed greatly touched and the next day a native came to the house of the misisonary bringing a little lamb in his arms, with the story that it was customary among their people, when parents lost a little one, for another mother who had a baby to lend the bereaved mother her own child, so that in her aching loneliness she might give her affection to the borrowed child and gradually accustom herself to her sorrow. As his wife had no child to send they had brought the lamb and wanted Mrs. Forder to give her time and devotion in caring for the lamb, thus easing the burden of her sorrow and loneliness. Thus the burial of the missionary's baby in that strange land opened the hearts of the people that had been sealed so hard and this beautiful instance shows that beyond the outer walls of superstition and evil there is a human heart after all that speaks the universal language of the soul. These and many other examples show that with an apostolic ministry the gospel of Christ can break even the walls of Mohammedanism and win those imprisoned souls to God.

CHAPTER XXVIII.

JERICHO, THE JORDAN AND THE DEAD SEA.

"A certain man went down from Jerusalem to Jericho." If he got there he certainly went down, for the descent from Jerusalem to the Dead Sea just beyond, is four thousand feet in a distance of about twenty-five miles, being an average of one hundred and sixty feet fall to the mile that the road must make.

Unfortunately, our journey was on about the hottest day of the summer. The wind was from the hot sands of the desert, and felt as if it was blown from a hot stove. The scorching sun beat down from a sky that offered nothing to temper its heat, but our spirits were as warm as the sun, and we made the journey with success and happiness.

Our first stop was Bethany, the home of Lazarus and his sisters, Martha and Mary. We visited the supposed spot where they lived and the tomb from which Jesus called Lazarus from death to life. In all the life of Jesus there is nothing more tender and touching than his connection with this home. It brings out the homelike nature of the Lord, and shows the kind of a friend and guest He was. Who can tell what He meant to this home and its three members, and who can tell what this home meant to Him? What will be their reward for giving Him a home when God makes up the count? The Master appreciated this home, for He did not have another like it.

Fresh to my mind came that beautiful eleventh chapter of John as we stood in Bethany. It has long been one of my favorite chapters, so full of real every day living interest and touches of heart and soul! I had often preached from it and tried to carry its message to the troubled and the struggling. Now it was a privilege to read it here in Bethany, and see the scene before me. One day over on the Jordan in a crowd, a man pressed in and said, "He whom thou lovest is sick." Of course that message would touch Him. Who has not felt the force of it in his own heart? "It was that Mary who anointed the Lord with ointment and wiped His feet with her hair whose brother, Lazarus, was sick." Yes, all the tender things they ever did for us come up before us when they are going through the shadows.

Then a strange thing happens. "He abode two days in the place where He was." Over there beyond Jordan two days busy with other folks, and his friend sick and dying, and these sisters brokenhearted. Why doesn't He come? Why does He wait so long? Why is His program, with its dates and numbers, not like mine? But we went over a verse. "Now Jesus loved Martha and her sister and Lazarus." Oh, that is the keynote to all the storms of life! If he loves us He will come—maybe not at the time we set, nor in the manner we desire—but in His own way and in His own time, He will come. Jesus turned His face toward that home. It mattered not that His disciples warned Him of previous plots to take His life back there. He would not let any danger deter Him when His friends were in trouble. He came walking, for He seemed to go that way over burning sands up steep hills, over rough places facing dangers and enemies for about thirty-five miles to help His troubled friends. Beautiful picture! And is it not true with us? Does He ever fail to come to help us in our trouble when we send for Him? Martha met Him down the road there before us, and "Mary sat still in the house." Trouble dazes and crushes some hearts, so that all they can do is to sit still in the house, while it drives others out down the road to meet the Lord. Jesus looked on them; on the grave and the heart-less mourners wailing around and "Jesus wept." Shortest verse in the whole Bible, but what a mean-ing. Why did he weep, Not from despair, or mourning. Maybe because of His sympathy for them and because death had come into the world, but surely because of the way they looked at death and His relation to it. "I am the resurrection and the life, whosoever liveth and believeth on Me shall never die." It was because their hearts did not take in this that He was weeping. Then He called his friend forth from the grave and turned him over to his loved ones. What if one would come to the ceme-tery to do that for us to-day? He is coming to do it tomorrow! Blessed be the thought!

On down the road which is very good, we drove toward Jericho. It was the way of the wilderness, and a more barren desolation would be hard to find. No house or tent did we see until about half way we came to a rock house called "The Good Samaritan Inn" because it is reported here was where the poor fellow fell among thieves. There is no doubt about the genuineness of the place, for there are many who claim the distinction of falling among thieves along here most any time, although we escaped because our party was too large and our guides and drivers too well armed for the sneaking cowards to attempt to harm us. We saw a number of them walking the road and sneaking along the ravines. In traveling these roads you must go protected or you can pay the Turkish authorities a ransom and they will divide with the thieves and you can go through unharmed.

We stopped awhile and refreshed ourselves and the horses at the "Good Samaritan Inn." It is occupied by kindly-looking Arabian sons of the out-of-doors who treated us with politeness and consideration. After doing all they could for our comfort at a reasonable price they favored us with the Bedowin dance given in honor of our party. I don't know how it compared with other dances, for I am not up on that form of depravity, but I don't think I want to see another one. The music was from drums made with a sheepskin on a pitcher, and bones whch caused a continual din that strained the eardrums. The dancers were men who carried their bodies through many contortions, and made many grimaces and muttered many things. But the chief feature of it all was the way they handled the long, sharp swords. They flourished them about their heads; dangled them upon their fingers, and whizzed them around and around, cutting the air so close to our heads and ears that we felt ourselves wiping the blood away. As we bobbed our heads to save our scalps, it seemed to amuse them more than it did us.

The last six or eight miles of our journey was through the plain so rich that if it was irrigated it would feed all that end of the world. It was here Sodom and Gomorrah, cities of the plain were destroyed for their wickedness and so complete was the destruction that nobody has ever located them. Some great volcanic earthquake must have destroyed the cities and changed things so as to form the Dead Sea and curse the land with salt and other solutions. The Dead Sea is in this plain. It is thirteen hundred feet below the level of the sea and at its deepest point is said to be almost as deep.

A few of us took a bath in the Dead Sea. We waded out into it as far as we could wade and then we waded further. Being the heaviest salt solution on the earth you cannot possibly sink in it. You can lie on your back and sleep and read floating about like a boat. If you stand up your feet will rise so high, pushing your body out of the water until you will fall on your head, getting your eyes, mouth and ears full of the water which is very unpleasant and painful. All you have to do is to tread water enough to keep your head out of it. The bath was delightful. No surf bathing I have ever experienced was equal to it, but after it was over trouble came. The salt and other solutions began to burn the skin and run about on it like grease. We felt as if we had been rubbed with red pepper and anointed with melted lard.

The Dead Sea is a beautiful body of water notwithstanding things that have been said about it. It is so clear that pebbles can be seen twenty feet deep. It has a beautiful sandy shore covered with pebbles, on which ebbs and flows a little tide. It is fifty-three miles long with an average width of ten miles. There is no life in it. No fish swims its waters, and all that are carried in by the Jordan soon die. We saw some dead fish floating on the waters. No living thing lives on its waves or along its shore. Beyond the sea high and rugged rose the blue hills of Moab, the land of Ruth. Further up the hills rose Pisgah and Mt. Nebo, where with an angel for an undertaker the Great Moses was laid to rest after looking over into the Promised land toward which he had so long been leading his people and into which he was not permitted to enter.

Back behind us rose the hill upon which Jerusalem sat and the green slopes of the Mount of Olives. As I stood there listening to the waves of the Dead Sea that washed the sands at my feet, my mind was calling up the tragic history enacted upon this plain as a theater. The scene was preaching great sermons to my soul. The cities of sin were gone, as they all must go. Where once surged the gay and sinful life of these rich cities of the plain now was desolaton and death. The river Jordan journeying through the hills of Canaan poured a great volume of fresh water into the Dead Sea, while from the hills of Moab lesser streams did likewise. This old sea swallowed it all and gave out nothing but desolation and death. It has no outlet save from evaporation. In spite of all the fresh water it drinks up it is never made fresh or sweet.

How like many lives is this sea? They devour all the rivers of life and blessings that flow into them from the hills of God and they give out nothing but poison and death. No life is in them or about them save the life of their own stagnated selfishness. All their ambition has been to get blessings and they have never heard God's command to Israel to "be a blessing." They are like one of our great Millionaires who undertook a few years ago to make a Sunday-school speech. He spoke of all the blessings he had received and said, "I have just been a sponge, drinking in blessings from God." Poor old sponge! How many there are in the world, just absorbing all about them and holding it until the life is squeezed out of them. They are Dead Seas drinking in all the blessings of God's rivers and turning them to salt. He must have been a sponge or he would not have said so. And yet what a reputation! What an accomplishment! An old sponge! How we detest and abhor them! What must God think of the sponges and Dead Seas in the human souls of this earth?

Leaving the Dead Sea we crossed the plain to Jericho where in the Jordan hotel we lodged after visiting the places of interest about the town. It would be hard to find a more desolate and filthy town than modern Jericho with its little black mud-huts where on the dirt floors live people, donkeys, goats, chickens, dogs and smaller fry, too numerous to mention. The name means fragrance, but it is

hoped the fragrance used to be better than it is now.
What a contrast between the present appearance
and that in the days of all its royal glory when it
was known far and wide as the City of Palm Trees
and was the winter resort of Herod, who leased it
from Cleopatra who received it as a gift from Mark
Anthony.

What a history Jericho has! That night after
a good supper I was unable to sleep from the flood
of history that beat at my door along with the jackalls howling under our window and the salt crusts
over my body and an oily substance that came from
the Dead Sea bath (which could not be washed off
for lack of water) along with scorching heat and
other "little things." So I reviewed before me the
history of the scenes old Jericho had known as I
lay awake.

Great and beautiful was this city of continual
summertime. It marked the first battle of Israel
after their entrance into the borders of their Promised Land. Seven times about the walls the host
marched and then blew their ram's horns and God
threw down the city walls. Rahab was saved by a
scarlet thread in her window because she had cared
for the spies who came to view the land. I could
almost hear the blast of the ram's horns. Here Zac-
cheus lived and somewhere nearby he climbed a
sycamore tree. Not our kind of a sycamore but a
tree whose limbs run near the ground and can be
easily climbed. Jesus called him down from the tree
where he had placed himself to get a view of Christ
and he seems to have been converted between the

tree and the ground. Here Jesus healed the two blind men recorded in Matt. 20:29-34.

The most interesting thing in Jericho to me was Elisha's Fountain. It is a large fountain or spring running out of a little hill with a stream strong enough to turn a mill. The surrounding country is supplied with water from this spring. All the rest of the water is brackish and this alone pure and sweet. The water runs a short distance and is swallowed up by the plain, but it shows what the country would be if it was watered. A beautiful oasis springs up about this spring. This fountain is conceded by Bible scholars to be the fountain Elisha healed with salt. 2 Ki. 2:19:22. "Thus saith the Lord, I have healed these waters; there shall be from henceforth no more death." And ever since this spring has been sweet and the others brackish.

Just beyond Jericho rise high mountains and the wilderness. It was perhaps there Jesus met his forty days' temptation after his baptism in the Jordan nearby. A projecting pinnacle is pointed out as the place where the devil took the Savior and showed him all the kingdoms of the world and the glories of them and offered them to Him for His allegiance. In the fertility and richness of this vast plain at that time it was a beautiful picture that met the eye from that mountain. But what was all the glories of the plain and its cities to Him who came to lay down His life for the world? It stirred my heart to think there in those hills my Savior faced the devil alone and weak from hunger for forty days to show us how to be victorious in temptation. Then came the blessed thought that when he was victorious and the devil left Him angels came and ministered to Him. They always do.

We visited the Jordan before our return to Jerusalem, and meditated on its banks on the history it has known. Wonderful river! What could these banks tell if they would? Near here Jesus was baptized by John the Baptist. Near here Israel, after forty years of wilderness wandering, crossed the flood into their long Promised Land, with only two of those who started from Egypt. How their hearts must have swelled with joy and peace as they crossed the river with the water standing up on either side and set foot upon the shores of Canaan! As they left Egypt, the land of bondage, the waters stood up and left a path for them and then rolled together behind them. Now at the end of forty years of trial the waters part again to let them pass over and enter their promised land. We bathed in Jordan's waters, and let our hearts roll on with its tide through the hills and the years. Some day we would stand upon the banks of another river on the shores of our Promised Land for which we had been marching and struggling through a wilderness for many years. Then there came ringing through our souls the old hymn we heard across the seas back home. From our earliest days we had heard it from happy souls who caught a vision of the other land. Many lips that had sung that hymn were hushed and many souls that had been thrilled by it have passed over the river and are resting under the shade of the trees.

So on Jordan's banks that day as the sun was going
down beyond the hills of Judea we sang:

> On Jordan's stormy banks I stand,
>   And cast a wishful eye
> To Canaan's fair and happy land,
>   Where my possessions lie.
>
> O the transporting, rapturous scene
>   That rises to me sight!
> Sweet fields arrayed in living green,
>   And rivers of delight!
>
> O'er all those wide extended plains
>   Shines one eternal day;
> There God the sun forever reigns
>   And scatters night away.
>
> No chilling winds or poisonous breath,
>   Can reach that healthful shore;
> Sickness and sorrow, pain and death,
>   Are felt and feared no more.

CHAPTER XXIX.

OVER THE HILLS TO NAZARETH.

Early in the morning of July 13th we drove out from the Damascus Gate and turned our faces over the hills toward the north, for the journey of eighty miles to Lake Galilee. We paused a little while for a parting view of Jerusalem and the hills about it. Our parting gave us a sad feeling. The several days we spent in the Holy City had drawn us to it and it made us sad to go. The rising sun over Olivet was filling the city and hills with light. Calvary, where Jesus died, lay barren in the sun. We cast a last look upon that hill and then on Olivet and Gethsemane as the carriages swung around a curve in the road and left the vison behind us.

We stopped at Mizpah. Here was one of the points where Samuel judged (1 Sam. 7:16) and here Saul was crowned king (1 Sam. 10:17). It was near here after Israel had defeated the Philistines Samuel set up a stone and called the place Ebenezer, which means "the Lord helps us." From this stone many churches in our own land received their name, and at many an old Ebenezer souls have been happy in the Lord. We also passed Nob, and Ramah where Samuel lived and where Jeremiah was cast in prison. We next came to Elbirah, said to be the place where the parents of Jesus first missed him, after they left Him in Jerusalem. We also passed Ai where Abraham once had his tent and where Joshua won such a great battle over enemies of Israel.

Our road also took us by Shiloh, noted because here the tabernacle was pitched and Israel camped. We tried to imagine how the scene looked. Also this was the seat of government of Israel at one time, and here the priest, Eli, lived and died. Here little Samuel was dedicated to God and began his service in the tabernacle and heard the voice of God call him in the night telling him what his work was to be. Here at Shiloh the trbies were gathered together. (Josh. 22). On this days' journey no place touched me more than Bethel. This pile of ruins has much rich history mingled with its dust. Abraham built an altar here and worshipped his God; here Joshua fought a great battle and won a victory for God and Israel; here Deborah judged Israel and closed out her eventful life; here the tabernacle was pitched; here Jereboam established idolatrous worship; here was the school of the prophets; and here the children mocked Elisha and the bears came out and devoured them. But Bethel is not noted for any of these events as much as it is for something else.

Here one day came a lone and way-worn traveler at the close of the day. No house in sight he ate a little bread and drank a little water from the small store he carried with him and laying his tired head on a hard rock he slept on the ground with the stars for a shelter above him. It was a dark and lonely time for him. He had been driven from home by trouble with his brother. His mother's diplomacy was sending him to her people to seek for a wife. To-night he was not only troubled with his own sin, but lonely on account of absence from his mother who petted him and his father who loved him. In that lone place that night God let down a ladder from Heaven and sent angels down its shining steps to comfort and help the lone and troubled traveler, as He will always do. So Jacob received a blessing, and learned that there was no place so lonely but that it was at the very gate of Heaven if we but knew it. He set up an altar to God and made a vow that if God would stand by him and bring him home in peace, he would be loyal to God and of all God gave him he would give back a tenth. He then changed the name of the place from Luz to Bethel which means House of God, and wherever the Gospel has been preached others have built God a house and called it Bethel until we can hardly find a community that hasn't a church by that name.

We lunched that day at a place by the name of Sabbonah. Our horses ate some food and we ate our lunch and drank some water from the well that was there. A large and mixed assembly gathered about that well. The maidens were there getting water for home use and some were washing their clothes. Our party of fifty Americans was there trying to get a drink; our Turkish drivers were there trying to water their two dozen horses; and from over the hills came armies of goats and sheep to get their noon-day drink. The scramble and clatter of this mixed host will hardly be forgotten.

A study of the shepherd life of Palestine and its relation to Bible teaching is very interesting. In the morning the shepherds can be seen on a thousand hills leading their flocks forth in search of good pastures. He inspects the pasture that there may be no poisonous weeds, snakes or wild beasts hiding there to damage his flock. The sheep know his voice and follow him. He does not drive them but leads them. He carries his club to defend the sheep and his staff with the shepherd's crook. With this he lifts up those that fall down and guides those who go astray back in the right path. At noon he takes them to water, "He leadeth me beside the still waters." He pours it from the well into a stone drinking trough so they can drink it or if it is a little stream, dams it with dirt that it may be still and deep enough for them to drink. At night he leads them to the fold, made of a rock wall that protects them. Standing at the entrance he inspects every sheep as it goes in. If one is faint he pours water from his waterbag into the cup that is tied to his belt and lets the sheep drink from his own cup. "My cup runneth over." If the ears, heads and legs are hurt from the briars and flies, he pours on the healing, soothing olive oil from his cruse. "Thou anointest my head with oil." As you see these pictures every day and everywhere in Palestine it throws a flood of light on the twenty-third psalm and the tenth chapter of John.

In the afternoon we came to Sychar and viewed the tomb of Joseph. His body is there embalmed with Egypt's art and some day will be viewed, when the Turks are driven out. Near here out on the plain is Jacob's Well. Jacob dug this well and used it for himself and flocks. Bible students have been puzzled because a well a hundred feet deep requiring so much labor should be dug by Jacob when nearby is plenty of running water. It is quite likely the people refused to allow Jacob and his vast flocks the use of their streams and forced him to dig wells to get water, for there are perhaps more disputes over the control of wells and springs in this land than anything else. Anyway the well is no fake. It is real and it is here, and quite likely it has not been moved from where it was. Being the only well anywhere around it is certainly the place where Jesus met the Samaritan woman, recorded in the fourth chapter of John.

It was a great privilege to drink some water from this well and read there the account of the Master's visit. Clearly rose the picture before us. Jesus was tired from his long journey and rested by the well while the disciples went into the town to buy their lunch, when this woman of the world came down to draw water, and he opened up her heart to her in such a way as to make her hurry back to the town saying, "Come, see a man which told me all things that ever I did. Is not this the Christ?" Drinking of the water of the well that day our eyes over and over rested on His words to the woman, "Whosoever drinketh of this water shall thirst again; but whosoever drinketh of the water which I shall give him shall never thirst, but it shall be in him a well of water springing up into everlasting life.

On our second visit we found a Catholic church being built over this well. It was almost complete and the well was at the altar. One consideration in building it was the revenue from tourists who will be charged an admission fee.

Late in the evening we reached the town of Nabulous, which is the modern name for Shechem. It is a town of 25,000 people, a large percent Mohammedans, but some Jews and Christians, and is located between Mt. Ebal and Mt. Gerizim. Here on Mt. Ebal Joshua built an altar unto God (Josh. 8:30) and the people with the ark of Israel were placed half on one mountain and half on the other, and repeated the laws of blessing and cursing until the hills rang. Here in Mt. Gerizim the Samaritans have worshipped since long before the time of Christ, (they claim since the days of Joshua). They compose a sect of about a hundred and eighty, all told. They accept only the first four books of the Bible and conduct their worship like the ancient Jews. They have a temple on Gerizim where they conduct much of their worship at the time of feasts and special occasions, and they also have a church down in the town. Here the high priest met us graciously and showed us the ancient scroll claimed to have been made by the great grandson of Aaron. It was marvelously new and well kept to be handled constantly without protection for several thousand years. The old fellow looked as if he hardly expected us to swallow the pill.

A number of tourists had arrived ahead of our party leaving room for only a part of our company in the hotel. The rest of us found quarters in a Catholic Monastery which Dr. Best very aptly named "Billy Goat Inn." The horses, donkeys and goats used the first story and we used the second. Our quarters and fare was not all that could be desired. The priest in charge of the livery stable was a talkative old monk who had more regard for ceremony than for cleanliness, and moreover he loved his ease and his wine. We found a company of mission teachers from Egypt en route to Jerusalem and found much interest in the report of their work. Sleep was not what it might have been. It was dog days and also dog nights and there seemed to be a canine convention going on in town with some difficulty as to selecting a chairman. Dr. Henry Van Dyke says there are a million dogs in Shechem and they howl all night. The word of a Presbyterian must be taken.

We found Shechem the first well-watered place we had seen except along the Jordan. There are a number of springs and streams which bless the land and cause to grow much fruit and flowers. This with the striking location between the two mountains make it a splendid location for a town.

Shechem was once the home of Abraham, and later on of Jacob. In later years Joshua wrought mighty works around it. It was set apart as one of the cities of refuge. Here Reheboam was made king. Later Abimelech destroyed the place. Later on it was rebuilt by Jereboam. The dust of Jacob and Joseph rests here, and here Jesus himself made visits.

As we drove out of Shechem early in the morning a crowd of lepers crowded about begging for backshish. So eager were they to get a few pennies that they paid no attention to the requirement to keep the distance, but crowded about our carriages in a way that was not comfortable. We threw a little money as far as we could and while the poor half-dead creatures scrambled for it we made our escape.

Our first stop of interest was at the town of Samaria. We felt our carriages in the road and a few of us went through the modern village, up the hill to the ruins of the ancient city, which was as great and gay as the modern town is poor and dirty. We were now in the territory that belonged to the tribe of Manasseh, having traveled yesterday through that of Ephraim. Here on this great hill that rises above the others round about was the proud and mighty city of Samaria.

From the ruins that now are seen the imagination can picture the great city that once sat upon this commanding spot, and ruled the land around. Standing in the ruins of Ahab's palace we looked far and wide over the holy hills; even out upon the waters of the Mediterranean Sea. It would be hard to find a place whose natural location and beauty was better suited for a city. It was called the "Crown of Pride of Ephraim, the flower of his glorious beauty which is on the head of the fat valley."

The city was built by Omri, king of Israel, and was the capitol of the ten tribes. It was besieged by Ben Hadad until an awful famine came upon it and the head of an ass sold for eighty pieces of silver, and mothers cooked and ate their own chil-

dren. 2 Ki. 6:29. Again it was besieged by Shal-
manezer, King of Syria, and the people were taken
and carried away to the cities of the Medes. It was
a city of wickedness and idolatry. Paul and Barna-
bas preached here as also did Philip, Peter and
John. There is no record of Jesus visiting the city
though it is likely He did, as it lay in His path to
and from Nazareth.

It would be hard to find the ruins of a city that
have known more blood and shame. Here Herod
lived in sin and luxury. Here in jealous rage he
slew his wife, Marianne, who haunted him until half
crazed, he lamented for her in awful agony when
his memory was not drowned by his indecent revel-
eries. Here he also strangled his two sons. Walking in the ruins of Herod's Palace where he lived in
sin and luxury I found a Roman coin that belonged
to his day. Perhaps it had been in his sinful hands.

But Samaria is best known as the home of Ahab
and Jezebel. Here this weak, depraved man and
this devil possessed woman—the meanest that ever
lived—wrought their devilment. Here Elijah contended with them and delivered the messages of
God. Here they both met their violent death-fitting
ends of their disgraceful careers. One day he went
out in royal chariot to battle, and came back with
his chariot wet with his own blood. One day Jehu
drove by and seeing Jezebel in the window ordered
her thrown down. Her body was dashed to pieces
and the dogs ate her flesh.

Just after passing Samaria we came upon the
new railroad, that is being built from the coast to

Jerusalem via Samaria. The most of the work was being done by women and girls, some of whom were as young as fourteen. In the burning sun they were carrying heavy burdens of stone, ties and rails; digging with picks and shovels; laying the rails and spiking them down, while Turkish soldiers uniformed and armed were seeing that the work was properly done. We also saw numbers of men building the carriage road through the country. This as well as the railroad is built by the Turkish government. Men were breaking rock all day in the heat for the sum of twenty cents.

Passing out of the hills we came to the plain of Dothan. It is a plain of beauty and productiveness and under modern agriculture like other sections, could produce wonderful crops. The plain was full of grazing flocks, as it was when Joseph came to the aid of his brethren here where they had come to pasture their herds. It was here the brothers sold Joseph to the Midianites and drenching his coat (his dead mother made him) in the blood of a kid took it back to his father with the story that a wild beast had devoured him. I was sitting in the carriage reading the account, "They lifted up their eyes and behold a company of Ishmaelites came from Gilead with their camels bearing spicery and balm and myrrh going to carry it down to Egypt. And Judah said unto his brethren, 'What profit is it if we slay our brother and conceal his blood? Come let us sell him to Ishmaelites.'" Gen. 37 26:28. Glancing up to get the setting of the story I saw a company of Arabians with a caravan of camels coming across the plain loaded with merchandise for Egypt. Looking at the dark faces of Ishmael's sons and the stately tread of the long train of camels I could easily imagine how the cruel brothers turned over Joseph to a similar company for a small sum of money and went home to their father with their lying tale, while the lad followed the camels over the hills to Egypt a slave but in God's providence to be their master as well as ruler of Egypt.

Passing from the plain of Dothan we came to Jenin where in the welcome shade of friendly trees by singing streams, we ate our lunch and rested from our journey. The real name of the place is En Gannim which meant fountain of gardens. It was given to the tribe of Issachar. Quite a little town has gathered about these fountains which are perpetual and abundant, but in Bible history the place has little significance and is mentioned only once. Our visit, however, was very pleasant because of the water and shade which are two comforts seldom found in overland travels in Palestine. Often the scarcity of water is a real hardship and at times it must be bought at a good price. On the second tour we found a railroad station at Jenin on the new road to Jerusalem and a village going up. It was now a British garrison with a company of soldiers. A monument here marked a battle with the Turks and not far away General Allenby's army captured 100,000 prisoners.

Another thing of interest at Jenin was the midday gathering of the flocks of goats and sheep for water and rest. Numbers of different flocks min-

gled together and lay down for rest after satisfying
their thirst from the streams. I have never seen
so many sheep and goats, and I was wondering how
the owners would ever get their own flocks separated from the others, but when the time came to
go back to the pastures with the herds, I saw the
Scripture again before my eyes. Each shepherd
called his own sheep by name and they arose from
their rest and followed him away, none lagging and
none going astray. Oh, that the sheep of the Lord
would do as well!

Surrounded on all sides by these flocks and their
shepherds, we found many things to interest us,
and we could have watched them for many hours.
In the midst of the flocks we saw two dark face
shepherds busily engaged in trade. It seemed one
desired to purchase an old bell wether from the
other's flock. They went over all the qualities of
the goat in question and waxed warm and emphatic
in their discussion. The purchaser seemed unwill-
ing to accept the statements of the owner until he
grasped his beard in his hand as though he meant
to pull it out, and looking him hard in the face pro-
pounded to him some more questions in Arabic. The
owner of the goat assented. The purchaser, per-
fectly satisfied, paid the price and led Mr. Billy
away by the ear. It is said an Arab will never tell
the truth until you catch him by his beard and swear
him by that. All other oaths are nothing, but he
will swear the truth by his beard. We saw it done
many times.

After leaving Jenin we soon came to Shunem,

the place where the "great woman" lived who built a room on her house and furnished it for Elisha. (2 Kings 4:8). Then turning a little northward we came out upon a hill from which opened before us one of the most thrilling views to be seen in Palestine. It is the plain of Esdraelon—which is also known by the name of Jezreel, Megiddo, or Armageddon. This plain attracts the traveler not only for the richness of its history, but also for its natural charm. The entire plain is made up of the four plains, Dothan, Megiddo, Jezreel and Sharon, which run together with lines of hills breaking through their lines at different places. These plains run from the sea to the Jordan, and embrace nearly fifteen hundred square miles. Their fertility is wonderful. It is claimed five or six crops can be raised in a year. Roving tribes now prey upon it, so that no crop is safe, and it is more a grazing and foraging ground of Bedowins than a home of farmers. If it was irrigated and properly culti-vated there is no limit to the harvests it would yield. In all the land there is no rain from April until November. Then it rains constantly until spring. In spite of these conditions good crops are raised, since the porous limestone soil absorbs the rain and gives it back in dews until the crop is made. Yet if the land was irrigated it would, of course, far exceed its present yield.

But the yield of history from this plain has been greater than would be the yield of grain under all the rains of heaven. This plain has been the battle-ground of the centuries. Being the natural meeting point of travel from all directions, and being well suited for a battleground, it has furnished a stage for many armies to meet and act out their bloody tragedies. Here King Josiah was killed fighting the armies of Egypt; here Gideon, with his three hundred, put to flight the Midianites (we walked beside the very brook where they drank and looked on their battlefield); here Israel met their miserable defeat under King Saul, and there before us, on Gilboa, he fell upon his sword. On a portion of this plain the dauntless woman, Judge Deborah, defeated the army of the mighty Sisera. So great has been its history in the wars of Palestine, that many Bible students have understood certain prophecies to refer to it as the Armageddon where the armies of the Lord and the devil shall meet in the last great battle to fight the final conflict for world mastery. It was nearby the decisive battle was fought in 1918 that defeated the Turks in Palestine and saved the land to Freedom and Christianity. Was not this the Armageddon of the Turks?

Just before us yonder stands Little Hermon and Mount Carmel, where a battle such as the world never saw before took place when Elijah, single handed, met Ahab and Jezebel with their four hundred priests of Baal, and vanquished them all and gained the day for God. On the top here he built his altar, and the Baalites built theirs. They called upon their God, and the old prophet grew sarcastic in his righteous zeal and told them to call louder, for their god was gone on a journey, was asleep or had grown hard of hearing. Then he poured water

on the wood of the altar that they might know he
had no magic fire, and turning his face up to God,
challenged Him to save His name. The fire came,
and the sacrifice, the altar and the water were all
consumed. Then he sent his servant seven times to
look toward the sea yonder for a cloud, for he was
claiming rain in the name of God to break the
drought of nearly four years. On the seventh journey the servant reported a cloud like a man's hand,
but it was large enough for the old prophet. He
ordered the people to hurry down the mountain that
they be not caught in the abundance of rain that
was coming from the Lord. It is thrilling anywhere
and any time to read the heroic deeds of the prophet
Elijah, but how much more so to read it at Mt.
Carmel?

And yonder is Mount Tabor, rising up in the plain
like a volcano, though not so pointed on the top. Its
top is covered with ruins of fortifications where it
was occupied at different times by Canaanites, Sara-
cens, Franks and Turks. It made a splendid fort
and gave command of all the surrounding plain.
The only living soul on the mountain is a monk, who
keeps a Catholic church which is in ruins.

We passed Endor, where Saul in his weakness
and sin, sought the witch at night to help him out
of his trouble, since he had cut off all access to his
God. And also the village of Nain, where Jesus
brought joy to the poor widow's heart and home by
meeting the funeral procession that bore the son to
his grave and restoring him to life and to his mother.
How Jesus must have been honored and loved in

that home! It would be interesting to know what became of this boy in after life. Did he become a great disciple? What became of all of those souls Jesus helped so much? If we read of them again their identity is not known. They must have stood by their Lord.

It was late in the evening when we left the plain and climbed the hills toward Nazareth. It was a steep, hard climb, for Nazareth is high up in the hills. When we reached the top we paused for a last view of the way we had come. The wide plain, with its flocks and caravans; Tabor and Carmel, and those historic hills so rich in Bbile stories standing there before us in the evening light made a picture never to be forgotten. Passing on around another hill, the town of Nazareth came suddenly upon our vision. What thoughts come to the heart when you come to Nazareth! Here Jesus, our Saviour, spent the years of his childhood and youth— years of which we know so little and have wondered so much. What meaneth these great silences in the life of our Lord? How did He spend them? What deeds did He do and journeys did He take about this place? Here He played as a child and roamed these hills. Later on He worked, for He was a working man, and with the hands that helped God make the world, He made things with Joseph's tools as He learned the carpenter's trade. Jesus Christ, the Saviour of the world, working at the carpenter's trade!

We found Nazareth a cleaner, nicer town than any we had seen. The houses made a better show-

ing, and the people looked happier, brighter, and
showed more strength of character. The boys were
bright, and the girls were pretty, and everybody
was friendly—so friendly that they were sometimes
troublesome. This is due to the fact that a smaller
per cent. of the inhabitants are Turks; and sec-
ondly, because Protestant missions are doing a
splendid work among the natives. Nowhere did we
see more fruitful evidence of missionary efforts.
Our hotel was a clean, pleasant, home-like place.
About its doors the women and girls, as well as
others gathered to welcome us and offer for sale
articles made by their own hands at very small
prices. They were persistent, but so pleasant and
charming that you could not turn them away. One
of them especially, named Marie, with her sweet
face, charming smile, big, dark eyes, and yet re-
fined manners, would win her way anywhere and
sell things to almost anybody. Those gruff travelers who turn away every other plea, usually surrender before Marie's smile and carry home some
lace work from her hands.

After supper, Philip secured for us an invitation
to a marriage, and we all went. It was in a home
not far from the hotel. We were very graciously
received and invited in. We were asked to take
our choice of sitting on our feet on the floor or
standing. We chose the latter, because we could do
it with more ease and comfort, and we could see
better. I am truly glad our young folks in this
country do not get married like they do over there,
both for their own benefit and for the benefit of

their neighbors. It takes a whole week to get through the ceremony. Nearly all night for that time the neighbors come filling the house and the yard, and the noise they keep up would put an old-time Southern serenade so far in the rear that it would never catch up. They have drums made of sheep skins stretched over jars, and other musical instruments too numerous and hideous to talk about. Whistles, flutes, stringed instruments like fiddles and banjos—only worse—tin pans, bones they beat together, and other things. These are kept going constantly accompanied with a continual moaning, chanting cry from the entire crowd. Many are dancing—the men and women separately. It consists mostly of whirling round and round on their toes or heels like a top, until they look exhausted and silly; but I am sure if I could do the trick at all I would look sillier than they do before I had gone half as far. This goes on for a week, and then the ceremony culminates with the religious rite that ties the knot. I know it is a relief when the couple are gone on their journey. My sympathy goes out to a family with half a dozen girls to get married. If there are old maids and bachelors in a land like that, who could wonder at it? Better be single than go through such torture.

The next morning we visited the places of interest about the town. Among them, the church which is said to be on the site of Joseph's home and his carpenter shop. While these places are uncertain, we did not let it detract from the charm of our visit, for we knew it was somewhere near here the Saviour lived with Mary and Joseph in their humble home, and near here was Joseph's shop where Jesus worked. There is one place in Nazareth, however, that is genuine, and over it the Catholics have not built a monastery. It is the Virgin's Fountain, the only source of water supply for the town. It has been here since before the days of Jesus. Here Jesus came for water for His mother, and here often He drank from the stream that flowed then, as it does now, to fill the pitchers of those who came to get its life. It was at this fountain, mentioned in Ben Hur, where the soldiers paused to get water on their march from Jerusalem to Rome with Ben Hur, the young Jew, who was condemned to the galleys for a crime he did not commit. Jesus was at the fountain at the time, and seeing the tired young Jew, he brought him some water from the fountain. All his life Ben Hur could never forget that water and the face of the one who gave it to him.

While visiting these scenes in Cana, some one stole my Bible from the carriage. It brought sadness to my heart, for I had lost a friend. With this Book in my hand I had come over the sacred places of the Holy Hills and read the account in the very places where they occurred. I had marked these passages and noted the dates of the visit. I had made many notes and impressions, as well as sermonic suggestions. Over the seas this Bible had been by my side. It was given to me by the Sunday-school of Thomas' Chapel on the Cartersville Circuit, my first charge in the Virginia Conference, and had been my companion ever since. I went on that day with a feeling of loneliness and constantly came to me the words I keep posted in the fly-leaf of my Bible:

"We've traveled together, my Bible and I,
  Through all kinds of weather with smile or with sigh;
  In sorrow or sunshine, in tempest or calm,
  Thy friendship unchanging, my life and my psalm.

"We've travelled together, my Bible and I,
  When life had grown weary and death e'en was nigh;
  But all through the darkness of mist or of wrong,
  I found thee a solace, a prayer or a song.

"So now who shall part us, my Bible and I?
  Shall isms or schisms or new lights who try,
  Shall shadows or substances or stones for good,
  Supplant thy sound wisdom, give folly instead?

"Ah, no! my dear Bible, exponent of light,
  Thou sword of the Spirit, put error to flight;
  And still through life's journey until my last sigh,
  We'll travel together, my Bible and I."

CHAPTER XXX.

ON LAKE GALILEE.

From Nazareth we turned our faces toward the Lake of Galilee, and winding through the hills, soon came to Cana, where Jesus attended the marriage and changed the water into wine. Passing on still northward, we came in the afternoon to the hill called "The Horns of Hattin," supposed to be the place where Jesus preached the "Sermon on the Mount." If this was the location, it furnished a splendid place for a pulpit on the spur of the hill, with the sloping green fields where the congregation could sit and listen.

Here we had our first view of Lake Galilee, and swinging down the road in a brisk trot our horses soon landed us on the lake shore. I hesitate to write of my impressions that day and night on Galilee. It stands out in my heart as one of the greatest days of my life, and as the days go on, memory seems to bring me closer to the life that throbbed in my heart that day.

It isn't the ruins that make the shores of Lake Galilee interesting. In the days of Jesus almost the entire lake shore was full of throbbing, thriving life. Nine flourishing cities were on the shore, and the busy life of fishermen and merchantmen kept the shore line and the waters the busiest place in Palestine. Now all these cities are gone, save dirty Tiberius, and so completely has been the destruction that there are hardly any ruins to look upon. Only in the last years were the ruins of Capernaum located and brought to light. All the boats but one or two have passed from the waters, leaving no wreck of their hulls on the shore. The teeming multitudes have passed away, leaving no graves to mark their resting place. The great fishing business is gone, leaving not a strand of a net on the shore. As though lifted up on the winds and carried out of the world, all the life, cities and people of those busy days have gone away, leaving no tracks behind them. So it is not in the life of Galilee we take interest, for there is no place quieter and more lonely, although it is just as great in possibilities now as it was in the days of Jesus. The waters are full of fish, which come in schools to the shore and to your boat side, and since Peter and John are gone, there is nobody there to catch them. Who ever heard of a Turk catching fish? To them that would be disgrace.

Nor is it in monuments and relics Galilee holds its charm. Strange as it may seem, modern genius and devotion has done no building here, but has left the spot untouched. The Catholics could not build a monastery over the lake, nor could the Turks cover it with a mosque, so it has remained untouched.

It is in memory's spiritual vibrations that the charm of Galilee lives. Coming back through the centuries, deeds done along this shore live as a film that runs its pictures before your soul. The breeze blowing over the lake is full of voices speaking; the flowers blooming along the shore line are full of faces looking; every wave that rolls over the waters and ripples on the shore brings boats of fishermen, some empty and some full; every rock has a history and seems to be a living form. A Presence strange and real broods over Lake Galilee. It greets you; it grips you; it calls you; it thrills you; it fills you; it puts its hand upon you and holds you.

We took a boat ride to the upper end of the lake to view the ruins of Capernaum, and on that trip we got an illustration of what the winds can do when they blow down the gorge and stir the waters of the lake until they seem to be mad. We were shaken by the waves and drenched by the spray, and when we reached the end of the lake the water was so rough the boat could not land, and the boatmen carried us out on their backs. When we started on that boat ride on the lake, Phillip put in our hand a card given by our hotel proprietor containing a song. Passing over the waves of the lake our party sang:

"Each gentle dove and sighing bough
  That makes the eve so blessed to me,
Has something far diviner now,
  It bears me back to Galilee!

CHORUS:

O Galilee! Sweet Galilee!
  Where Jesus loved so much to be;
O Galilee! Sweet Galilee!
  Come sing again thy song to me!

"Each flowery glen and mossy dell
  Where happy birds in song agree;
Thro' sunny morn their praises tell
  Of sights and sounds in Galilee.

  O Galilee! Sweet Galilee!
    Where Jesus loved so much to be;
  O Galilee! Sweet Galilee!
    Come sing again thy song to me!

"And when I read the thrilling love
  Of Him who walked upon the sea,
I long, oh how I long, once more
  To follow Him in Galilee!

  O Galilee! Sweet Galilee!
    Where Jesus loved so much to be;
  O Galilee! Sweet Galilee!
    Come sing again thy song to me!

Jesus did love to dwell in Galilee. He loved it because of its beauty and charm, but He loved it more
because the people were here. The struggling,
troubled, hungry, suffering, sinful people were here
in multitudes, and His heart drew Him here with
them. He did not withdraw from men, save for rest
and prayer, nor did he seek the exclusive classes. He
sought the masses. Where they were He went. His
burdens were theirs. Their troubles were on His
heart. These things brought him to Galilee. Here
were the masses, the working, struggling folks, and
He loved them.

When we returned from our boat ride we found our quarters in the Hotel Tiberius, in the town by that name. It seems strange that the only town that has survived the storm of the centuries since the days of Jesus is this town that bears the name of its founder, one of the vilest of Roman rulers. And stranger still, modern life has actually cast aside the name Galilee for this beautiful lake, so closely linked with the life of Jesus, and given it the name "Sea of Tiberius." All the Christian world ought to rebel against such a shame and see that it bears the name Galilee. The town of Tiberius is as dirty and ugly as a town can be. Missionary work under the Free Church of Scotland has been going on here for over twenty years, but there is a great deal to be done yet. Tiberius is so full of fleas that it has long been called the home of the "King of the Fleas."

Our hotel was a clean and comfortable one, kept by German-Americans for the benefit of tourists. We were hungry when called to the table, and the supper they served us was a good one and well prepared. The following is the menu:

Soup with Sagon.
Fried Fish from the lake.
Croquets.   Vegetable Marrow.   Tomatoes.
Roast leg of Lamb.   Potatoes.   Nature's Salad.
Pudding.   Raspberry Tart.
Bread.   Butter.   Fruit.   Coffee.

Brother Williams and myself were assigned to a room on the third story, the only room on that floor. Our room opened on a porch facing the lake, which we had all to ourselves up there away from the crowd. Who could sleep a night like that? The moon rose over the hills of Bashan and sent down upon the waters of Galilee a silvery charm. The wind had ceased, the waves were still, and everything about the lake as quiet as though asleep, yet in all that quietness and peace, living forms came to us out of the night, and voices strong and loud were calling to us over the waters.

Out there on the waters memory sailed a boat. A company were coming from the other side. Peter and his friends were handling the boat, and they knew how. A storm arose. The wind roared. The waves dashed as if in the lake a demon seemed to writhe. The Master was asleep and they awoke Him with the question: "Carest thou not that we perish?" He arose from the rest He was getting in the quiet of the waters after a trying day, and with His quiet, peaceful face looked at the storm. When His lips spoke "Peace, be still," the storm king cowed, rolled up his winds and went away, for what storm can go on when His lips speak "Peace be still"? Many sinful, troubled souls have heard that voice, and the raging storms that shook their hearts have felt the calm of peace. Our souls, in the quietness of that night, were singing:

Master, the tempest is raging,
 The billows are tossing high;
The sky is overshadowed with blackness,
 No shelter or help is nigh!

"Carest Thou not that we perish?"
  How can'st Thou lie asleep
When each moment so madly is threatening
  A grave in the angry deep?

"The winds and the waves obey My will,
  Peace, be still Peace, be still!"
Whether the wrath of the storm tossed sea,
  Or demons or men or whatever it be,
No water can swallow the ship where lies
  The Master of ocean and earth and skies;
They all shall sweetly obey Thy will,
  Peace, be still! Peace, be still!

But hark! I see another boat, and over the waves
it is coming through the night. This time the Master was not on the boat. On the other side the lake
that day He had fed five thousand men, besides
women and children (Matt. 14), from the fisher
boy's lunch, showing us how He can help us out of
hard places when we trust Him, and also how we
can do big things for God on small capital. Night
coming on, He sent the disciples back across the sea
in their little boat about their own affairs, and He,
feeling need of refilling his soul with spiritual stores
after His exhausting labor, went alone in the mountain to meet His Father in prayer. But His eyes
looked out in the night and watched the little boat
as He does every little boat in which a child of His
sails the sea of Life. Ah! the little boat has struck
contrary waves, as our boats so often do, for there
are so many contrary waves everywhere. They

rack every heart and shake every soul. We can't sail far without striking contrary waves. Yonder is the little boat tossing as though it must be swamped. Now it rides high upon a wave as though it will be dashed to pieces. Now it sinks down in the trough of the sea as though it has gone to its grave forever. In the face of that storm the skill of John and strength of Peter are nothing, and Jesus is not in the boat! Ah, if He were here! But so often when we need Him most He seems so far away.

But look! yonder in the night He comes. His white form is walking on the angry waves; his face is looking through the storm. He had no boat to bring Him, nor would He tarry to launch it, but He is coming! He is coming! Through the storm He has seen His children in their trouble, and He has come to their help. And "when He entered the boat the wind ceased." Of course it did. Can the winds and storms shake a heart when He has entered it? Yonder comes the boat with the master Pilot in the bow, and in safety it touches the shore. As the boat came in our souls again were singing:

> "When at last I near the shore,
>   And the fearful breakers roar,
> 'Twixt me and the peaceful rest,
>   Then while leaning on Thy breast,
>   May I hear Thee say to me,
>   'Fear not, I will pilot thee.' "

But as I looked behold across the lake I saw coming shoreward another boat. It was not a boat of apostles and saints but fishermen, and they had no Master with them, for He is dead now. The night was gone and the day had come. Over the hills of Bashan the sun was coming up to travel the sky-path I had watched the moon move in. The boat sat light in the water and by that and the tired disappointed look on the fishermen's faces I judged they had toiled all night which was the time the fish will enter the nets and caught nothing. They were busy with the oars, though their movements were mechanical and listless. They said nothing as fishermen do who come in with nets that are empty. No boat was ever launched on the waves for such a momentous trip. The church of the King was in that boat, and the fate of the Kingdom depended upon its journey. Jesus was dead and the disciples had laid down their affairs of church and taken up their nets to fish. Suppose the boat sinks. Or suppose this fishing business is successful and becomes their life work instead of preaching?

But they did not succeed. Their nets were empty but their hearts were full. The greatest blessings sometimes are in empty barns, empty nets and adversity. The heart is not apt to be full when the hands are full. We pray for those who are in adversity, but those who succeed need our prayers more. In failure men will seek God. In success God must seek them. We have never known what blessings our failures and troubles have been to us. The Disciples were better off than if their catch had been good. They were in a better position to meet their Lord. Christ had called them to be Apostles and now they found that they failed at fishing. Their hearts were troubled and their minds went back as minds do when we fail. They go forward when we succeed, and backward when we fail. As Peter put his great shoulders forward against the oars he made a motion with his head and said, "Right over there is where the Master saved our boat from sinking, John, remember?" John, who was guiding the rudder, brushed a tear from his eyes and answered, "Yes," and pointing to the Gadara hills, said, "And yonder He healed the man of evil spirits, and fed the multitude."

A voice from the shore called, "Boys, have you caught anything?" A natural question always asked a fisherman, and one a man with empty nets dreads to hear. Peter muttered, "Nothing." The voice from the shore again called, "Let down your nets on the right side of your boat." Thinking he had seen a school of fish working in the water they let down their nets on the right side. Ah! All night they had been fishing on the wrong side. There is so much effort on the wrong side— the side Christ does not want us to work on. They made a pull at their nets and felt the tug and jerk of fish against the meshes, a feeling a fisherman delights to feel. And then they drew in the biggest haul they ever made. John looked up at the white figure on the shore and said, "It is the Lord." Why did he say it? Because there was something in the way the big fish came in that net and pulled against it. And then the heart of John knew his Master's voice. When Peter heard that he jumped in the sea and made for the shore, leaving boat and net. He had denied his Lord, now he had come to own Him.

"But when the day was breaking Jesus stood on the beach, but the disciples knew not that it was Jesus." Yes, he was on the beach waiting at the end of their weary night. He stands on every beach in the night like the great lighthouse that He is. He guides the little boats over the waves to Him. He had come down there just to watch their boat come in—to guide it in. He was interested in His children and His church in that little boat. Beautiful and tender is this touch of life. Suppose He had not been on the shore that morning? No, they didn't know Him. Often we fail to know Him, so bent are we on our trades and our troubles.

I saw them land their fish and beach their boat at the Master's feet, fishing as a business ended with them forever. I saw them sit down to eat their morning meal with the risen Lord. The morning light was gliding the hills with gold and throwing a heavenly charm over the lake. I heard the Master say to Peter, "Simon, son of Jonas, lovest thou me more than these?" And over the lake I heard Peter answer, "Yea, Lord, thou knowest all things, thou knowest I love thee." And seeing them all upon the shore together my soul again burst forth in song:

My soul in sad exile was out on life's sea,
   So burdened by sin and distress
Till I heard a sweet voice saying, "Make me your
    choice,"
   And I entered the haven of rest.

I've anchored my soul in the haven of rest,
  I'll sail the white seas no more;
The tempest may sweep o'er the wide stormy deep,
  But in Jesus I'm safe ever more.

With the coming of the glorius day that followed that memorable night, we had our breakfast and took our boat for a cruise along the lake. Oh! the history dear to every Christian's heart that this lake and these hills have known! What stories they could tell if they would speak. Is it any wonder voices are in the air and faces look from everywhere, and the breath comes fast as you walk these shores and ride these waves? That morning in the sunlight a few of the events in the life of Jesus enacted in this sacred place came up before us, but they were only a few. The most of the activities of Jesus recorded in the Bible occurred on and about the lake and in Jerusalem, but how many deeds these hills and shores hold secret that have never come down to us?

Yonder on the lake shore is Magdala, the home of Mary Magdalene. Along this shore Jesus chose eleven of His disciples, all but one coming from Galilee, the other, Judas Iscariot, coming from Judea. Here on one side the lake on the green grass He fed the five thousand and on the other side the four thousand. Here He healed a lame man. Here He cured Peter's wife's mother of the fever. Here He healed the man with the withered hand. A man who was dumb saw him and spoke. A ruler's daughter was brought to life when she was dead.

A leper who met Him with faith went away with life. A woman with an incurable disease for thirty-eight years touched His garment and He touched her soul, and sent her home whole. The Centurion nobleman, who came in behalf of his sick servant, was rewarded with his servant's health. And the Scripture mentions a lame man who saw His face and rose and walked; and a palsied man let down through the roof that got up and carried His bed when he saw the Master's face. It also tells us that here He spoke the parable of the Sower and many more like it. It gives an account of His meeting the demon possessed man in the rugged hills of Gadara and cast the devil into a herd of two thousand swine who rushed into the sea and were drowned. I wondered how those hogs were gotten out of the sea?

And I remembered hearing a good old Virginia friend of mine teaching this lesson once. A lady asked him of he thought the devils were drowned with the hogs. "I don't know for certain," he said, "but I do know this, if they were drowned they have never been missed." I could almost hear those Gadarenes ask Him to leave their land when He destroyed their hogs. It made me think of some folks back home. I had seen the church of Jesus Christ drive the greedy hogs of Avarice out of a state that they might no longer devour the helpless and the weak in their troughs, their hoggeries, the saloon, the gambling den, the sweatshop of child slaughter, and the brothel. And when the swine keepers saw their herd drown in the sea of oblivion and public condemnation they tried to run the Church of Christ and its servants out of the community. I heard the devils beg Christ to let them go into the hogs. A strange request, but devils must have something to get into and destroy. It is worse than hell for a devil to have no bodily form in which he can ride down to hell and lash it and gash it, and poison it and stain it, and gorge it and damn it.

As soon as an evil spirit destroys one body by the burnings of sin, it seeks another forthwith. Perhaps an evil spirit's standing with the Arch fiend at the judgment will depend upon the number of bodies and souls it has destroyed; just as the standing of a German submarine commander with the Kaiser depended upon how many boats loaded with helpless souls they sent to the bottom of the sea. If a devil can't get a human form to ravish, it will take a hog, a dog, a horse or even some object that has no life. A runaway train, machinery, a gun, a river, a stove, a knife, are these not at times dwelling places of demons? So Jesus let them go into the hogs because it was against the law to keep hogs in this land.

I saw the place—imagined I saw it—where Peter at the command of Jesus caught a fish with gold in his mouth with which he paid the Lord's tax and his own. I saw the place where Jesus pushed the boat from the shore and using it for a pulpit preached to the congregation on the shore. I caught a crab from the waters of Galilee, though wise men say they do not live in fresh water. I picked up from the shore beautiful small white shells such as I never saw before, and brought them home. We crossed over the lake, landed near the outlet of the Jordan, bathed in the clear blue waters, and taking a last look over the scenes Jesus loved so well we climbed up to the station of Sanak and boarded the little train whose nose was turned toward the hills of Bashan, while clear and sweet came the voice of John G. Whittier ringing in our souls:

Faith hath still its Olivet,
And love is Galilee.

CHAPTER XXXI.

DAMASCUS AND THE LEBANON MOUNTAIN.

Our little train steamed and snorted up the hills and through the ravines of Bashan like Bashan's bellowing bulls. Bashan means soft, sandy soil and after you climb to the top of the great plateau you may think it well named. It is a fertile land and some of it well watered. Our journey all day lay through the hills and plains of this land that was given to the tribe of Manasseh, and then we entered the land of Syria which is not really Canaan, not being a part of the Promised Land occupied by the children of Israel. While this land is not considered Palestine proper it is so closely related to the rest af the Holy Land and so links its history with that of Israel that it is generally classed with it.

The greatest city in Syria is Damascus. It is the oldest city in the world and one of the most interesting. They tell a story there that once upon a time three Knights came riding over the plain on fine Arabian steeds and gallantly and proudly entered the city. So charmed were they with the city that they each desired to take the name for his horse; but waxing into a warm dispute over who should claim this honor they submitted the case to a smart lady they chanced to meet. She sat as judge hearing each press his claim and then she rendered a decision to the effect that each had equal right to the name, but it would not do to name all the horses Damascus, so they must divide the name one would be Dam, the other Ass, and the third Cuss.

They tell another story of Mohammed, the prophet of Islam, who came this way to enter the city. Passing over the barren plains he looked upon the gardens and streams, and all the fruit and powers of the city as he rested on a hill. So overcome was he with the beauty and charm of the city that he turned away with a sigh saying, "Man cannot have but one Paradise and I want mine in the other world, not this one."

The city is beautiful, though its beauty is made more striking because it is the only city in this part of the country, and nestles in an oasis in the midst of barrenness. To enter it you pass over barren plains that make a striking background, bringing out the beauties of the place. The thing that makes Damascus beautiful, yea, that gives its existence is the Abana River. It hurries down from the Ante Lebanon mountains ten miles away as though it must waste no time in bringing its waters of life to Damascus. Just before reaching the city it slows its pace and from one narrow stream it divides itself into seven that flow through this oasis, and Damascus with beautiful flower gardens, and gardens full of fruit, sits like a queen not upon seven hills like Rome, but upon the banks of seven streams. After giving Damascus its beauty and life these streams soon disappeared in the sands as though the work was done and like man when his task is finished find their grave in the sands.

Naaman, the mighty Syrian (2 Ki. 5) lived here and when a little maid in his home who had been brought from the land of Israel as a captive learned her master had leprosy and could get no cure she told him a prophet back in Israel could heal him. He made the long journey with what feelings we do not know, but he went seeking health, and a man will go to the ends of the earth on a slight hope for that. The prophet told him to wash seven times in Jordan, and Naaman grew furious, saying, "Are not Abana and Pharpar, rivers of Damascus better than all rivers of Israel?" It gives us pain to say it, but it is true. Abana is more beautiful than Jordan but not better. At last the proud old fellow was humbled and obeyed, coming from his Jordan bath healed of the dread disease. They showed us the home of Naaman, where a leper colony is maintained to care for those afflicted with the disease he had. Strange but fitting memorial.

We visited the Street called Straight. It is full of bazaars, dogs and donkeys, but it is beyond and above all those things for which this street is renowned. It marks the place of the conversion that changed Saul of Tarsus, the persecutor, to Paul the apostle, the persecuted. He was smitten blind on the road into the city and conducted here to this street to the home of Judas where through the prayers of Annanias he found his sight and his Saviour. Every Christian feels like pausing here, for there is no event in the church since Pentecost that meant as much as the conversion of Paul, the mightiest apostle the Church of Christ ever had.

We had a pleasant hotel in Damascus and found some pleasant American travellers there. Our fare was very good, especially the fruit which was plentiful and delicious. It did much to offset the ever-present mutton. We visited the points of interest in the city, including the mosques, the grave of the mighty Saladin, the greatest Turk that ever lived, for it was he who conquered all this land for Mohammed more than seven hundred years ago. We enjoyed excursions in the streets where it seemed we found more pups than we did in Constantinople. Our ladies had one privilege we could not enjoy, they visited the harem of one of the rich men, and brought back glowing reports of the gorgeous quarters, and the charming wives. We were left out, for no man, not even near kin, can cross the threshold of the harem. But we didn't care. Who would want to go to an old harem? They were not ahead of us. We could go to our lodge and they couldn't.

Before we left Damascus we climbed a high hill that overlooked the city and gazed down upon it, and beyond the city we looked out upon the wide ocean of sand. Caravans of camels were coming over the sand dunes. They looked like ships sailing over the waves of the sea. Others were going out. Thus they carried on the commerce of the world back beyond Babylon and Bagdad into regions unknown and unexplored by civilized men. For the wide stretch of those unknown sands we call desert because we don't know what it is. It is full of sons of Ishmael, roving desert men. No man owns that land. No man has ever conquered it or them and the prophecies of the Bible say no man ever will. They send horses, sheep, grain and other things out to the world and from the world they get some things, but the world has little they want. They live in tents of goat's hair which the Bible calls the black tents of Kedar. God said of him before he was born, "He will be a wild man, his hand will be against every man and every man's hand against him; and he shall dwell in the presence of all his brethren." Gen. 16:12. "I will make of him a great name." Gen. 17:20. These Ishmaelites have brought down the Abrahamic teachings and in many respects have been truer to their origin than the Jews. Religion is making slow but sure progress among them. The Standard Oil Company has decided to put a lamp in all the tents of Ishmael and the Church of Christ ought to put the light of Christ in all their tents. When the children of Ishmael and Isaac turn to Christ it will be a great victory. A careful study of these strange Bible people is interesting and well worth the time.

Damascus there below us taking in and sending out these ships of the desert seemed a big seaport in this ocean of sand. Strange did it look that day. Torn by strife and war, sacked and pillaged, made horrible by massacre of Christians, beseiged by armies, with no defense it has lived on as a city since before the days of Abraham, and it will be a city when God calls time on the world.

To the southwest rose Mt. Hermon, its head ever white with snow, over ten thousand feet above the sea. It is generally agreed by Bible students now that on the side of this mountain was the scene of the transfiguration. You cannot get away from Mt. Hermon anywhere in this part of the country. It even stands as though white with age looking down upon you from the eternal snows while sometimes you are burning in the sun.

From Damascus we journeyed up through the beautiful valley of Coele, Syria, rich in lands and fruits with the Lebanons on one side, and the Ante-Lebanons on the other, lifting their snowy heads high toward the skies, while down in the valley we felt the burning heat of Syria's sun. Our journey for several miles was along the banks of the Abana and Pharpar, whose cooling streams of clear water rushed over the rocks between banks heavy-loaded with fruits and flowers.

The Moslems claim that it was from this very dirt God made Adam, and we passed through the place they call the Garden of Eden, and saw the very tree on which the fruit grew that tempted mother, Eve(?) Further on we came to the grave of Noah. It is two hundred feet long, yet the Turks claim the old fellow was so large that he is greatly cramped for room, and had to double up his knees and put his feet straight down. If his sons and their wives were of equal proportions the ark was a whopper. But we banished these foolish Turkish legends from our minds and gave our minds to more profitable reflections.

In the evening we came to Baalbeck. Here we were to spend the Sabbath, and it was indeed a fine place to spend it. In front of us were the Lebanon mountains with the far-famed cedars of Lebanon, waving their branches toward the skies. Here was the place whence came the timbers of the temple in Jerusalem. Before our hotel stood the stately ruins of the temple of Baalbeck, the grandest ruins of the world. It would be impossible to give anything like a clear description of these ruins, which are on such a mammoth scale that even when you read volumes on its history and structure you are stunned when you pass over its fallen stones to find it so much grander than you thought.

Its history goes so far back in the dawn of history that like Egypt it is lost in the dawning of the ages. Every civilization has built more to it. You can clearly trace the works of Solomon, the Romans, Greeks, Crusaders, Christians and the Turks besides those who come before all these. It is the Baalgad mentioned in the Bible (Josh. 11:17 and 13:5). It meant the city of The Sun, where from earliest times people worshipped Baal, the sun God. Solomon was led off by some of his wives who were Baal worshippers and used his skill to add to the glories of Baalbeck.

While I cannot attempt anything like a description or a history of the ruins there are a few facts I desire to record. The temple covered about two hundred thousand square feet, being five hundred feet long and four hundred feet wide. It had about one hundred and twenty great pillars, many of them red marble, which are said to have come from Egypt as no such stone has been discovered elsewhere. Many of these pillars are over nine feet in diameter and over sixty feet long. How they were ever brought up into these mountains and put in place is a mystery too great for me.

But the thing that dazed me more than anything I saw was three huge stones in the wall of this temple. One is sixty-four feet long, thirteen feet thick and seventeen feet wide. Another is sixty-three feet and eight inches long with the other dimensions the same as the first, while the other is even sixty-three feet with width and heighth the same. These stones are about ten feet from the foundation and are put together with such precision that a penknife blade will not go between them. There is a stone down in the quarry a mile away where these came from that is greater still. It is fourteen by seventeen and sixty-nine feet long, weighing about one thousand tons. It is left in the quarry unfinished. Either the workmen struck or the machinery broke down, either of which would not seem improbable. This temple when finished, and covered with gold, must have been a grand sight standing there upon the high hill facing the sunrise. It could be seen for miles and must have made a great impression on those people who were so easily led to idolatrous worship.

Some of our party almost lost their wits trying to think how these great stones were moved a mile up hill and put in the side of the wall, along with unravelling some other mysteries of the building. Expert engineers of our time have not been able to bid for the contract. We exhausted all the theories we could think of and they all seemed inadequate. It seemed to me something had to be done to relieve the anxiety of some of them, so I gave notice I had worked out the theory beyond all doubt. It was a heathen temple and the Lord didn't have anything to do with it. Man couldn't build it, therefore the devil did it. It had been a long time since I studied Logic, but I thought I would risk this. The devil wanted to build him a temple over here that would rival Solomon's in Jerusalem, so he got a big crowd of little devils and middle-size devils to help him, and they dug out these big rocks and pillars and some pitched them up there, while others caught them and put them in place like men laying brick. My theory seemed more plausible than any advanced and was accepted. Before I took leave I purchased from the learned French Professor who had charge of these ruins a book he has written on their history, and in reading the theories advanced as to the construction, to my surprise I found that before the days of Christ it was believed the devil did build it.

Our Sabbath was profitable and interesting meditating in such scenes, and walking beside these flowing streams in the midst of fruit gardens under the shadow of Lebanon. Poor would be the heart that such a Sabbath would not bless. After supper we met in the hotel for a religious service. It was my privilege to preside over this service while Dr. Best preached an excellent sermon.

On Monday we went to the station for our last days journey to the sea. I was thinking of the days ahead of us when on the Mediterranean, fruit would be scarce and mutton plentiful, so Brother Williams and myself purchased from a man at the station a basket of the largest and most delicious

CHAPTER XXXII.

COMING HOME THRU CLOUDS OF WAR.
(August 1914)

Rev. W. E. Gibson, D. D. and myself left our party in Rome and headed homeward. We had heard grave rumblings of war. The others begged us to stay with them and go on to France. The plan was to colonize when travel ceased and call for Uncle Sam to help us. But we were bent on going. Somewhat dazed we told them goodbye, and went to the ticket office to have our tickets endorsed. We were to sail on a German boat. Imagine our surprise when we were told no German ship was on the seas. France, Russia and Germany were at war and England was likely to act at any minute. The ships of these nations were all ordered interned where they were and their flags were off the seas.

While we stood dazed trying to take this in, an American woman rushed by and demanded twenty seven tickets to America. She had a party of teachers, who must get home for school. I waited for I too wanted to go home and I thought if that sister went, I would swing on to her apron string or anything else I could hold and go with her. The ticket man told her she could not go unless she got on the Conopic, an English boat in Naples, one hundred and fifty miles away. She was due to sail tomorrow at 5:30 P. M. She might intern or she might go to England.

"Wire down there for our passage" cried the school marm as tho it must be done.

apricots I have ever seen. The basket was a nice one, made in the Lebanons, and held about a peck. We ate those apricots and will never forget them. The basket I brought all the way home and have it on the table now. The price was two francs—forty cents. We divided with some of the ladies who were threatened with seasickness.

We told Philip and his brothers good-bye. and it seemed like parting with brothers. They took the boat for Joppa and we boarded a ship by way of Egypt. The sun sank lower and lower beyond the waters of the Mediterranean casting its soft mantle of evening light upon the Lebanons and the shore-line of Palestine. For a little time the land seemed transfigured in the twilight as we gazed on it from the deck of our boat, thinking of the things we had seen and felt, and the history that land had written.

Then the light faded, the night came, and the stars came out, the land faded from our eyes but not from our hearts. The breath of the night was on our faces, the waves were singing at our boat side, as our ship turned her nose to the out-bound seas and set her strength to the wheel. Our journey in Palestine was ended. No, it had just begun. Until we land on the Primised Hills of Everlasting Life our hearts will travel those paths over and over again.

"There is no use madam, the Government has confiscated the wires. If I could wire, they would not hold passage for you. There are fifty thousand folks who will want to go on that boat by tomorrow. Your only hope is to go to Naples and try."

"When does the train go?"

"At 10. It is 9:40 now."

"I can't get my party together."

I heard no more. I caught Gibson by the coat tail and yanked him out into the street. We caught the first cab driver we could find, yelled "Macaroni depot" in his ear and gave him two francs. He broke the speed limit and dumped us in the station. We yelled, "Cook, Cook," and the agent of Thomas Cook & Sons, the tourists' friend came. We gave him money to buy our tickets and tipped him. As the wheels of the Naples train began to turn, he shoved us in a section of a car occupied by two American ladies and a handsome Italian lady. We leaned forward to help that train make time. The glorious history of these hills and the processions that long ago moved on the Apian way were not in our meditations.

Before the train halted by the beautiful Bay of Naples, we hit the ground running. We stormed another cab driver, put money in his hand and made him understand. He seemed to think our mission urgent and he gave old Dobbin gas and opened wide his excelerator. We entered the German Steamship office and asked for money back on our tickets. Strange to say, we got it. I have never heard of anyone else who did.

Then we hurried to the English office nearby and got in line. They were coming from Dan to Beersheba and all of them wanted to go to New York. When our turn came he asked us what he could do for us. We told him nothing under the sun unless he could sell us a ticket out of Italy on the Canopic. As we spoke, we could see her swinging on her anchor, the Union Jack flying in the breeze and a boat and a flag never looked so beautiful. Our flag was not there and our hearts went out in admiration for the British Flag. Great Old Flag! The Germans never did drive it off the seas. The whole world—America included, owes much to the British flag.

The ticket agent said he was not sure he could get us on the boat. It was now beyond its capacity. He looked over the list once and found nothing. Our hearts were sinking and all the music we could think of was, "My Country 'tis of Thee, Sweet Land of Liberty." He looked again and his pencil halted almost at the bottom of the last page of the sailing list.

"I want to accommodate you gentlemen but the only place we have is a room that is already occupied by a gentleman, who travels our line every summer. He is very particular about rooming by himself and purchased passage with the understanding that he was to have the room to himself. It is a small room and if you can make it satisfactory with him, I will sell you a ticket."

We assured him he could trust us to fix the matter with that gentleman, and we were not concerned

about his name or his nationality. We got the
tickets and got aboard. We found the room which
was about half as big as a half grown pantry. We
put our goods where we could and took charge.
After a while, the occupant came in. We advanced,
introduced ourselves and told him this was our room
to New York and we would be glad for him to share
it with us provided he had no other place.

We did not have room to go to bed at the same
time and had to do it on the installment plan. Having
been raised in the country, the place everybody
should be raised if he can possibly arrange it, I
like to go to bed early and get early. (In the country
we do not retire and rise, we go to bed and get up)
so I drew the first shift. Gibson came next and the
new man last. He was a Quaker preacher and his
name was Welch. He must not be confused with the
Methodist Welch heretofore and hereinafter mentioned. He was not kin to the other Welch but
was just as expert in some lines as the Methodist is
in others. When I learned he was a Quaker
preacher, I knew trouble was ahead. I believed in
pouring for Baptism, Gibson believed in dipping
and Welch didn't take any kind. Gibson believed
in close communion, I believed in falling from Grace
and Welch believed in wearing his hat in the house,
and in doing when the spirit moved him. To mix
such a conglomeration in a pantry room for ten
nights in time of war is enough to cause spontaneous
combustion. Just as well try to mix the germs of
Germany, the microbes of Iceland and the atoms of
the atmosphere in a bottle and expect to keep in

the stopper, as to but these three in a little room to sleep and expect things to stay normal. And Tommy son, things did happen. It was as spicy a pudding as ever you tasted. If you listen I will tell you.

Old Vesuvius was belching out fire against the Italian sky as we set sail. The stokers struck for the war was on and if a boat sinks what chance does the man at the furnace have? They were persuaded to return. Folks offered thousands of dollars for standing room on the boat. An Italian Count stole on and hid himself until we were well out at sea. A wealthy couple who went over with us and lived in style in Paris went back in the steerage. A man purchased passage for his wife, sending her to the children while he remained behind.

The first bulletin on the wireless the first morning told us two submarines were behind us and had blown up a transport, carrying a thousand soldiers. The next told us submarines were working on the ocean front. The next morning the board said, "Owing to the gravity of the situation, the captain deems it best to withhold further information. England declared war yesterday." Lights were ordered out and the ship crept out on the wide old sea in utter darkness. When we went to our bunks to sleep, we felt a torpedo might summon us to the judgment before morning. Looking back, the hardest thing on me was wondering about the folks at home. I wired my wife I was on the Canopic, but would she get it? What worries the home folks must face! Two things did not fail me—the Grace of God and my sense of good humor.

That Quaker could do more things, going to bed and getting up than any man I ever saw. I did not know there were so many things in the catalog. He went to a wall pocket at the foot of my couch and fumbled after the blacking and the brush tickling my toes as he did it. Among my peculiarities is, I do not like for people to tickle my toes when I am trying to go asleep. When he blacked his shoes, he replaced the outfit and tickled my toes as he did it. He then went to the head of my couch where he kept his toilet articles. He got out his clothes brush scratching and fumbling as he did it. He brushed his clothes, creased and folded them and gently placed them under his bunk. He went back to the wall pocket, got out his shaving outfit. His razor was an ancient type and his stropping process was enough to break up the peace of a department house. He stropped and soaped and shaved. Then he got out of that pocket, three different tubes of concoction to put on his face. One I suppose was to prevent chapping, one to prevent wrinkles and one to preserve beauty.

I am not finding fault with him for using these. He needed them. If there is anything on earth men and women can do to improve their faces, they ought to do it. If some of them have two faces, they ought to wear the other one.

Then he brushed his teeth and washed out his mouth with three kinds of anti-germ killing sanitary preparations. Then he brushed the few remaining hairs that remained on his pate, soothed and fertilized them with three persuasive fluids he hoped would coax them to linger a few more moons. Next he took from under his bunk a portfolio and brought out some things he said were landscapes he painted in northen Italy, for he said in addition to being a preacher, he was an artist. And when a preacher takes to art or golf, you better sing an offertory and let the ushers pass the plates. The things may have been landscapes, but in the dim light allowed us, they looked like billy-goats. After this, he said his prayers, as every saint and sinner ought to do in time of peace as well as war, and then at last he went thru some bodily manipulations called physical—or silly culture and got in bed. It took him one hour and fifteen minutes to render the program without any encores.

But the worst of it was, he gave us a matinee at 3 A. M. That is where and when I bucked. It is where and when the Methodist and Baptist's faith combined to persecute the Quaker. I said to Gibson the next morning,

"If that fellow thinks we are going to submit to that matinee, the telephone girl gave him the wrong number."

"I will stand by you in anything you do to him unless you kill him," said the Baptist.

"Leave it to me," I answered. "If he starts the matinee tonight, something will happen on the high seas."

About 2:30 A. M. he started the first number on the matinee program. It was his physical exercise. Then he came to the second number. He sat down on his feet, took out his portfolio with a hideous rattling of stiff paper and began to look at his landscapes. No light was on save the moon shinng in the porthole and gleaming on his bald head that looked like a Bermuda onion in an Italian restuarant. I quietly removed my blanket, got myself up so I could act and without his knowing, I had moved, I leaped down upon him, got him by his night shirt collar and yelled like a Camanchee Indian ready to tomahawk him and wear his scalp away on my belt. He leaped up and yelled, "Have the Germans got us?" and went in his bunk with such a vim, he almost went thru the wall. I turned about a time or two, muttered something, kicked up my heels and got back in bed. The next morning, he awoke looking at me and asked me if he could get up. I told him he could, and he dressed and got out in seven minutes. That night he poked his head in the door and asked if he could go to bed. I told him he could and he got in bed in seven minutes.

He suddenly concluded I was in the habit of having fits which is true. It was on this trip down in Egypt, I contracted the habit of having fits. I was riding in a carriage with a lady and two gentlemen when we came to a dirty street full of bad looking characters. They blocked the traffic and besieged us. Some of them looked like canibals and did like they wanted to use us for a picnic stew. They surrounded us, begging, pleading, muttering. They tried to get in our carriage and got their hands in our pockets. We begged and threatened but it seemed to do no good. I had learned they were very susceptible to supernatural things. Anything spooky got on their nerves. I suddenly wondered what they would do if I had a fit. I knew if I didn't have one the lady would and I wanted to get ahead of her. I was raised in a southern atmosphere that will make a man do anything for a lady, so I had the fit. I rolled my eyes about like a sick calf, chewed my tongue and slobbered like a mad dog, growled like a wild beast and pulled at my clothes like a lunatic. It worked, for they cleared the street and left us free to go our way. After that when they needed me, they called for me to have a fit and it worked. It will always work. If you have any undesirable company, you try this on them some day and you will see how well it works.

But I am not as naughty as all of this sounds. I have a true and tender heart. A few nights after this, I was awake thinking of my sweetheart and the little ones across the wide waters. I remembered that the last letter said the little girl said, "I dot no daddy now. He went over the big boshen and big fish et him up." I heard the waves rolling by the boat side as she plowed westward thru the death infested sea and the song they seemed to sing was, "I am nearer my home today than I have ever been before."

Just then, I heard Welch groan like he was sick and I put my hand out in the dark to touch him. He yelled and Gibson said,

"Shake him. He has a nightmare."

I shook him with both hands and he yelled still louder. Gibson was up and helping me. We shook him and beat him, thinking if we did not awake him, he would die. Some girls in the next room began to cry and ask if the Germans had captured the boat. Some folks came running in and made a light. At last he was awake and he fell back on his pillow saying,

"It was awful. It was awful."

"What was it?" asked Gibson.

"An old bull was after me, running me around a tree," he said, "And when you hit me, I thought he had hooked me clean thru."

Then I laughed. I had not laughed much for several days for there had not been much to make me laugh. I cannot keep well long without laughing. Now I forgot mines and submarines as I saw a Quaker preacher running around a tree in his night clothes and a mad bull hot on his trail.

Our wireless man picked up a message that two German war ships were waiting for us at the Azores. We changed our course, went one hundred miles north and beat them in the race for American waters. The New York office wirelessed for us but we could not answer. Then the report was started that the German warships had captured us and carried us to Germany as prisoners of war. This was wired to my home in Richmond and for five days my wife believed it. But in seven minutes after I was on American soil, I had my phone ringing in Richmond and my loved ones knew I had

safely landed. Down into old Virginia I came my
heart singing with Van Dyke,

"Home again! home again! America for me,
My heart is turning home again to my own
Country;
Back to the land of room enough
Beyond the ocean bars,
Where the air is full of freedom
And the flag is full of stars.

DEPARTMENT OF STATE

Washington, June 15, 1921.

*To the Diplomatic and Consular Officers of the
United States of America:*

Gentlemen:

At the instance of the Honorable Claude A.
Swanson, Senator of the United States from the
State of Virginia, I take pleasure in introducing to
you the Reverend J. M. Rowland of Lynchburg, Virginia, who is about to proceed abroad.

I cordially bespeak for the Reverend Mr. Rowland
such courtesies and assistance as you may be able
to render, consistently with your official duties.

I am, Gentlemen,

Your obedient servant,

HENRY P. FLETCHER,
Acting Secretary of State.

COMMONWEALTH OF VIRGINIA, UNITED STATES OF AMERICA.
GOVERNOR'S OFFICE

Richmond, June 11, 1921.

To Whom It May Concern:

Reverend J. M. Rowland, of Lynchburg, Virginia,
proposes to take a party through Palestine, Egypt
and Europe this summer for the purpose of travel
and study, returning via London for the World
Methodist Conference.

I desire to commend Reverend Mr. Rowland, who is a Methodist minister in Virginia, and a gentleman of high character and distinguished attainments, to officials and those with whom he has to do during his trip.

WESTMORELAND DAVIS,
Governor of Virginia.

BISHOP'S ROOM
PUBLISHING HOUSE M. E. CHURCH, SOUTH
Richmond, Virginia, United States of America

May 27, 1921.

Rev. J. M. Rowland, the pastor of the Rivermont Methodist Church, of Lynchburg, Va., is personally known to me, and is altogether reliable. It is his purpose to conduct a party through Palestine, Egypt, and Europe, and he asks me, as one of the Bishops of the Methodist Episcopal Church, South, and as Secretary of the College of Bishops, to commend him to the Government authorities as a reliable citizen and minister. Rev. Mr. Rowland can be fully trusted as a patriotic American, and as an honorable gentleman. Any statement he may make can be relied on.

COLLINS DENNY,
Secretary of the College of Bishops, Methodist Episcopal Church, South.

TRIBUTE FROM THE PARTY.

WHEREAS our party of sixteen, Wicker Tour No. 4, 1921, have travelled together most pleasantly and profitably from New York, visiting Baal-Bek, Damascus, the Holy Land and Egypt, and

WHEREAS we are now about to separate after six weeks of happy comradeship

THEREFORE BE IT RESOLVED:

1st. That we thank our capable friend and conductor, Rev. J. M. Rowland of Lynchburg, Virginia, for the efficient and courteous way he has managed the excursion of Tour 4 through these countries and that we congratulate him upon his success as a director.

2nd. That we extend our thanks and appreciation to George Jallouk, the best of Oriental guides, for his unfailing courtesy, thoughtfulness and we especially express our appreciation to him and his good wife for their hospitable entertainment of our party at their home in Jerusalem.

3rd. That a copy of these resolutions be forwarded Dr. J. J. Wicker, and a copy to Rev. J. M. Rowland, and a copy to George Jallouk.

W. H. T. SQUIRES, Sec'y.

Done by Unanimous vote

Cairo, Egypt, Aug. 10, 1921.

OUR 1921 PARTY.

Rev. J. M. Rowland, Editor Richmond Christian Advocate, Conductor of the Party, Richmond, Va.

Rev. W. H. T. Squires, D. D., Pastor Knox Presbyterian Church, Norfolk, Va.

Rev. E. R. Welch, Pastor Chestnut Ave. Methodist Church, Asheville, N. C.

Rev. A. L. Stanford, Pastor Main St. Methodist Church, Gastonia, N. C.

Rev. C. M. Pickens, Pastor First Methodist Church, Morganton, N. C.

Rev. T. J. C. Heath, Pastor Zion Methodist Church, Norfolk, Va.

Rev. A. P. Ralledge, Pastor Methodist Church, Elkins, N. C.

Miss Estelle Warlick, Professor Bible, Davenport College, Lenoir, N. C.

Mr. F. D. McKenney, Furniture Dealer, Petersburg, Va.

Mr. J. N. Jarrett and wife, Vice-President Imperial Insurance Co., Raleigh, N. C.

Mr. J. P. Jarrett, retired business man, Raleigh, N. C.

Miss Oliver Widdowson, Missionary, China.

Miss Emma Horning, Missionary to India.

Mr. A. W. Short, merchant, Bloxom, Va.

Mr. I. G. Jenkins, Y. M. C. A., Sect'y., Detroit, Mich.

EUROPEAN SECTION OF THE PARTY.

This party joined our party at Naples and continued with us the rest of the tour through Europe.

Rev. J. J. Wicker, D. D. Evangelist and Director of the Wicker Tours.

Mrs. J. J. Wicker, of Richmond, Va.

Rev. G. T. Rowe, D. D., S. T. D., Book Editor Methodist Church, South, Nashville, Tenn.

Rev. J. H. Barnhart, D. D., Pastor West Market Methodist Church, Greensboro, N. C.

Rev. V. V. Curtis, D. D., Pastor First Methodist Church, Greenwood, Miss.

Mr. J. A. Dornan, merchant, Richmond, Va.

Mrs. J. A. Winston, Richmond, Va.

Mr. W. Winston, Richmond, Va.

Mrs. M. E. Gathright, Richmond, Va.

Miss Wingo, Richmond, Va.

Miss Margaret Webb, Atlanta, Ga.

Miss Pauline Jones, Portsmouth, Va.

Mrs. B. O. Gratz, Lexington, Ky.

DATE DUE

GAYLORD | | | PRINTED IN U.S.A.